Vernacular buildings in a changing world: understanding, recording and conservation

D1338972

Vernacular buildings in a changing world: understanding, recording and conservation

Edited by Sarah Pearson and Bob Meeson

CBA Research Report 126
Council for British Archaeology
2001

Published 2001 by the Council for British Archaeology
Bowes Morrell House, 111 Walmgate, York YO1 2UA

British Library Cataloguing in Publication Data
A catalogue for this book is available from the British Library

ISSN 0589-9036
ISBN 1 902771 19 2

Typeset by Archtype InformationTechnology Ltd, www.archetype-it.com
Printed by Pennine Printing Services Ltd

The CBA acknowledges with gratitude a grant from English Heritage towards the publication of this volume

Front cover: 9–9a West Street, Faversham, Kent (photography courtesy of Sarah Pearson)
Back cover: Squatter's cottage, Chobham in Surrey, taken 1975 (photograph courtesy of Bob Meeson)

Contents

Part IV: The records

Part V: Conclusions

List of abbreviations

ADS	Archaeology Data Service	OASIS	On-line Access to Archaeological Investigations
AIP	Archaeological Investigations Project	PPG 15	Planning Policy Guidance Note 15: Planning and the historic environment
ALGAO	Association of Local Government Archaeological Officers		
BIAB	British and Irish Archaeological Bibliography	PPG 16	Planning Policy Guidance Note 16: Archaeology and planning
CBA	Council for British Archaeology	PRO	Public Record Office
EH	English Heritage	RCAHMW	Royal Commission on the Ancient and Historical Monuments in Wales
FAC	Field Archaeology Centre (Manchester)		
GMAU	Greater Manchester Archaeology Unit	RCHME	Royal Commission on the Historical Monuments of England
HEIRNET	Heritage Information Resource Network		
		RICS	Royal Institute of Chartered Surveyors
IFA	Institute of Field Archaeologists	SCAUM	Standing Conference of Archaeological Unit Managers
IHBC	Institute of Historic Building Conservation		
		SMR	Sites and Monuments Record
ICOMOS	International Council on Monuments and Sites	UMAU	University of Manchester Archaeology Unit
LBC	Listed Building Consent	VAG	Vernacular Architecture Group
LPA	Local Planning Authority	VCH	Victoria Histories of the Counties of England
MBC	Metropolitan Borough Council		
NMR	National Monuments Record	WEA	Workers' Education Association

List of illustrations

List of tables

List of contributors

Malcolm Airs, Reader in Conservation and the Historic Environment at the University of Oxford and Chairman of the Institute of Historic Building Conservation

Nat Alcock, Reader in the Chemistry Department at the University of Warwick; also a recognised authority on vernacular architecture and an independent building historian

David Baker, Consultant for Historic Environment Conservation, formerly Head of the Heritage Group, Bedfordshire County Planning Department, Vice-president of the Council for British Archaeology

David Clark, Associate Tutor in Architectural History at the Oxford University Department for Continuing Education

Kate Clark, Head of Historic Environment Management, English Heritage

Nicholas Cooper, Architectural Historian, formerly of the Royal Commission on the Historical Monuments of England

Anna Eavis, Head of NMR Services, National Monuments Record, English Heritage

Jane Grenville, Department of Archaeology, University of York

Barry Harrison, Architectural and Landscape Historian, formerly Senior Lecturer in History for the School of Continuing Education at the University of Leeds

Robina McNeil, County Archaeologist for the Greater Manchester Archaeology Unit, University of Manchester

Bob Meeson, Historic Buildings Consultant, formerly Senior Archaeologist in the Department of Planning and Development, Staffordshire County Council

Richard Morriss, Historic Buildings Consultant, Richard K Morriss & Associates

Mike Nevell, Research Manager at the University of Manchester Archaeology Unit

Sarah Pearson, Architectural Historian, formerly of the Royal Commission on the Historical Monuments of England

Edward Roberts, Honorary Research Fellow in the School of Humanities at King Alfred's College, Winchester

Humphrey Welfare, Director of Projects in Archaeology and Survey, English Heritage

Acknowledgements

The primary thanks must go to the contributors, without whose voluntary commitment this report would not have been possible. Under the direction of Malcolm Airs and the editors, the Department for Continuing Education at the University of Oxford is acknowledged for hosting the conference at which most of the following papers were given. The conference was the first of a series organised jointly by that Department and the Vernacular Architecture Group, whose support is warmly appreciated. Subsequently, Humphrey Welfare offered continuing practical assistance and encouragement, and Kate Sleight and Jane Thorniley-Walker steered the final text to publication.

We are grateful to those who supplied or permitted the use of illustrations, as credited in the text.

The publication was made possible through a generous grant from English Heritage.

Sarah Pearson & Bob Meeson
January 2001

Summary

The principal architectural component of the built landscape is comprised of vernacular buildings, whose value to everyone is increasingly recognised. At the same time there is a growing awareness that their historic integrity is being eroded. Based largely on a conference at Oxford in 1998, this Research Report is relevant to all who are concerned with the future of vernacular buildings in England and Wales. It explores many of the current issues facing those who study small historic buildings, and who are concerned with their conservation.

Firstly, the discipline is set in its historical context, exploring the many ways in which building recording has been or can be approached, whether from an academic point of view or for practical and conservation purposes. The need for better-informed conservation and planning decisions has led to a significant increase in the amount and type of building recording undertaken. Informed conservation requires an understanding of particular buildings, their contribution to local distinctiveness, and well-researched general knowledge. Two papers by professional consultants indicate the problems encountered and the range of uses to which such work may be put.

It remains a high priority to continue to explore the wider development of historic buildings academically, and to that end new research techniques and applications, such as tree-ring dating, are developing. The role of education is explored, particularly in the light of major changes in university organisation and the introduction of information technology. The crucial part played by independent voluntary building recording is also illustrated.

Once records are made, the ways that they can be stored and accessed is a matter of considerable concern, particularly as the volume of information continues to grow while the resources of national and local repositories remain relatively static.

The papers are widely divergent in their themes and approaches, but there is considerable agreement on the issues that need to be addressed.

Résumé

La principale structure architecturale du paysage construit est composée de petits bâtiments historiques ; leur valeur universelle est de plus en plus reconnue et pourtant, en même temps, il y a une prise de conscience croissante de la mesure de leur disparition. Se référant largement sur une conférence à l'Université d'Oxford en 1998, ce compte-rendu des recherches intéressera tous ceux qui sont concernés par l'avenir des bâtiments traditionnels en Angleterre et au pays de Galles. Il explore de nombreux problèmes actuels auxquels font face ceux qui étudient les petits bâtiments historiques et qui sont concernés par leur sauvegarde.

Tout d'abord, cette discipline est placée dans son contexte historique, explorant les nombreuses manières dont a été abordée, ou pourrait être abordée, la documentation sur les bâtiments, que ce soit d'un point de vue universitaire ou à des fins pratiques et pour la sauvegarde. Le besoin de décisions de sauvegarde et de planning mieux informées a mené à une considérable augmentation de nombre et du type de bâtiments sur lesquels est entreprise une documentation. La sauvegarde informée exige une compréhension de bâtiments particuliers, de leur contribution au caractère distinctif local et des connaissances générales bien recherchées. Deux communications écrites par des consultants professionnels indiquent les problèmes rencontrés et les divers usages auxquels pourrait se prêter ce genre de travail.

La poursuite des démarches en ce qui concerne le développement des bâtiments historiques sur le plan universitaire reste une haute priorité et, à ce but, de nouvelles techniques de recherche et de nouvelles applications, comme la dendrochronologie, se développent. Le rôle de l'enseignement est exploré, tout particulièrement au regard de grands changements dans l'organisation de l'université et de l'introduction de la technologie de l'information. Le rôle crucial joué par la documentation bénévole indépendante est également illustré.

Une fois la recherche documentaire terminée, il faudra se soucier des différents moyens pour la ranger et pour y avoir accès, étant donné, particulièrement, que le volume de l'information continue de croître alors que les ressources des dépôts nationaux et locaux restent relativement constantes.

Les communications ont des thèmes et approches très différents mais elles s'accordent quant aux problèmes qu'il convient d'aborder.

Überblick

Die vorherrschende architekonische Struktur der Bau-Landschaft besteht aus kleinen, historischen Gebäuden, deren Wert zunehmend Anerkennung findet, währenddessen sich ebenfalls das Tempo eines bausubstantiellen Zermürbungs-Prozesses ins Bewußtsein rückt

Der folgende Forschungsbericht wendet sich an all diejenigen, die sich vom Werdegang traditioneller Gebäude in England und Wales betroffen fühlen und basiert größtenteils auf Konferenz-Inhalten der Universität Oxford aus dem Jahre 1999.

Vielen gebenwärtigen Angelegenheiten wird hier auf den Grund gegangen. Sowohl diejenigen, denen kleine, historische Gebäuden am Herzen liegen, als auch die an ihrem Erhalt interessierten sind angesprochen.

Zunächst einmal wird die Disziplin im historischen Kontext gesetzt. Auf vielen Wegen wurde sich den Methoden der Gebäude-Aufzeichnung genähert. Diese werden hier erkundet, sei es auf akademische Art oder aber aus praktisch veranlagten oder erhaltenden Motiven.

Die Notwendigkeit, besser informierte Planungs-, wie Gebäude-Erhaltungs-Entscheidungen zu treffen, hat zu einem bedeutsamen Anwachsen von Gebäude-Aufzeichnungen geführt, sowohl bezüglich der Anzahl, wie auch der Methoden. Den 'besser informierten' Erhaltungsmaßnahmen muss ein Verständnis bezüglich gewisser Gebäude-Typen vorausgehen und darüber, wie sie zu einem unverwechselbaren Erscheinungsbild eines Orts ihren Beitrag leisten. Zudem ist ein breites Allgemeinwissen dafür essentiell.

Die Aufzeichnungen von zwei professionellen Beretern zeigen Probleme auf, mit denen bereits umgegangen wurde, aber auch die Breite des Nutzungsspektrum dieser Art von Arbeit.

Das Weiterverfolgen der Entwicklung historischer Gebäude aus akademischem Blickwinkel bleibt weiterhin Priorität und für diesen Bereich werden Forscungstechniken- und Anwendungen, wie z. B. das Auswerten der Jahresringe von Bäumen, weiterentwickeit.

Die Bedeutung von Bildung wird erforscht, speziell die grundsätzlichen organisatorischen Veränderungen im Universitäts-Apparat, wie auch die Einführung der Informations-Technologie betreffend.

Der ausschlaggebende Part, den unabhängige Voluntäre bei Gebäude-Aufzeichnungen spielen, wird ebenfalls dargestellt.

Solbald es fertige Aufzeichnungen gibt, stellt sich die Frage ihrer Verwaltung und des Zugangs zu jeweils benötigtem Material, besonders, da das Informationsvolumen weiterhin anwachsen wird, während die Ressourcen lokaler und nationaler Bezugsquellen relativ unverändert bleiben werden.

Die Berichte weichen in ihrem Themen und Vorgehensweisen start voneinander ab, dennoch ergibt sich ein beachtliches Maß an Übereinstimmung hinsichtlich der Themenauswahl.

Preface

Small buildings, in their infinite variety, constitute a core part of the historic environment and fittingly formed the focus of the conference, organised by the Vernacular Architecture Group and the University of Oxford Department for Continuing Education. The proceedings from that conference constitute the core of this volume.

The familiar and comfortable forms of vernacular buildings are indissoluble from perceptions of regional character and from the spirit of place of villages, market towns, and scattered rural communities. They are thus an integral part of our cultural consciousness, firing the inquisitive imagination and stimulating a great deal of investigation in the second half of the 20th century. Although small buildings within the vernacular tradition are readily recognised and appreciated by the wider public, their huge numbers and their extraordinary diversity of form, development, structure and materials make informed assessments especially difficult. In parallel, the very popularity of these buildings has exposed them to restoration and alteration that is well intentioned but often ill-informed, a dichotomy that has posed particular challenges to those responsible for their conservation.

The conference published here illustrated how the huge body of evidence potentially available is gradually being unlocked and acted upon. In this the involvement of the Department for Continuing Education was particularly appropriate as so much recording – by groups or by dedicated individuals – has stemmed from extra-mural courses. The framework that they have provided, and the enthusiasm that they have channelled and nurtured, have generated much of what we know today. The research that spins off from these courses is a powerful testament to the value of 'life-long learning'. This study of buildings for their own sake will continue unabated, but recent years have also seen a continuing shift from the recording and analysis of individual buildings to the provision of wider understanding, through syntheses of building-types or through regional studies. This is now being taken further to the active use of that new knowledge as the informed basis for conservation.

The actual recording of a building calls for a variety of skills, and while both the activity and the result are satisfying in themselves they form only the first step of a longer process. Dissemination and accessibility – whether by publication or by deposit in a public archive – soon become essential. However, the inclusion of buildings in local Sites and Monuments Records is still patchy, and even the information collected by and for the use of planners in district councils has rarely been made available for wider public use. At a national level, however, the databases are being thrown open through emerging electronic access to the Listed Building System and to the Images of England (the latter being set to provide an online photograph of every listed building in England).

Signposting the existence of records of building analyses represents a continuing and developing challenge: to ensure that those who need the information, now or in the future, can find it and make use of it. Such signposting greatly assists the creation of syntheses, enabling the record of a particular building to be linked to others and put in context so that robust statements of significance may be made. In treating small vernacular buildings, the construction of this wider picture can be crucial for conservation officers in local authorities in the management of change – whether they are dealing with individual buildings, streetscapes, or conservation areas, or with the production of Local Plans or design guides. Ideally, both specific and contextual information should be available as early as possible so that they can influence the plans for works. This is infinitely preferable to the conservation officer having to react – much later in the overall process – to inadequate applications for listed building consent. It was particularly noticeable at the conference that much of the discussion centred on the timely use of records in planning procedures.

Taking the wider view, it is essential that the advances in knowledge that stem from the recording of individual buildings (reinforced where appropriate by sophisticated surveying or by dendrochronology) are passed on. Heightened public awareness, altered perceptions, and further professional training schemes will greatly strengthen the whole business of architectural conservation. Convincing owners and curators of the significance and value of particular features or building-types, or of the long-term benefits of making use of traditional materials, will provide a sound basis for the invaluable, everyday actions in conservation that will do more than anything to protect and to sustain our stock of small historic buildings.

English Heritage is particularly glad to support the publication of the papers from this very successful, enjoyable and stimulating conference.

Humphrey Welfare
Director of Projects in Archaeology and Survey
English Heritage

Introduction

The conference papers on which this book is based grew out of a recognition that the study of vernacular buildings, as practised between the 1950s and 1980s, had changed significantly by the 1990s. During the earlier period, and beginning from a state of almost total ignorance, the primary aim was to discover how many small historic buildings survived in Great Britain, identify their type and dates, show how those of one region differed from those of another, and note the changes in design, structure and planform that occurred over time. For many years this remained the main preoccupation of researchers, whether professionals or amateurs.

By the 1990s, it was generally recognised that historic buildings were a major cultural resource which was being relentlessly damaged, sometimes through over-enthusiastic and uninformed restoration. The perception that they must be understood in order to be properly conserved led to the introduction of government guidelines aimed at securing better-informed conservation. This in turn led to an increase in detailed recording, and brought people with different backgrounds and skills into the field. There is an urgent need to get across the role that recording can and should play in conservation, not simply in order to mitigate loss, but to instruct all who are involved in proposed work – whether as owners, agents or managers – as to what is important about a building before decisions are made about its future. At the same time, there is still more to be discovered about the buildings of particular areas, periods or types, and new techniques and approaches are changing both our understanding of them and their continuing use. Finally, there is the question of what happens to all this knowledge once acquired.

There is room for a wide range of skills and approaches in the study of small buildings, and this book seeks to draw together specialists from different backgrounds who make or use records of vernacular architecture. They range from academics to government employees, from professional consultants to interested volunteers, and their work reflects the variety of current interests and concerns.

Part I: Background, objectives and methods

1 Exploring the issues: changing attitudes to understanding and recording *by Sarah Pearson*

The last few years have seen a number of books and conferences devoted to the recording of buildings, most notably the volume entitled *Buildings Archaeology: Applications in Practice*, published in 1994 following a conference on recording held by the Institute of Field Archaeologists in 1993 (RCHME 1991, Wood 1994). Thus it may be argued that another is not required. But most books have dealt with larger buildings, or at least with all buildings, and have been primarily concerned with methodology. Although in theory the methodology of recording all buildings may be the same, historically those who have engaged in the study of small buildings have had a distinctive approach, perceptibly different from that used for other buildings. The last few years have seen this beginning to change, largely because of a growing interest in conservation. For a while this resulted in an unfortunate confrontation between different attitudes, which was particularly marked in the late 1980s and early 1990s. It focused on issues such as levels and methods of recording, and led people to take up entrenched positions. Thankfully, this is changing, and one of the purposes of this book is to identify the various presuppositions and to discuss the changes, and the challenges that have come with them.

Buildings Archaeology was largely concerned with record-making for the management of historic buildings. Indeed, David Stocker actually called his introduction: 'Understanding What We Conserve', and made the point that this is an appropriate approach for members of the IFA, increasing numbers of whom are recording smaller buildings. But this has not been the only, nor even the main reason, why people have studied smaller buildings – the word 'study' rather than record is used deliberately, for this book is not just about the practical recording of individual small buildings; it is about understanding all aspects of the study of small or vernacular buildings, which means also paying attention to the human, social and cultural importance of historic buildings, as has recently been discussed by a number of writers (eg Grenville 1994, Palmer 1994, Johnson 1994, Gould 1995).

Historical background

The rise of recording historic buildings in the sense that we know it today began among architects in the early 19th century. The publications of John Britton on castles, and even more importantly the works by Thomas Rickman on the stylistic development of churches, had a tremendous impact (Britton 1807–26, Rickman 1817). Rickman classified features and styles thereby providing a framework which could be used for dating purposes. During the first half of the century numerous local and national archaeological and historical societies were founded, both catering for and stimulating the rising interest in ancient monuments of all kinds; and from 1842 Robert Willis, Jacksonian Professor of Natural and Experimental Philosophy at the University of Cambridge, was publishing his pioneering structural analyses of medieval cathedrals and other buildings (Willis 1972, see also Pevsner 1972). Thus a great deal was going on among the educated public at this time. But none of this was officially recognised.

On the Continent, governments were quick to accept their responsibilities, and already by the early 19th century they were taking an active role in the identification, protection and recording of historic monuments in their care (Brown 1905, 11, 76–96, Harvey 1961, 1972, 27–8); but shamefully, in Great Britain, despite pressure from architects and antiquarians, the state played little part (Miele 1996, 20). In 1846 two architects, Edward Blore and William Twopenny, were invited to draw up a report for the Commission of Woods and Forests on the preservation and repair of ancient buildings and works of art belonging to the Crown. Their report starts by recognising the increased interest of the public in historic monuments and their preservation, but notes that 'unfortunately the progress of knowledge has not kept pace with the increase of zeal and admiration', which they felt was a pity, since there was scarcely a village without some historical remains, and injudicious repair was 'often obliterating every trace of originality and not infrequently changing the character of the work which they profess to preserve'. To counteract this, they said, the government should be setting a good example in its treatment of Crown properties. It is worth quoting their recommendations in full, since they are as apposite now as they were when written:

We . . . suggest that before any repair be executed . . . careful drawings . . . should be made which would assist the Commissioners in determining as to the value and extent of the repairs to be sanctioned, and also afford evidence of the state of the building . . . before the repair in contemplation was executed. These drawings should be carefully preserved and would in time form a collection of great value and interest, and their utility and interest would be greatly increased if they were rendered accessible to the public by depositing them in the British Museum where they might be made the foundation of . . . a public collection of drawings of antient buildings and other works of art in this country.

The necessity of careful reports to the Commissioners by competent persons of the actual state of the work proposed to be preserved, and if necessary repaired, before it is touched is so obvious that it seems hardly necessary for us to mention it, but we venture to suggest that great care should be taken in the selection of those persons upon whose fitness for so important and difficult a duty so much will depend. To be qualified for this duty it is not only necessary that the persons employed should be possessed of skilful practical knowledge but that they should also have a right feeling of respect for antient art, which feeling should be supported and enlarged by a good knowledge of different styles of art which have prevailed through successive periods. (3 January 1847, PRO *Works* 14/131.4)

The report was politely acknowledged as interesting, but it led to no action by the government. Thus, despite the fact that by the 1840s many of the major aspects of recording, that is, structural analysis, accurate drawing, typological classification, assessment and survey in advance of restoration, and preservation of the results as a corpus for future research, were being discussed by architects and antiquarians, England had to wait for several decades for legislation to protect its ancient monuments, and even longer for the state to acknowledge the importance of an inventory or of recording.

Concern over the destruction of unprotected historic buildings led to the founding of the Society for the Protection of Ancient Buildings in 1877, and in due course, and under pressure from various sources, the Ancient Monuments Act was passed and the post of Inspector of Ancient Monuments established in 1882 (Saunders 1983, Champion 1996). But this dealt with only a handful of monuments, and although the Office of Works was responsible for the care and repair of a number of state-owned buildings, this did little to alleviate the problems about which people had been campaigning. One of the tasks which was seen as essential was to know just which buildings were worthy of protection and repair. Where were they? How many of them were there? An inventory of the nation's historic buildings was required. Since the government did nothing, in 1894 C R Ashbee set up the Committee for the Survey of the Memorials of Greater London, to compile a register of notable buildings in London, and alert and educate people to their importance and interest before it was too late (Hobhouse 1994). The problem was not, of course, confined to the capital, and so, when the Victoria History of the Counties of England was begun in 1899, again as a private enterprise, it began the task of systematically describing, and in some cases illustrating, the more important buildings in each parish that it tackled (Pugh 1970).

Ultimately, and very belatedly, as is the way of governments, the Royal Commissions were set up in 1908 to make inventories 'of the ancient and historical monuments and constructions connected with or illustrative of the contemporary culture, civilization and conditions of life' in each of the three countries, 'from the earliest times to 1700'. The idea was that the inventory would form the basis for legislation relating to protection, for legislation could not be enacted until the government had some idea of the quantity and quality of the country's historic monuments. It was thought that this would be a task of a few years, and the Commissions were asked both to publish inventories, and to recommend those monuments most worthy of preservation. The character of the work stemmed from a very 19th-century attitude to both history and officialdom, which can be summed up by comments made by David Murray, president of the Archaeological Society of Glasgow, who in 1896 had called for the formation of something like the Commissions, staffed by official surveyors 'competent to observe and record, with no theory to support or evolve', who would make a 'correct and impartial record of facts' (Murray 1896, 29, 36, 71). This was the official approach of the Commissions from 1908 until the 1970s, and it is small wonder that in the early years they produced few bright and lively minds, the great exception being Sir Alfred Clapham, Secretary of the English Commission, who, however, still simply used his staff as rather low-grade research assistants. The work consisted primarily of verbal descriptions augmented by measured plans of churches and a few important houses. At the time this approach was deemed adequate, as can be seen from the fact that no less a person than Grahame Clark (1934) praised the Commissions for doing a marvellous job of mapping antiquities to a very high standard.

However, the Commissions were not, despite pleas from eminent academics such as Baldwin Brown (1905), properly tied into the legislative process or the protection of sites. In addition, as the date range of monuments considered of historic interest extended, and the diversity of those considered important increased, progress became ever slower and the inventories could not possibly provide the background to the legislation that had been intended. Thus, after the Second World War the government had to set up another process of inventorisation, the listing of historic buildings. Again, it was decided to give this responsibility to a different department, and these decisions have left a legacy of fragmentation of responsibility which still applies in Scotland and Wales and has only been clarified in England since the Royal Commission and English Heritage (as it has become) merged in April 1999.

The beginnings of the study of vernacular architecture

After the Second World War interest in smaller buildings increased, and some people began to think about them in new ways. The first volume of Sir Cyril Fox and Lord Raglan's *Monmouthshire Houses*, which appeared in 1951, was the first publication to illustrate this new approach, and in 1952 the Vernacular Architecture Group was formed to provide a forum for the exchange of ideas about smaller buildings. These studies were question-led, which was a far cry from the 19th-century ideal of inventorisation. People wanted to know not just what buildings there were, but how style, construction and plan forms evolved; and, as stated in the first volume of *Monmouthshire Houses*, the authors 'considered that this enquiry could be carried out by archaeological methods' (Fox and Raglan I, 1951, 10). Buildings were analysed structurally, and relatively simple measured drawings, sections as well as plans, played a prominent part in survey.

Monmouthshire Houses set the tone for a number of regional surveys of vernacular buildings. Such studies were usually topographically based, but their approach differed fundamentally from that of the inventories, for they were directed to buildings of a particular period or type, and in the best examples their purpose was to record in order to answer historical questions about both the buildings and the societies which gave rise to them (eg Brunskill 1974, Harrison and Hutton 1984, Alcock 1993, Giles 1986, Barnwell and Giles 1997). They did not include very detailed measured surveys because this was not considered necessary for the purpose in hand. This point cannot be stressed enough: the detail of the record was commensurate to the task. It was more important to cover the ground and gain an overview than to survey any individual building in more detail than was necessary. Fox and Raglan described their approach as archaeological, and they were not alone in this. As W A Pantin wrote in 1958, when describing the same sort of method, it was 'a process which may be called excavation above ground' and it was important to build up 'a body of generalised knowledge ... [which] in turn helps us to understand and diagnose individual specimens'. These workers, and others like them, were not just recorders; they were historians who wanted to use buildings as primary sources to explore certain aspects of history. Pantin, in the same paper, was at pains to emphasise the importance of studying buildings and documents together. Many of the practitioners were amateurs, in that they gained their livelihood in other ways, and this is how a great deal of the best work in this tradition has been, and is still being, done. It is typical, for example, that in the 1990s, when Mick Aston of the University of Bristol required a survey of historic buildings to be undertaken for his archaeological project on Shapwick in Somerset, he approached the Somerset Vernacular Building Research Group, whose excellent report was published in 1996 (SVBRG 1996). In this volume Nat Alcock discusses the role of the independent recorder.

In addition to regional topographical surveys, attention began to be paid to various aspects of the construction of smaller houses, in particular by J T Smith of the English Commission (eg Smith 1955; 1958). The approach was again one in which the purpose was to understand evolution. To start with, it was overall structural form that was examined. Later fieldworkers, particularly Richard Harris and the late Cecil Hewett, in their different ways have taken structural analysis a stage further, and brought the understanding of timber framing to a very high level of precision; but their work is more closely affiliated to the kind of detailed survey I will consider shortly, than to the work of those who practised the historical approach.

Meanwhile, the trend towards greater inclusiveness compounded the problems of the Commissions. Not only were increasing demands made upon the English Commission, but it also became obvious that the pursuit of the complete record was a chimera (Fowler 1981, Croad and Fowler 1984). The job was taking far too long, and by the late 1960s it was clear to some of the more forward-looking staff in the English Commission that an approach conceived before the First World War, and doggedly pursued with little modification, had become outmoded. Architectural scholarship had moved on, and much of the verbal description was irrelevant. Eric Mercer and J T Smith felt that the greatest failure of the Commission was, that despite all the detail that was now included, the volumes failed to provide an overall picture of the architecture of a county and its development, nor did they show in what way the buildings of one county differed from another (unpublished Memorandum to the Commissioners, 1969). In other words, if the listing of individual items was taking place elsewhere, the Commission should at the very least be providing the overview. In line with current thinking outside the Commission, the approach they suggested was typological and historical. What was required was analysis and understanding, the evidence for which would then be presented through discussion and illustration. The emphasis was still on traditional buildings of the 18th century and earlier, for the present interest in later industrial and institutional buildings had not then begun.

It was to be another ten years before such views prevailed in the Commissions, although the publication in 1975 of Eric Mercer's *English Vernacular Houses*, signalled the first signs of change. This book summed up, albeit from a very personal point of view, the current state of knowledge about vernacular houses. It was not published without dissent, for some Commissioners felt that this sort of volume was wholly inappropriate to a government body, smacked too much of research, and detracted from the Commission's main task, which was the inventory. However, one can now see it as the forerunner of the kind of studies, subsequently undertaken by the Commissions, and latterly also funded by English Heritage, which are now regarded as essential prerequisites to the protection of complex or inadequately understood building types. As such they are thought to qualify for government funding.

Listing buildings

The Commission's inability to complete its task led to the setting up of a new process of inventorisation, the listing of historic buildings. This is not the place to go into the history of listing in any detail, but it is worth mentioning it for several reasons. In the first place, this process also proved inadequate and had to be revised on more than one occasion. Secondly, by the time the national resurvey of England was complete in 1992/3 it comprised more than half a million individual buildings, and had taken 500 man years of fieldwork – and that of course was not the end (Robertson *et al* 1993, 91–2). Thirdly, the resurvey employed a great many people who have continued their careers in historic buildings and are among those recording today. Initially, listing focused on inventorising individual buildings, but modern listing, which is still continuing, is as much concerned with understanding categories of building, and with complexes, ensembles and landscapes – very much more difficult concepts to get to grips with for the purposes of protection. This is also very similar to the sort of recording latterly undertaken by the Commissions.

The decline of detailed records

During the immediate post-war years, what was being done in the way of recording historic buildings as part of the conservation process, as advocated by Blore and Twopenny in 1847? The answer is, very little, and it is worth considering why this should have been so. In recent years those who have written on the recording of historic buildings, particularly churches, have pointed to the dearth of detailed recording undertaken in the early-20th century. Richard K Morris has quoted the views of Francis Bond who, in 1906, saw the second quarter of the 19th century as a golden age for the serious study of church architecture (Morris 1994). Bond adduced various reasons for the decline, ranging from the difficulties of getting to the buildings, the lack of teaching and of accessible records, the competing claims on archaeology of exotic sites in foreign places, and the tendency towards periodisation.

However, one may wonder whether Bond was not too close to the problem to see two of the main reasons why ecclesiastical buildings were no longer being studied and recorded with the same enthusiasm as before. The first was a widespread feeling that most of the work had already been done. Most of the major monuments had already been surveyed, and a number of important books on architectural development had been written – it is, for example, instructive to notice how many of Bond's illustrations were reproduced from 19th-century sources. The second is that the main effort was confined to churches, and that architects, who had been the principal recorders during the 19th century, were no longer required to design ecclesiastical buildings.

The Gothic Revival was over, and with it the need to understand both the overall form and the details of Gothic buildings. Indeed, as the modern movement got under way, Gothic buildings were beginning to cause shudders of distaste. Such recording as was done by architects was more likely to be devoted to country houses, as in the work of Reginald Blomfield or Albert Richardson. In general, however, the detailed understanding of past styles was seen as less essential, and the 'archaeological' or historical approach to buildings was viewed very cautiously by architects. Although they still studied the buildings of the past to learn about good construction, it was no longer thought either desirable or necessary that earlier styles should be reproduced (Powys 1937, 35–42). Architectural schools continued to teach their students to draw important historic buildings – it was not until the second half of the 20th century that this aspect of their curricula finally disappeared; but their hearts were no longer in it as they had been a hundred years before, and the one profession which was well-equipped to undertake measured survey (even if this was not usually analytical in the modern sense), was largely lost to the cause.

In a sense it could be said that the dearth of recording in the first half of the 20th century was brought about by the withdrawal of the architects from active participation in the recording business. Who was to take their place? The only group of people who were trained to make drawings to the requisite standard were archaeologists. When one thinks about it now, it is small wonder that they moved in to fill the void; but this did not take place immediately, for the 30 years after the Second World War were a bleak time for historic buildings. They were more likely to be demolished than restored, and it was not until the interest in conservation became more widespread from the 1970s onwards that anyone saw the need for detailed recording.

Once the listing of historic buildings got under way, permission had to be sought for the demolition of a listed property. Not only was this a form of control over what should occur, but it meant that information about what was proposed could be made centrally available, and this provided the opportunity for records to be made. It was out of this situation that the Commissions' involvement in recording threatened buildings arose, but these records, like their other work, were interpretative accounts of the historical development of buildings, and were not meant to be an integral part of the process of restoration. Throughout this time the issue of accurate recording in advance of restoration remained badly neglected. In state-owned properties it was accepted that details would be lost during restoration work, and therefore that a record was essential, not really as an aid to restoration but for historical reasons or, as Sir Charles Peers admitted, for 'mere self-defence' (Peers 1931, 320). Outside this category, detailed analytical recording of the fabric was rare, and received no encouragement from the state.

In private practice, few architects specialising in the restoration of buildings were concerned with recording as they worked. Very little space, for example, was devoted to the topic in John Harvey's book on building conservation. He simply advised architects to take photographs and draw 'at least a ground plan'; from this, historical development could be studied and structural weaknesses identified (Harvey 1972, 89). That a great deal more could be learnt from the detailed analysis of a structure, and that this might prove valuable to the restoration process itself, was not discussed. Signs of change began in the early 1970s, when Harold Taylor asked for better surveys of Anglo-Saxon churches, resulting in pioneering exercises in intensive recording at places like Rivenhall, Brixworth and Deerhurst (Taylor 1972); and Richard Harris started calling for the detailed recording of timber-framed buildings (Harris 1977). However, it was to be some time before this approach was being widely advocated.

The advent of archaeological recording

The pace of change increased in the later 1970s when the Department of the Environment funded the first thorough archaeological and documentary investigations of its own properties, such as that at Audley End, undertaken by Paul Drury (Drury 1980). The novelty of the approach even for a monument as major as Audley End, may be gauged by the fact that such studies were still, in the 1990s, referred to as exemplars (Howard 1994). The notion that recording should be an integral part of all historic building restoration was not acknowledged by anyone until 1985 when English Heritage (as it had then become), made recording a condition for its grants for restoration. The lateness of this date is worth bearing in mind. The wheel had gone full circle. What Blore and Twopenny had felt to be self-evident 140 years before, had at last been officially recognised.

These detailed studies were originally undertaken by archaeologists. When they moved into building recording in the 1970s and 80s they were quite clear in their own minds that they were doing something new, namely that by employing techniques derived from excavation they were providing records of buildings to a higher level of detail and precision than were currently being undertaken by anyone else, and that through such recording they were discovering new facts about the buildings concerned. Initially, since their techniques were time-consuming and expensive, the work of archaeologists was largely confined to buildings of national importance. Also, their advent in the world of standing building recording caused a lot of tension and aggravation, and it is easy to see the reasons why. They designated their own work as 'archaeological', and that done by others as 'art-historical'. Not un-

naturally this caused fur to fly, particularly since the majority of those already engaged in building recording did not see themselves as art historians; nor would they be accepted by that profession as such. Archaeologists also saw themselves as part of a 'tradition' going back to Willis in the mid 19th century. Although Willis was neither an architect nor an archaeologist, and analysed structures in a way unknown to his architectural contemporaries, his approach was in fact closer to that of the architects of his period than to that of contemporary archaeologists. Those archaeologists who followed, such as St John Hope, were considerably less rigorous in their analysis. Thus it is somewhat dubious whether there was a 'tradition' as such. In fact, in the middle of the 20th century Willis became the prophet of medieval architectural historians decades before he was discovered by archaeologists. Nonetheless, it is undoubtedly the case that detailed recording by archaeologists has not only made an immense contribution to the quality of interpretation and restoration of individual historic buildings, but has also pervaded the whole subject, increasing standards of understanding and analysis throughout the discipline. This is wholly to the good.

From the other side of the divide, however, archaeologists were justifiably seen to be lacking historical architectural background, which sometimes meant that they took a sledge hammer to crack a nut – discovering from an exhaustive survey what more experienced recorders could have told them in a tenth of the time; and their historical knowledge was often rudimentary, which left them unable satisfactorily to place their buildings in an acceptable historical or typological context. This last problem perhaps arose because they did not actually see this as part of their job – although others disputed the value of such a narrowly defined brief. It is also possible that to begin with the fight for accurate recording to be recognised as an integral part of conservation led archaeologists to brush aside the fact that recording previously had other aims, or to recognise that those other aims were still valid. One would like to think that we have got beyond these divisive views, and that all practitioners are learning to employ an appropriate mix of archaeological, architectural and historical analysis.

Closer investigation of what has happened during the 20th century would no doubt reveal that the situation was considerably more complex than the simple picture outlined above. Virtually every statement made in this paper could be qualified, and David Stocker has already pointed out that the aims of art historians, as he terms them, and archaeologists are much closer than the stereotypes imply (Stocker 1992). Indeed, the inadequacies of the stereotypes become apparent when an archaeologist can write of Mark Girouard's *Life in the English Country House*, that it 'has claims to belong to archaeology as much as to architectural history' (Fairclough 1992, 352).

Conservation and recording

In the last ten years the archaeological approach to recording has become more important as the impetus to understand and record buildings before they are altered or restored has gained momentum. Not only English Heritage but bodies like the National Trust, which used to be somewhat cavalier in their approach to the buildings they owned, are now extremely responsible, and a great deal of high quality analysis and recording takes place on major monuments before work is done. In 1994 the introduction of PPG 15 – outlined in David Baker's paper below – brought the concept of recording to the attention of all local authorities and extended it to the whole range of listed buildings. PPG 15 encourages local authorities to require an appropriate level of information prior to restoration or alteration, and while this is pursued with differing degrees of rigour, there is no doubt that the practice of requiring records is growing. Previously, recording was something the owner grudgingly submitted to – it might waste a bit of time, and time was money – but those who did the work were paid for by the government. Now, as in dirt archaeology, the owner or developer may be required to provide the record as part of his application. To date, most recording of this kind has been associated with larger and more important buildings, but gradually the pressure to see this as an essential part of the conservation process is filtering through. One of the problems with getting the message across to those who deal with smaller buildings lies, as discussed by Kate Clark, in the shortage of basic training that is currently available for those who handle the actual conservation of historic buildings, be they planners and conservation officers, architects and surveyors, or owners and developers.

The fact that the 'developer' of a small building may be a private individual of limited means can cause problems. Richard Morris (1997) has drawn attention to the fact that in some high-powered circles conservation is beginning to be seen as too intrusive and as having 'gone too far'. If true, then there may in due course be a backlash from the present situation, and if so, we may see the owners of small buildings joining the rebellion, since the matter so directly touches their private pockets. Responsible conservation officers obviously bear this fact in mind, and therefore tailor recording requirements to what is essential to inform the decision-making process and any subsequent works.

The records

The new situation raises the question of what the role of these records is, whether it is worth making partial records, and what happens to them once made. Are the records made in response to PPG 15 intended only to inform the restoration of that building, thereafter to be consigned to the file for future reference next time the building has a face lift? Are they to help the conservation staff of the authority increase their knowledge and understanding of local historic buildings? Or can they also serve a wider purpose, available to students and used to educate the general public in the character of the buildings of an area? These are issues that Kate Clark, Robina McNeil, Bob Meeson and Richard Morriss look at from a number of angles.

As Anna Eavis then goes on to ask, where should the completed records be kept, and how can they be made accessible? Traditionally, the National Monuments Records in England, Wales and Scotland were the recommended repositories. However, the number of records is increasing rapidly and, like all major archives, the NMRs have had to review their collecting policies. They are often likely now to recommend that records should be deposited locally, and anyway this is probably where they are likely to be of most use. Are the County Archives or the County Sites and Monuments Records even the correct place? If the material is to be used for managing the heritage at district level, how useful is depositing records in a county SMR? Should they in fact be retained at district level? This would be the most convenient for the local conservation officer, but his or her office is probably not the best place for the conservation of records, and is hardly suitable for public consultation. In the long term the problem may be solved by the general introduction of compatible databases taking both text and images. But not only are resources and suitable software so far lacking, but many local authorities have probably not even begun to consider this as a desirable aim. Finally, if, in the interests of education, the knowledge gained from such recording is to reach a wider public it needs pulling together, synthesising, and making available. Who is to do this, in what form, and how will it be paid for?

Research and independent study

In dirt archaeology, the influence of PPG 16, which came into force some years before PPG 15, has been profound. Many of the results have been excellent. But some have been questioned, notably by independent archaeologists such as Martin Biddle and Richard Morris, who have deplored the decrease in emphasis on research and the marginalisation of the voluntary sector. Since building recording is not destructive and since the background of recorders is so varied, a similar distinction between professionals and volunteers is unlikely to take place at present, although it is certainly something that should be guarded against in the future. A greater danger for building recording lies in the related issues of research and publication. Despite the fact that there is an ever-increasing number of conferences, the papers of which are frequently published, and many articles are written for specialised journals such as *Vernacular Architecture*, published work tends to be small in scale, and few if any seminal articles have appeared in the last few years. More people than ever before may be finding their livelihood in this field, but with central funding firmly focused on management and conservation, there is a real danger that thinking on the subject will lag behind practice.

One of the problems for the study of vernacular buildings, in marked contrast to buried archaeology, has always been the limited involvement of universities. As Barry Harrison indicates, continuing education has traditionally had a valuable role in helping people to understand their local environment. Meanwhile, David Clark takes up Kate Clark's concerns and shows that it also has a place in training the professionals of other disciplines who are involved with conservation to appreciate the importance of understanding small historic buildings. But while the interest is certainly there, this is a fast-changing field which is having to respond to the reorganisation of the university structure and the rapidly developing requirements of the conservation world, so there is still much to be done.

In full-time university education the subject has been badly neglected. Until recently historic buildings were only studied either as great architecture within art-historical courses or, occasionally, in a structural context, as in the Manchester School. Today, small or vernacular building studies may be taught in schools of archaeology or building conservation – as at Durham, York and Bournemouth. But, as Jane Grenville indicates, there are still very few academics in the field, and some among them are more concerned with practice than with history or theory. Thus the major institutional input into the subject has always been from government, through the Commissions, and what are now English Heritage, Cadw, and Historic Scotland. Not unnaturally, this has meant that the emphasis has been on the practical application of the subject, rather than on developing its intellectual basis. Initially this emphasis meant that the desire to catalogue was disproportionally prominent at the expense of understanding the material. Today it results in a preoccupation with management needs. Conservation, both for individual monuments and whole areas, has become a major issue. This has led the government to introduce the new controls over the management of the historic environment, and the statement that we need to understand what we conserve is becoming a commonplace. We recognise that understanding includes the need to record, and thus for the first time the detailed recording of physical fabric has a practical application and public money may be spent upon it.

This is excellent news, but at the same time it is unfortunate that there is still little money for the overarching research which is an essential element of the process. During the listing resurvey the best listers acquired unrivalled knowledge of the buildings in their region. This included theories about structure, form, function and development. Quite rightly, such knowledge found no place in the lists themselves, but unfortunately it was seldom thought

worth paying extra to capture that knowledge before the listers were swept up in their new lives – as English Heritage inspectors, Commission investigators, conservation officers, or historic building consultants. This is as much a loss to those who manage the buildings of the area as it is to historians or the interested public. Nowadays, thanks to the enlightened policy of thematic listing, the general research which underpins listing is more likely to be published, but publication is still not an inevitable outcome of more detailed recording. The results of the recording of many important small buildings should be published, although they may well not be because the money to pay the recorder to take time off from recording to think, research and write is not forthcoming. This problem has bedevilled dirt archaeology in the past, and there is a danger, in this new world of historic building consultants, that it will prove a stumbling block in this field as well. As a case in point, two contributors to the conference which gave rise to this book were unable to find the time to turn their excellent contributions into publishable papers, and Richard Morriss, who kindly stepped into the breach, finds that as a consultant he has little opportunity to undertake any wide-ranging research (p 72).

Likewise, very little money currently goes towards large-scale research projects on traditional small buildings. The Commissions in Scotland and Wales and the new English Heritage in England are largely occupied with working on other kinds of buildings, and are anyway tending to concentrate their limited funds on quick and practical results. English Heritage supports some relevant research, such as the recent work on historic thatch, and on tree-ring dating softwood. But most government-sponsored research is not concerned with what one may term 'traditional' or vernacular buildings, for they are thought to be better known and in some basic senses better understood than the majority of industrial and institutional buildings. Also, where publicly funded, such research is usually devised with management aims in mind. The 'pure research' which Jane Grenville has termed 'blue skies' research is, if not actually frowned upon, at least not thought to be the business of government (Grenville 1994). Occasionally a major research project undertaken simply to advance knowledge rather than to serve an immediate practical end, attracts other forms of funding. The most notable recent example is the project on cruck construction, funded by the Leverhulme Trust and discussed by Nat Alcock, below, but this is rare indeed. The subject is the poorer for this, for all disciplines need new ideas and new directions, and they are unlikely to come from projects which have conservation as their main aim. It is instructive to think how very much less would be known about the dating of medieval timber buildings if it were not for a number of tree-ring dating programmes which did not have management or conservation as their primary aim, such as the Leverhulme study, the Royal Commissions' work in Kent and in Wales, and

10

projects such as those in Shropshire and Hampshire, which are financed by the heroic fund-raising efforts of private individuals.

However, as Edward Roberts shows, tree-ring dating is not, or should not be, an end in itself. History is not just about looking at individual, or even groups of, documents or buildings and publishing them with a commentary; it is about interpreting the past for the present, and to remain alive it requires publications by high quality thinkers with vision. As Pantin wrote 'it is important to build up a body of generalised knowledge [which] in turn helps us to understand and diagnose individual specimens'. That comment is as applicable today as it was in 1958. In addition we need the new ideas and theories which are likely to come from academics, or at least from those with time to sit and think. In a paper to the Vernacular Architecture Group a few years ago Matthew Johnson asked why it was that no new national synthesis of vernacular building had been published since Eric Mercer's *English Vernacular Houses* of 1975 (Johnson 1997). The answer is perhaps two-fold. In the first place academics in the field are few, and outside the universities no one now will fund the research and writing of such a synthesis. Secondly, the sheer amount of data which it would now be necessary to absorb before writing a ground-breaking synthesis is likely to put off all but the most determined researcher. In the long run this is definitely not good news for the viability and health of the subject.

Is it, in fact possible to separate out 'pure research' in this field? Is it not the case that almost all well-thought-out, serious research is likely to lead to increased understanding, and will therefore inevitably have a management spin-off in the long run? Work on tree-ring dating shows how this can occur, and other, less obviously relevant studies, such as that on textile mills in West Yorkshire (Giles and Goodall 1992), have had a significant effect on management and conservation policy. The greater our general understanding of buildings and their development, the better we will be both at educating others and conserving the heritage in a meaningful way for the future. The historical approach remains an important adjunct to the practical application of recording. In the next century the approach will obviously be different to that taken in the 1950s – the

subject would be the poorer if it were not. Recently, some academics have been calling for more attention to human, social and cultural aspects of vernacular buildings, and this may also include being less insular and learning from what takes place in other lands and cultures. The government's stated aims include making the heritage more accessible to the many. This means not just conserving buildings or opening them to the public, but understanding them and communicating that understanding so that the public come to have a better and more integrated appreciation of what the heritage is and its value to society. This is far more all-embracing than simply managing. Management is a means to an end, not an end in itself.

Conclusion

The picture, therefore, is one of hope and fears. On the one hand, there is generally a greater appreciation of heritage than in the past, not least among the owners and occupiers of historic buildings, while better analysis and recording, undertaken by more people and to higher standards, means that buildings are being understood and conserved far more adequately than previously. But on the other hand the daunting accumulation of information and emphasis on management and conservation has led to a downgrading of the research which is so vital in maintaining those high standards. It is here that the roles of both academics and those who study buildings for love are essential. There is room for, and a role for, everyone, and the sooner this is officially recognised the better.

Acknowledgements

This paper has its origins in work undertaken for RCHME in connection with a book on recording historic buildings which was never completed. I am grateful to my former colleagues, in particular John Bold and Hugh Richmond, for their support and encouragement at that time. More recently the paper has benefited greatly from the constructive comments of Peter Kidson and Bob Meeson.

2 Out of the shunting yards: one academic's approach to the recording of smaller vernacular buildings *by Jane Grenville*

Introduction

The Scottish poet, Norman MacCaig, wrote a rather bleak little poem called 'An Academic' in which he describes an emotionally desiccated figure obsessively measuring the immeasurable and reducing great literature to 'a do-it-yourself kit/ of semantic gestures'. The third stanza reads:

> . . . Trains
> have to reach their destinations.
> But yours, that should be
> clattering and singing
> through villages and landscapes, never
> gets out of the shunting yards.
> (MacCaig 1969, 61)

I was asked to write about new approaches to the recording of vernacular buildings for this volume. This inevitably led to a massive writer's block, for we all know that there is nothing new under the sun, and I can perform no peculiar magic to transform the field. But MacCaig's image of the academic engine stuck in its shunting yard seemed to describe not only my own despair, but also the impasse that building recording appears to have reached. For many years we have been exhorted that what we need 'is not so much better recording as better ideas' (Smith 1989, 20), to 'cook the cake' of our raw data in order to say 'interesting things about the men, women and children who inhabited the houses we study' (Johnson 1997, 13). Yet somehow, with a few honourable exceptions, the train remains stubbornly stuck in the sidings. Syntheses and explicitly theoretical approaches attract criticism from the recording fraternity for being too broad brush in their approach, too little concerned with the detailed evidence of the buildings themselves. Building reports, by contrast, are criticised by the synthesisers for their tendency to add yet more undigested facts to a rising tide of data. This chapter is an attempt to couple the engine of theory demanded by Smith and Johnson with the long train of existing data and recording techniques so that together they may indeed clatter and sing through villages and landscapes.

What follows owes much to my colleagues at the University of York, both in the Department of Archaeology, where a major research interest is the relationship between archaeological fieldwork, theoretical approaches, analysis of data and final synthesis in a comprehensive and credible report, and in the Centre for Medieval Studies, where interdisciplinary work is the norm and the practical problems it raises are constantly reviewed. The archaeologists Kate

Giles, Steve Roskams, Rochelle Rowell, and historians Jeremy Goldberg and Sarah Rees Jones, will all recognise echoes of conversations we have had, while Martin Carver, the Professor of Archaeology at York, has been very generous with his time and particularly with his ideas, which I have borrowed in abundance for this paper. The tables reproduced later are adapted versions of an original idea of his and I am grateful to him for allowing me to steal his intellectual property so shamelessly. Perhaps the greatest debt goes to those students who have had the courage to put the vision into practice and produced the case studies with which I have illustrated the points I wish to make. The projects I discuss are not concerned exclusively with small vernacular buildings – churches, monastic structures and medieval guildhalls will all make an appearance. That in itself is perhaps a matter of interest. Even now, research interests continue to revolve around higher status structures. But my point is that the kind of recording strategies and analytical paths followed are, or at least could be, equally applied to smaller buildings.

Lastly in this introduction, I wish to consider the different constituencies involved in the recording of smaller historic buildings, for they are disparate. What follows in the body of the chapter is, I hope, of central importance to all, but the different intellectual cultures of each group leads, I fear, to a certain mutual suspicion. The first and largest constituency is probably that of the amateur recorders, working on a voluntary basis, often in groups formed at county level or as a result of adult education classes. While it is, of course, dangerous to generalise, it seems that their interest springs initially from an intellectual hunger for local history, archaeology and what in America would be characterised as folk studies. This is intellectual curiosity at its purest, a simple desire to know more about one's historical and topographical context. The work is interesting and wide-ranging and crucially, much, though by no means all, of it is published and fairly widely accessible through the pages of *Vernacular Architecture*, the county archaeological and local history journals and locally-focused monographs. Often empirical and descriptive, it is not used as much as it might be in broader syntheses and some of the research questions posed in this chapter might form suitable starting points for such work.

The second group is that of the professional recorders, those operating within heritage agencies at national and county level or in archaeological units, and those individuals or small firms who have responded commercially to the requirements of PPG

12

15 for the adequate recording of buildings in advance of alterations. Normally working in situations equivalent to rescue or commercial evaluation in subsurface archaeology, the constraints and motivations here are different. Whilst all these people have a genuine and fundamental interest in the past, their immediate preoccupations may be more mundane: an ex-student of mine remarked that although I had spent a year drumming into her that the three most important factors in the design of a recording project were research, research and research, the hard truth out in the commercial world was that they were money, money and time (insofar as it is money). I take the point, but maintain strenuously that the money that society is putting into the recording of buildings (willingly or unwillingly) demands a return in terms of an interesting and demonstrable narrative about the building. Developers and householders genuinely want to know what we have learnt as a result of our researches.

Lastly, there is the tiny group, in which I place myself, of those who are paid to undertake research and who choose the vernacular building stock as the research base. Based mainly in higher education, these few have other more arcane constraints, little understood outside the increasingly bureaucratic world of contemporary academia. Dedicated research funding is available only on a competitive basis from the Arts and Humanities Research Board and projects must have clearly expressed, identifiable and achievable goals which will be of use to the wider research community. Funding is not the only problem: fieldwork opportunities are increasingly squeezed by the constraints of time spent in teaching and administration. So the outlook for major long-term projects is pretty bleak, but it is important to note that the system forces us constantly to reconsider our research input and output. The necessity to do so ensures a continual reevaluation of research aims and agendas. It may well be that this is the new function of academic archaeology: to define and debate research agendas for the use of the wider research community, rather than to carry out that research on a large scale. Time will tell whether this is a sterile navel-gazing exercise or a fruitful means of imposing some intellectual rigour on a drifting empirical project.

The past in the present: contemporary matters and the research agenda

Academics often talk of 'the research agenda', by which is meant the areas of interest that are shared by researchers in a particular area. Bob Meeson (see p 32) alludes to the unfashionableness of research agendas, which perhaps reinforces my point that different constituencies within this broad group of researchers are led by different imperatives. Research agendas, so termed, may be out of favour outside academia but within it, no research agenda

means, quite simply, no research. If one cannot demonstrate a broad question or set of questions that one wishes to answer by undertaking a survey, then one cannot gain financial support or the intellectual backing of one's colleagues. We have to look for the bigger picture. Areas of interest shift from decade to decade, and it has been argued that such shifts reflect only the political, economic and social conditions of the researcher's day. I want to take a few moments to consider this proposition, for it has, in my view, led to some highly questionable intellectual positions.

In vernacular building studies, as Johnson has pointed out (1997, 16), we can use the approaches of earlier writers such as Addy (1898) and Innocent (1916) to identify the preoccupations of the time. Addy, for instance, had a close interest in the cultural affinities between Britain and Germany, a strong relationship in the 19th century, about to be burst asunder in the 20th. Innocent's concerns with craftsmanship and materials are a reaction to the technical developments of his time: 'the old methods of craftsmanship are vanishing with the changed conditions of education and industry, and it is a matter for regret that they cannot be adequately described in writing' (1916, 281).

So how far do wider contemporary social concerns impinge on the research agenda? The first part of Table 2.1, which we use at York to stimulate debate among students regarding the relationship of the present to the study of past, is the result of many classroom conversations. It is endlessly amended and revised. It is easy to see how some issues have translated directly into the academic world – feminist studies, for instance, rose in the humanities in the 1970s and 80s in step with the Women's Movement and the relationship is obvious, as is its modification to 'gender studies' in the 'caring 90s'. Does a current concern in historical research with masculinities reflect the anti-feminist backlash? Not all current economic and political issues impinge so directly upon the choice of research topic, but their influence on the attitudes of the researcher must be acknowledged as Johnson has pointed out: '...this awareness of our own subjectivity is the final element of our loss of innocence: the innocent belief that we can study the past independently of our own world' (1997, 16). The view that the past is capable of independent study is, he avers, 'arrogant'. It is difficult to disagree, although the point is hardly a new one – as long ago as 1961 E H Carr made the case convincingly in his classic textbook of historical method, *What is History?*, and scientists have long been concerned with the 'observer effect' in experiments. Yet it is a view that has recently been taken to its logical extreme with some curious results. A more recent textbook on methodology in history, Keith Jenkins' *Re-thinking History*, takes a post-modern stance and states that 'when we study history we are not studying the past but what historians have constructed about the past. In that sense whether or not the people in the past had the same or different natures to us is not only undecidable but also not at issue. In

Table 2.1   Themes in archaeological research

Contemporary social concerns	Archaeological concerns
Economic systems and fairness Taxation and resource distribution	Is there a factual past?

Nationalism/Devolution/Relations between Britain and
  Europe
Racism
Religion/ideology
Gender issues
Town/countryside divisions
	What provokes change or encourages continuity
	Why are societies and subsets within them different
	  from one another?
	How does material culture enable us to understand
	  economy, social organisation, power, belief?
	Does material culture carry meaning as well as
	  function? How might we interpret this?

Fashion/peer group identity	

Notes
Material culture is a phrase that I shall use repeatedly throughout the rest of this paper – it is entirely familiar to archaeologists, but may not be so widely used in other fields of historical research, including the recording of small buildings. Quite simply it refers to the physical things that a society produces – the objects and buildings that every society surrounds itself with, and which may be functional, or symbolic or both.

that sense the past doesn't enter into it. Our real need is to establish the presuppositions that historians take to the past' (1991, 47). Such a nihilistic and truly arrogant view, that the only subjects worthy of study are ourselves, suggests that we might as well leave our studies there, in the first half of Table 2.1 and abandon all hope of using our evidence to understand the lives of those in the past.

There has, in fact, been much discussion in archaeology over recent years to echo Jenkins' view, and challenge the idea of a factual past. Whether or not the past actually happened has absorbed a good deal of academic archaeological thinking over the last fifteen years or so. This seems to me to be something of a waste of time. For me, there is no doubt that the house in which I am sitting was built and that that event took place at some time in the past. We cannot recapture that event, although we may try to reconstruct it with greater or lesser success. That success depends upon three things: firstly the quality of the evidence of the past event, secondly, the effectiveness with which we frame our questions about the event, and thirdly, to some extent bound up with the previous point, our awareness that our views of the past are mediated by our contemporary condition. Some typical questions asked by archaeologists are suggested in the second part of Table 2.1. What provokes change or encourages continuity? Why are societies and subsets within them different from one another? Are economics the driving force of society? How does material culture enable us to understand economy, social organisation, power, belief? Does material culture carry meaning as well as reflect function? If so, how might we interpret this? Which questions we choose to ask may indeed reflect upon ourselves and our circumstances, but this surely enriches rather than impoverishes the field and we should perhaps not spend too much time ticking one another off for failing to conform to one or other school of thought. What we *do* need to beware of is the collection of data for data's sake. The framing of questions enables us to gather data in a focused and useful way.

To provide convincing answers, such questions must be matched to evidence of sufficient quality. To say that 'there can be no final single "right" or

"wrong" interpretation' (Johnson 1997, 15) is to stretch a point, for while it would indeed be unrealistic to subscribe to any single explanation, there can be no doubt that some interpretations are, quite simply, wrong – that the evidence to support them is absent or too weak to carry the weight of the argument. The way in which we gather data, transform them into evidence and then provide an explanation (a process sometimes undertaken in reverse order) is the subject of the next section.

The archaeological process

Table 2.2 illustrates the intellectual processes of archaeology. We are driven to investigate by the imperative of intellectual curiosity or by the requirements of the conservation process. Something new is discovered, for example, a firehood in an ostensibly mid-18th-century polite farmhouse; or the opportunity arises to revisit some of the medieval townhouses of York last inspected by the RCHME in the 1960s, armed with new research on late medieval urbanism, and new questions about the social use of space to answer; or a listed building is to be altered, and recording in advance of the work is specified. The value of an historic building may be recognised principally by the general public as aesthetic or as adding to a sense of place, and only secondly as a source of information about the past. Nevertheless, there is a fairly widespread eagerness to understand more about buildings and their history, as anyone who has taken a party around an historic town centre and counted the number of 'extras' who tag on to the group can attest. A major discovery or extensive survey can usually generate at least a paragraph and a photograph in a local newspaper and the knowledge gained adds to the value that the local population ascribes to its surroundings. By adding to our knowledge, investigation and explanation may have a direct impact in planning terms – a building becomes listed, for instance. Additionally or alternatively, the work may alter perceptions of the building, or its type, or its setting, or the history of those who have used it, and thus feed back into the loop to

Table 2.2   The archaeological process

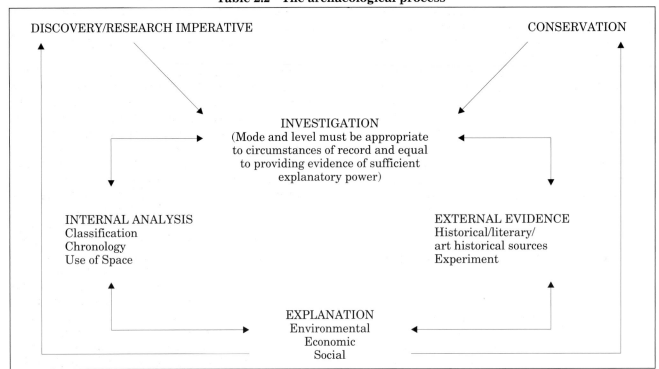

update research agendas and generate new questions. The process of investigation is not, then, an introspective one, for the benefit of a small but dedicated community of enthusiasts, but one which has an impact upon the appearance of towns, villages and landscapes.

Crucially for this argument, the process may be turned on its head and the relationship between explanation and investigation reversed. A researcher, very often one who is operating within my third grouping of interested parties either as a student or a member of staff within an educational establishment, appears with an explanation, a theory requiring proof, a new way of looking at the past that demands some data to test its efficacy. The theory may be drawn from another discipline, and sociology, anthropology, geography and architecture have all figured prominently over the last decade or so, or it may have been generated internally within archaeology or vernacular buildings studies. What is required is a suitable case study against which to test it. The research agenda, then, is clear. The danger, as has been observed by others before, is the temptation to shoehorn the evidence to fit. Rules of evidence are critical here, and the way in which we analyse or draw parallels from other types of data ought not to transgress those rules (see below).

It is in this division between investigation and explanation that a false dichotomy seems to me to have arisen. A theoretical engine chugging comfortably through an intellectual landscape without a train to pull looks pretty redundant to the majority of trainspotters. Yet for the vocal minority, a set of carriages set out for all to see and identify and name and classify holds no dynamic interest in the absence of an intellectual destination and an engine to pull it

there. The criticisms on either side are fair. The issue, the new approach (if it can be said to be new, which I doubt) is to encourage both sides to think of their enterprise as incomplete without the other. Observations require explanation and that may be sought in many ways (see *Explanation* below), but explanations that lack evidence of a load-bearing nature to support them remain ultimately unconvincing. This chapter will now look in turn at each of these four areas of endeavour – investigation and explanation as the two principal operations and the analysis of built fabric and its comparison with other forms of evidence as the tools with which to couple the two.

Investigation

The process of investigation is dictated to a large extent by the mechanism through which it was commissioned. My ex-student's three imperatives of money, money and time spring to mind, for often funds are limited and time is shorter, as occupants not unreasonably require the use of their sitting room or shop or workshop or whatever. The circumstance of the record is important but it should not be the sole determinant of a recording strategy. Beside investigation in Table 2.2, and linked to it in a dynamic loop, is explanation, for how one interprets a structure depends on the quality of information gathered. The clearer one is before one starts about the questions asked, the more appropriate will be the level of data collection. I would argue that most recorders are aware of this consciously or unconsciously. How else do we make those daily decisions about what to leave out of the record? The reason that information about scribing on timber frames has so often been over-looked in the past is not that it was not noticed, but that it was not sufficiently understood to be seen to be significant. Now that it is, it is routinely recorded. Builders may remove sections of stone wall that are critical to our understanding of a structure while we are off-site. Their bewilderment at our dismay is genuine – to them it was, after all, just a stretch of old wall, and not a structurally efficient one at that. It is the questions that we wished to ask of it, the research agenda, the pre-selected areas of investigation that make the destroyed evidence so important. That is not to suggest that we should ignore the element of seren-dipity so often present in recording; it would be foolish to see a research agenda as a straitjacket that rules out of court the chance or inexplicable discovery, but the reflexive relationship between data and explana-tion should always be maintained quite explicitly in the researcher's mind.

Case study: the church of St Helen, Skipwith, Yorkshire

In a field project undertaken for the MA in the Archaeology of Buildings at York, Richard Peats undertook to reconstruct the interior appearance in the 15th century of the parish church of St Helen at Skipwith, just south of York (Peats 1998 and forth-coming). The church is well-known for its Anglo-Saxon tower and its chancel of *c*1300, declared by Pevsner to be 'one of the most noble . . . of the East Riding' (Pevsner and Neave 1995, 687–9). Peats' interest was not so much in the architectural history of the church as in the understanding of the use of the interior as a space for worship and ritual within the liturgy of the pre-Reformation Catholic church in England. His recording methods were tailored to suit. He produced a plan of the church, analysed and phased it in the traditional way and then turned his attention to specific evidence for former structures, now removed. Rather than drawing entire elevations stone-by-stone, their outlines were produced using a combination of photographic techniques and theodo-lite survey. They were drawn up in AutoCAD, with the results stored digitally by the computer for repro-duction at whatever scale and projection might be required. Within these, where evidence for earlier structures remained as blocking or refacing, detailed stone-by-stone surveys were undertaken by hand and the information digitised and added to outline elevations. These were then elided to provide a three-dimensional model of the church, and the evidence of one elevation matched with those adjoining or oppo-site to allow a convincing reconstruction of the position of the rood screen, the partitions to the chantry chapels and a possible altar beam in one of the side chapels. Alterations undertaken in the me-dieval period were identified (for instance, it was possible to see that the position of the altar beam had been changed) and a three-dimensional reconstruc-tion of the interior of the church was produced,

looking from various different angles within the building. The impressive results were clearly pre-sented (see Figs 2.1, 2.2) so that on the strength of the drawings alone, alternative explanations could be proffered.

The project triumphantly showed that a combina-tion of outline and detailed recording, when coupled with a fearless use of the computer to provide the tools for reconstruction, can deliver a real insight not only into the way in which a building has developed, but also into the ways in which it was used and how it appeared to those who used it. Recording strategies were pitched to answer those specific questions, and appropriate computer draughting was used to further the understanding of the results. There is plenty more, of course, that we could ask of Skipwith church, and the potential for further study remains. But within the time- and budget-limited constraints of a summer research project, excellent results were achieved. The lessons learnt are transferable to the study of small vernacular buildings. For instance, if one were interested in the changes to internal domestic space and its use, one could record in detail all evidence for early fireplace positions and removed partitions, leaving other features such as the origi-nal timber frame or mass construction wall recorded in plan only. The plan should be sufficiently accurate to allow others, more interested in the initial con-struction of the building, to return to add the necessary detail, but for the purposes of the ques-tions asked, detailed recording could be limited to immediately relevant features. One does not have to record everything within a building to the same level of resolution, but one does have to know *why* one is recording at any particular level.

Explanation

It is the aim of research to uncover new facts, new material, new observations and *explain* them (Phil-lips and Pugh 2000), and it is the act of explanation that raises research above mere data-gathering. So while it may be interesting to know, for example, the dates of all the early aisled halls in England, it is far more interesting to attempt to explain their form, distribution and chronology. In order to explain we must generalise, test our generalisations against further evidence, refine them and present them. While there are many schools of thought regarding the most appropriate overarching theory into which explanation may be fitted (and most of them end in -ism) it seems to me that there are three major areas into which they may be classified: explanations which ultimately depend upon environmental factors, those which see economics as the prime mover, and those which take social imperatives as the mainspring.

Environmental explanations were central to the thinking of prehistorians who developed what is known as Systems Theory in the 1960s and 70s. Soci-eties and economic systems were seen as complex

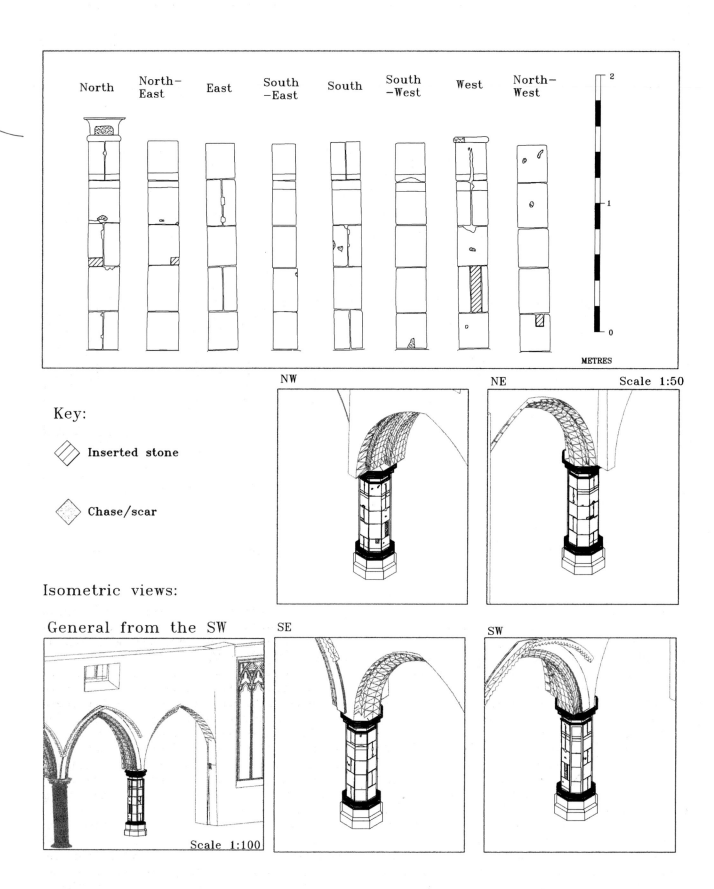

Figure 2.1   St Helen's church, Skipwith: the north-east column: hand recording added to AutoCAD 3-D model (Drawn by Richard Peats)

Figure 2.2   St Helen's church, Skipwith: reconstruction of the nave and chancel based on detailed recording (Drawn by Richard Peats)

interlinked equilibria, where changes in one area must necessarily lead to adjustments in another, but wholesale change was explained only by factors external to the system, namely climate and its effect on the availability of resources. Many explanations of the disastrous events of the 14th century in Europe rest on such environmental explanations, with worsening weather and poor harvests blamed for famine conditions and a weakened population, and the numerous epidemics of which the Black Death was but the worst. Environmental explanations find their way into the study of historic buildings in providing reasons for the choice of materials, design, roof pitch and so forth. There can be no doubt that an understanding of how buildings stand up and how they combat the climatic conditions of the areas in which they stand, is crucial to an overall comprehension. The criticism of environmental explanation is that external factors can present constraints for builders, but they rarely impose a single solution as we can easily observe by noting different house types and construction within the same community. Sometimes environmental explanations are totally com-

pelling – there can be no other reason for the end of Pompeii, for instance – but what they do not tell us is why people lived (and indeed continue to live) on the slopes of live volcanoes.

Economic reasons may bring us nearer to the truth here. If the administration of resources might be seen to lie at the heart of individual and collective action then certainly archaeology and vernacular buildings studies, as the investigation of physical remains, lend themselves to the analysis of material conditions. In a world where house prices and mortgages form a major preoccupation of a large part of the population it is easy to see how an understanding of housing as principally a manifestation of an economic system might predominate. Such a theoretical stance may take a relatively simplistic view – that the perceived quality of housing reflects the economic status of its occupants: castles for the rich and hovels for the poor. Or it might lead the researcher to a more complicated and intricate argument about changing economic conditions over a long period of time, and the relationship of the housing stock to wealth, as for instance in Currie's classic discussion of rates of attrition in vernacular housing (Currie 1988). Economic constraints may well be among the reasons for occupying marginal zones, such as the slopes of volcanoes or inhospitable uplands, but there are those who find such explanations ultimately unsatisfactory since economics, the conscious organisation of material resources, may be seen as a specifically human and cultural phenomenon.

There is an argument that economic systems are merely subsets of social systems and that ultimately all explanation of human behaviour must rest in the social world, the world created by human invention, the perceived environment. 'Human beings, in contrast to other social animals, do not just live in society, they produce society in order to live' (Godelier 1986, 1). Not only do we produce society: we create societies in boundless variation. How we understand those societies and how we understand material culture and social structure in the light of one another has been a central question in archaeology almost since the birth of the discipline. Within the study of buildings, questions of ethnic identity, nationality, craft competence, family and household relationships and power relationships more generally have all demanded attention and continue to do so. In this mode of explanation, social variation holds the key, if only we could understand it. Furthermore, in much recent work, material culture has been understood not only to reflect social structures and norms of behaviour, but also actively to *structure* them – things and buildings play an active part in maintaining or overthrowing rules and accepted behaviour. For instance, Johnson (1993) has argued that the closure of open halls at the end of the medieval period not only reflected but actively hastened and reinforced social change through the physical as well as social separation of masters and servants. Such an explanation contrasts interestingly with that of Hall (1983, 99–100) who sees rebuilding and the closure of halls in 17th-century south Gloucestershire as a clear response to changing agricultural markets and their fluctuating profits.

These, then, are the three main areas within which I would identify most modes of explanation. Rarely are they mutually exclusive, although often one reads polemics which suggest that they are, with environmental and economic stances being accused of determinism and social explanation being seen as ultimately relative and unprovable. Coupling the engine of explanation to the carriages of data depends on the efficacy of coupling hooks, the methods which we use to translate data into explanation. These take two distinct forms – the analysis of the buildings themselves, which I have referred to as 'internal analysis' and the use of material from related fields, which I call 'external evidence'. Their success depends upon the rigour with which they are applied, the quality of the data and whether they can stand up to the rigorous analysis and the robustness of the explanation provided. It follows that data collection, analysis and explanation are interdependent, not independent, functions.

Internal analysis

How are facts and observations about a building turned into evidence, into planks in an argument about the past? Much intellectual endeavour, whether academic or not, is spent in trying to 'make sense' of things and the first thing we do in the tradition of western Enlightenment thinking is try to classify and to generalise. We have a certain set of implicit intellectual rules about this: like must be classified with like, as much to draw out contrasts as similarities, and the classes themselves must be compatible. So for buildings, we classify fabric, plan form, constructional techniques, architectural style, symbols and so forth. Chronology often acts as a starting point for analysis and in archaeological thinking, the constructional details provide the key here. A thorough understanding of building techniques in both timber and mass wall construction allow us to carry out the equivalent of a stratigraphic analysis in excavation. If we can identify the primary and secondary events (major construction phases and minor alterations), we can isolate at least a relative chronology. Stylistic and typological details can help us to provide approximate dates by analogy with other buildings of known date that display the same features. There is an interesting issue raised here by Meeson in this volume in relation to Handsacre Hall, an aisled hall in the Midlands, which has delivered a late-12th-century tree-ring date for the curved tenon braces. This is regarded by many as an implausible date – it is simply too early for this technology. If we are looking for 'new' approaches, I would argue that in this area there is a good deal to be done. Ian Tyers' work on checking stylistic typologies against newly derived dendrochronological dates is an admirable start and his results make interesting reading, as much for the wide coincidence between the two methods as for the more dramatic instances, such as Little Sompting and Greenstead-juxta-Ongar, where the tree-ring date is significantly removed from the earlier estimate (Pearson 1997, 32–3). But we should remember that dates are simply a framework, an essential tool in the business of writing history – without them we cannot establish causality, progression, development. If we take them as ends in themselves, then we are reduced to a train-spotter mentality and the debate about who has the earliest aisled hall is, as Meeson points out, desperate and sterile. But the possibility that there is an early use of tenoned joints in the context of Handsacre should require us to reconsider our evidence for craft transmission and the development of competences and to look at those things in the context of other evidence, not least the well-preserved timbers from the London waterfront excavations. Our battery of new approaches should include a willingness to confront uncomfortable and difficult evidence and assess it with an open mind, even if that forces us to rethink long-accepted theories of the development of construction. This is not the first time that the advent of an absolute dating system has ruffled feathers in the archaeological pigeon loft: the celebrated Australian archaeologist Gordon Childe felt that the advent of radiocarbon dating invalidated much of his pre-war work, and the first radiocarbon dates have themselves been revised in the light of calibration against dendrochronological dates.

The importance of chronology, both absolute and relative, lays a particular duty on the recorder to observe and understand the constructional details of the building and to interpret its sequence closely. How this is achieved has been the subject of one of the most vigorous of methodological debates in the field, namely whether or not it is appropriate to apply stratigraphic analysis, as developed in field archaeology, to the interpretation of buildings. In a paper in *Vernacular Architecture*, Ferris (1989) suggested that a stratigraphic approach should enable a more methodical, thorough and less subjective approach to building recording. He did not, as he has been characterised, offer the opinion that the analysis of buildings may (or, indeed, should) proceed in the absence of any critical judgement. Much of the subsequent argument (Meeson 1989, Smith 1989, Wrathmell 1990, Ferris 1991) centred around either specific methodological points or broader matters of interpretation. I argue that stratigraphic analysis is a useful tool, but that like all tools, it is most effective when used appropriately. A careful and abstract approach to the sequencing of buildings, rather than one which relies upon discursive observations and notes, may indeed enable us more effectively to identify the phases in the history of a building. But such phasing should not be seen as an end in itself – it should be specified where research aims demand (and time and money allow) the answering of specific and detailed questions about the building, its use and its comparanda which depend upon a close chronology of its origins and alterations. Stratigraphic analysis may be a new (or perhaps now not-so-new) approach, yet it is not the universal panacea that archaeologists in the 1980s might have hoped. But its effectiveness, when carefully deployed in the pursuit of accurate relative chronology, is undeniable.

Case study: Stoneleigh Abbey

Rochelle Rowell, faced with the task of unpicking the chronology of the gatehouse at Stoneleigh Abbey, Warwickshire, as part of her doctoral studies on monastic hospitality, found that a strict stratigraphical approach was the only reliable way to unfold the complexities of this multi-phase stone building (see Figs 2.3, 2.4). Identified in the Victoria County History as 17th-century, and by Pevsner and Wedgwood (1966, 408) as partly 14th-century but otherwise Elizabethan, the building is in fact almost entirely medieval with some later alterations to windows and doors. By identifying building breaks, cuts and fills, and by characterising different sections of masonry and providing all these features

with stratigraphic numbers, Rowell has been able to take a logical and thorough approach to the building, identifying phases and linking different areas of the structure together within them. Anomalies arose which had to be resolved, among them the difficulty in assigning a date to the east gable wall – the realisation that this was the *earliest* structure on the site, dating probably from the 1270s, provided the key to the understanding of the rest of the building as 14th century, while stratigraphic analysis of the west end confirmed that the later structure was the result of two building campaigns. Such analysis is a means of imposing rigour and logic on the business of sorting out a three-dimensional puzzle of which several pieces may be missing. It is applicable to mass wall structures both large and small and may be used most fruitfully in the investigation of complicated, much-altered, multi-phase buildings, a description which would fit many a smaller vernacular farmhouse. Whitehough, near Leek, visited by the Vernacular Architecture Group during its spring conference in Staffordshire and Cheshire in 2000, represents one such building, which is difficult to understand by eye alone (see Fig 2.5).

One mode of analysis which demands a really close understanding of chronology is that of the use of space. Buildings are a highly sophisticated manipulation of three-dimensional space and an analysis of the disposition of that space can greatly enhance the researcher's understanding of the building and the way in which it is used. There are many forms of spatial analysis, although the term has become almost synonymous with one particular technique, that of justified access analysis, or gamma analysis, as developed in the 1970s at the Bartlett School of Architecture by Bill Hillier and Julienne Hanson in connection with contemporary design (Hillier and Hanson 1984). Put very briefly, access analysis redraws the floor plan of a building to reflect not the spatial layout of rooms, their relative positions and sizes, but rather an abstract conception of the means of access through a building. This results in a diagram that bears no physical relation to the building at all, but rather consists of a series of circles (representing rooms) and lines (representing access to them, normally in the form of doorways) that tell us something about access patterns, which may then be interpreted to suggest the openness or exclusiveness of a given plan. This in itself does not offer a simple reflection of social practice but it provides an alternative means of enhancing our understanding of buildings and how they were used. Other types of spatial analysis include Frank Brown's (1990) morphological approach to plan analysis which explores the variations in room disposition and the factors of size, access, aspect and location that constrain the final choice, or the structuralist division of space into representations of binary opposites so favoured by prehistorians and ethnographers (Bourdieu 1973, Waterson 1997, Hingley 1990). Even a fairly unsophisticated exercise such as tabulating the relative sizes and length–width ratios of open halls can

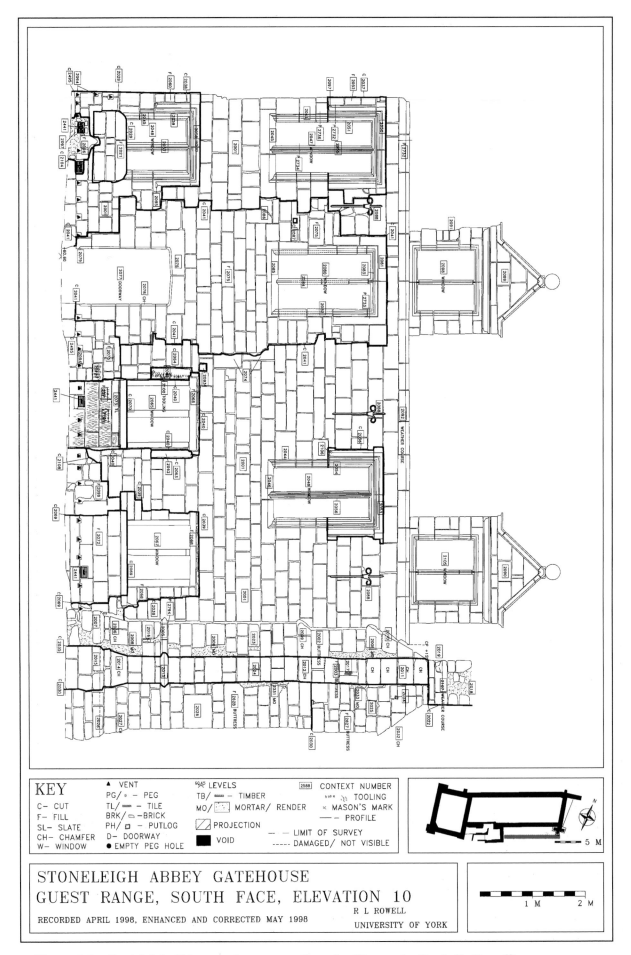

KEY

▲ VENT
PG/ ◦ – PEG
C– CUT   TL/ ▦ – TILE
F– FILL   BRK/ ▱ –BRICK
SL– SLATE   PH/ ▫ – PUTLOG
CH– CHAMFER   D– DOORWAY
W– WINDOW   ● EMPTY PEG HOLE

⁵⁰⁴⁵ LEVELS
TB/ ▬ – TIMBER
MO/ ▤ – MORTAR/ RENDER
▨ PROJECTION
■ VOID

2588   CONTEXT NUMBER
〰 TOOLING
✕ MASON'S MARK
— – PROFILE
— LIMIT OF SURVEY
----- DAMAGED/ NOT VISIBLE

5 M

STONELEIGH ABBEY GATEHOUSE
GUEST RANGE, SOUTH FACE, ELEVATION 10

R L ROWELL
UNIVERSITY OF YORK

RECORDED APRIL 1998, ENHANCED AND CORRECTED MAY 1998

1 M   2 M

Figure 2.3   Stoneleigh Abbey gatehouse: stratigraphy (Drawn by Rochelle Rowell)

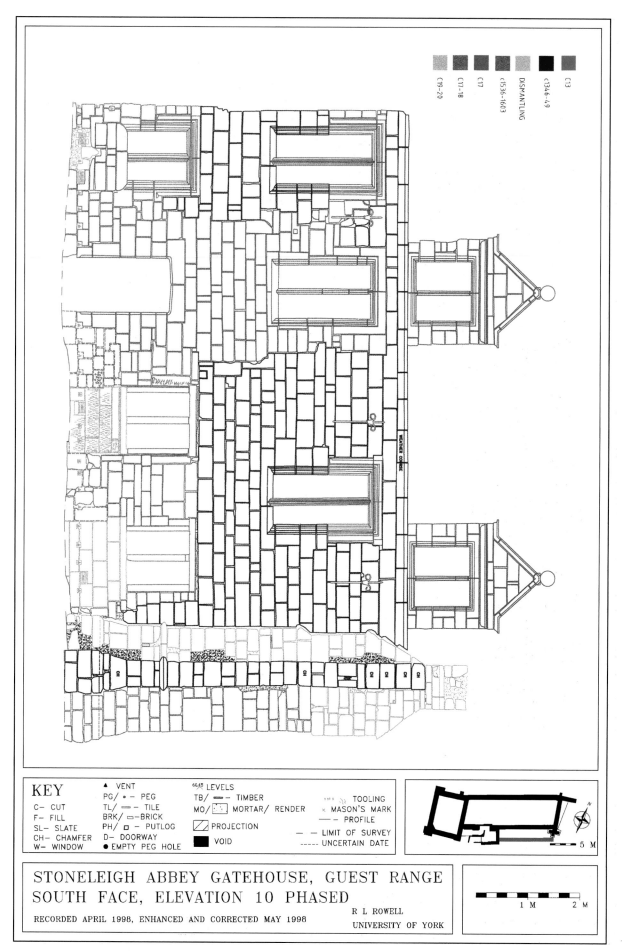

Figure 2.4   Stoneleigh Abbey gatehouse: interpretation (Drawn by Rochelle Rowell)

Figure 2.5   Whitehough, Leek, Staffordshire

produce some surprising results (Grenville 1997, 106–10). Amos Rapoport has provided some useful conceptual frameworks for considering space as systems of settings containing systems of activities (Rapoport 1990). All of these methods are just that – methods of analysis, tools to aid explanation, and not explanation in themselves. Which to choose may well depend upon the types of questions that are framed in the search for explanation, or, as in the case of my own work on halls, an idle experiment may yield unexpected patterns which demand explanation. Again, as with classification and chronology, the effectiveness of this type of analysis in aiding explanation depends upon the robustness of the evidence to which it is applied, the accuracy with which it is implemented and its appropriateness to the problem addressed.

Case studies: Bowes Morrell House and 7 Shambles, York

An example of an interesting attempt to apply formal spatial analysis to a small vernacular building is Nicolette Froud's study of Bowes Morrell House (111 Walmgate), York, a 15th-century house close to Walmgate Bar, one of the main city gates (Froud 1995, Grenville 2000). The building is L-shaped, with a single-bay hall parallel to the street, a range containing a shop running at right angles to it, and a

three-bay range behind. Through the careful recording of all the evidence within the timber frame (including empty mortises, nails, subsequent cuts for doorways and paint traces), the work demonstrated successive phases of subdivision of the ground floor of the building. Absolute dates for these changes could not be assigned, in the absence of datable features or newly introduced timbers, but the relative sequence was established with a reasonable degree of confidence. The changes were then mapped as access diagrams which highlighted the fact that the shop, originally an integral part of the complex, had been isolated in the first phase of alterations, and that gradually the hall and cross wing had been subdivided to provide ever smaller separate spaces. This process of enclosure had taken place over a total of six phases of alteration, and had not been a simple progression – walls were removed as well as inserted (see Fig 2.6). The investigation demonstrated the flexibility of the timber-framed building, and the use of access analysis demanded a rigorous approach to the observation of evidence for internal change. Without it, I suspect, a vaguer statement about the 'closure' of the building might have been made and the focus of the work would have been fuzzier.

Another type of formal analysis of structures is concerned with the relationships suggested by carpentry techniques. This is an area that has been considered by Richard Harris in his influential 1989 article on the grammar of carpentry. Here he identified four

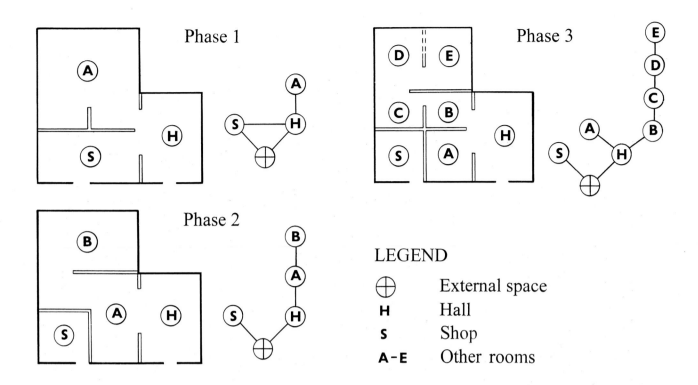

Figure 2.6   Bowes Morrell House, Walmgate, York: phase plans and access (After Nicolette Froud)

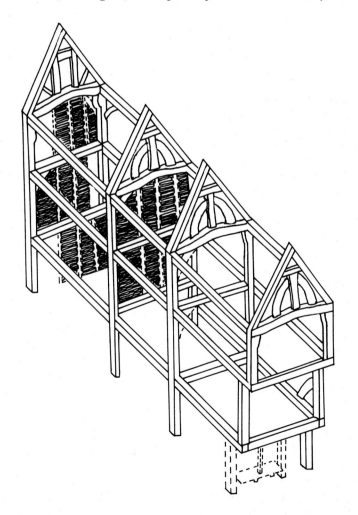

Figure 2.7   7 Shambles, York: the timber frame (After Rosemary Hayden)

major aspects of English medieval carpentry which seem to be ubiquitous, but which do not present obvious functional explanations:

1) the use of the tiebeam lap-dovetail joint
2) the bay system as it relates to plan and structure
3) the rules governing the position of the upper face
4) the rules governing the conversion of trees to frames

He suggested that the reasons for these rules were cultural rather than functionally practical and likened their use to a linguistic grammar, arguing that 'building and language are comparable in that they are both cultural activities devoted to a practical end. They have to satisfy practical demands, but these demands do not themselves define the end result. The culture does that.' (Harris 1989,1). This idea, that a cultural meaning may be embedded within the construction technique of a building, was pursued by Rosemary Hayden in her investigation of 7 Shambles (1995), a 15th-century shop and house, probably belonging to one of the butchers who dominated the narrow city centre street (see Fig 2.7). Here a careful observation of former internal subdivisions, combined with access analysis and recording of the structure of the external walls suggests that circulation patterns around the building were cued by the orientation of the braces (triangular strengthening timbers between the main posts and beams) in the side walls. On the ground and uppermost floor, the braces faced to the south-west, but on the middle floor they pointed north-east. This corresponded with the lines of access through the house, which were deliberately set to run along alternate sides of the building. Furthermore, two different types of roof structure (crown posts at the front and queen posts to the rear) were recorded, but detailed observation of the building sequence showed clearly that these were contemporary. Both would have been visible within the rooms they spanned, and the two rooms were not interconnected. The crown posts would also have been visible from the street to those looking into the building. Access patterns suggest that the rear room was a lower status sleeping area. Both roof truss types function equally efficiently, so what seems clear here is that their meaning differed. Crown posts indicate the high status of the front room which was relatively inaccessible, yet highly visible. This may not be so much a case of the desire for privacy on the part of the owner, as a wish to be *seen* to be exclusive.

External evidence

The tools of explanation are not limited to internal analysis alone. We may look at the associated evidence of other disciplines working with other types of evidence and we may use our own contemporary observations by setting up experiments that attempt to reproduce the actions, if not the thoughts, of our subjects. To take the analogy of a criminal investigation, the internal analysis of the evidence could be likened to the investigation of material by the Scene of Crime Officer and by forensic specialists, while the interdisciplinary work is equivalent to the taking of statements from witnesses, with all the implications for extracting bias, self-interest and forgetfulness that the police have to take into account. In this analogy, experimentation is the equivalent of the reconstruction of the crime, set up to jog memories, or in the case of archaeology, to highlight practical aspects that might otherwise be overlooked. Thus the work of Harris and others in dismantling and reerecting timber-framed buildings has much to tell us about the constraints and possibilities of medieval carpentry, but interestingly has led to some less functional insights about the way in which craftsmen transmitted meaning through their work (Harris 1994).

The use of historical, literary or art historical sources has a long pedigree in the study of smaller historical buildings. Likewise, archaeological evidence has been taken by scholars in other fields to illustrate their arguments. Archaeologists, over the last twenty years, have expressed reservations not only over the way in which evidence from different disciplines has been used in conjunction, but also over their perception that the impetus for the research agenda has come from the historians, that archaeology is seen as the 'handmaid' of history and that it is time for archaeologists to strike out and establish their own agendas in response to the particular strengths of the material record (Rahtz 1980; Gilchrist 1993, 8–15; Austin 1990). Such work has led to a healthy reassessment of the contribution of the discipline of archaeology, particularly its role in generating explanation.

Case study: medieval guildhalls

Kate Giles' work (1999a and b, and forthcoming) on the medieval guildhalls of York and their postmedieval transformations has provided an excellent example of an integrated, truly interdisciplinary approach. Recorders of vernacular buildings can scarcely be accused of being unfamiliar with the written sources: the use of wills and probate inventories, hearth tax returns, estate records and maps, enclosure acts and their associated maps, tithe material, building contracts and independent surveys (Part VIIIA of the successive volumes of the Vernacular Architecture Group's *A Bibliography of Vernacular Architecture* has always been 'Documentary sources and approaches'). The novelty of Giles' approach lies in her determination not to be content with the view that documentary sources and buildings illustrate one another in a straightforward fashion. Rather than describing buildings and understanding them more fully through recourse to the documentation, she sees both forms of evidence as keys to the understanding of social change insofar as 'medieval and early modern people *represented themselves* through texts and artefacts' (Giles 1999b, 87, my italics). Her theoretical position, based on the work of sociologists Pierre Bourdieu and Anthony Giddens, is that societies operate by certain rules which are transmitted from generation to generation, but which may change, either as the result of deliberate rebellion or subversion, or, more subtly, through the accumulation of minor changes to social practice that occur when individuals react in a way that shows that they understand what is required of them (they are, to use the jargon 'knowledgable agents') and are able (or not!) to manipulate the situation to achieve their ends. Place, familiar and unfamiliar, has an important role to play here. Suppose we wish, for whatever reason, another person or social group to change their behaviour. We may challenge them in unfamiliar and intimidating surroundings and achieve our aim by coercion. Or we may deliberately choose to persuade them gently, setting them at ease in a situation that is familiar and reassuring to them. Either way, buildings and spaces within them are playing an active role in building the social situation – they are not simply a stage on which unrelated social actions are played out, but are either carefully chosen and manipulated or exercise an unconscious influence on behaviour. This is the essence of Giles' argument about the way in which guildhalls were used from the 15th to the 17th centuries. The building now known as the Merchant Adventurers' Hall was built between 1357 and 1369 by the religious fraternity of Our Lord Jesus Christ and the Blessed Virgin Mary, and known as Trinity Hall. The fraternity's function was religious and social, operating in varying degrees as a burial club, paying for the funerals of and saying masses for the souls of its deceased members (a crucial function in a society whose religious sensibilities were dominated by a belief in purgatory), and as a hospital, at once performing good works and providing a supply of paupers whose prayers were extra efficacious in the speeding of souls through purgatory. In addition, the fraternity acted as a social and political network – the fraternity feast had practical political as well as paraliturgical functions (Giles 1999b, 92). A change occurred in the following century: the fraternity of Our Lord Jesus Christ and the Blessed Virgin Mary seems to have coexisted in Trinity Hall with the craft guild of the mercers. Granted, the personnel may have been much the same, but the aims and organisation of the two associations differed. So did the craft guild impose its new identity on the guildhall? Far from it – in an apparently deliberate attempt to maintain authority by associating with the older organisation in its original and unchanged space, the craft guild used a familiar and understood past to legitimise its position as a political power in the city. It was not until the Reformation, and even then, probably not for a generation afterwards, that the physical appearance of the guildhall began to change. Initially relying on a sense of continuity with the past, the craft guilds (still in existence long after

the abolition of the religious fraternities and the denunciation of the concept of purgatory) retained the guildhalls in their medieval form. Towards the end of the 16th century, however, changes were made. Among the most significant, in Giles' view, was a 'shift in emphasis from the interior open spaces of the guildhall itself to the exterior facades of the buildings and the way in which these were seen by York's citizens'. New wings were added and with them came classical architectural motifs and decorative bargeboards. In the 17th century, one of the guildhalls (St Anthony's) was entirely encased in brick. Giles suggests that this is connected to a change in perception from a medieval mindset, in which the bodily experience of space was paramount, to an emphasis on the eye and the gaze. She suggests that this may be connected with 'the cultural, ideological and political movements of the 16th and 17th centuries in which emphasis was placed on the external expression of the inward self' (Giles 1999b, 97). Other changes included the subdivision of the open halls, now used for secular functions, for smaller meetings of governing bodies and for storage of goods. The hospitals, while continuing in use, were now split from the halls in terms of access, and the documentary sources are clear about their function as a place of last resort for the *deserving* poor, and not for any indigent. The buildings remained, and remained recognisable, harking back to the past to reinforce the ancient authority of the guilds that occupied them, but they changed, and those changes both reflected and powered changes in social organisation and political influence within the city and in English society more widely.

Giles' work has depended on a very close reading of both buildings and texts, and on a willingness to use the two not simply to illustrate or explain each other, but rather to ask broad questions about the way in which societies transform themselves and the role of built space within those transformations. Such work demands a good knowledge of contemporary historical research and the differences of opinion amongst historians (Evans 1997). To dig deeper than the simple illustrative and descriptive potential of both written sources and material culture may demand a familiarity with some of the more arcane theoretical research in history, sociology, anthropology and human geography; but I suspect that a really good theoretical position is characterised by its simplicity and elegance, and that it is therefore possible to accept ideas about material culture as an active agent in social affairs, rather than simply a passive reflection of them, without necessarily embracing the jargon that such theory has generated, and which is so alienating to many with an interest in vernacular architecture. Using the records we make of vernacular houses to help us to understand wider social change is essential as Harrison noted in his review of Johnson's (1993) pioneering attempt to do just this (Harrison 1994). I am not sure that the message has yet penetrated, and until it does, we must continue to call for the integration of buildings, landscape studies and written sources to extract social meaning from the evidence of the past.

One attempt to do this is currently being developed in the Centre for Medieval Studies at the University of York. Within the Centre, postgraduates learn the basic rules of each discipline and are encouraged to look across disciplinary boundaries in their search for explanation, by means of team-taught interdisciplinary seminars. Such work inevitably has led the teaching staff to consider the resonances within their own fields of research on medieval townhouses, on the household as a literary device and historical unit, on the development of civic structures in the later Middle Ages, and so forth. We have created the Urban Household Project 1350–1550 to provide a forum for discussion and find that as a group, rather than trying to answer one another's questions directly, we are modifying and recasting them. One colleague, a historian who studies the living and working conditions of single women in the 15th century, asked me 'What kinds of houses did single women live in?' and I had to reply that this was a question beyond the scope of archaeological investigation. But if we modify that to the question that another historian posed, namely 'Is there evidence from the archaeological study of the townhouses of medieval York to suggest that segregation of servants began in the later 15th century?' then we may be able to get somewhere, and by extension of the question (since many servants were single women), we may be able to place some of our spinsters within larger households. But, as with Giles' and Johnson's work, the aim is more than the simple illustration of hypotheses developed within the discipline of history. Rather, by introducing the theoretical postulates concerning the social use of physical space, we hope to modify and qualify historical approaches. The interdisciplinary group as a whole is concerned to gain a fuller understanding, based on both written and material evidence, of living and working conditions in the medieval city, and that understanding derives as much from the dissonances between our categories of evidence as from the coincidences. After all, what people do and what they say can be very different, and understanding motives often depends upon understanding that disjunction.

Conclusion

In this chapter I have sought not so much to break new ground, as to try to couple up recent advances in approaches to and techniques of recording buildings (the train of MacCaig's poem) with the change in the type of questions that are being asked of the material past (the engine of theory). In neither field have I broken new ground, but I hope that the recorders of small buildings will have gained something from the juxtaposition of these thoughts. I advocate targeted recording, using the computer as a tool for interpretation rather than simply as a glamorous method of displaying results. Furthermore, I argue that the use of stratigraphic analysis is not everywhere necessary or appropriate, but that we should recognise the circumstances in which it *is* helpful and use it to its fullest to tease out the relative chronologies of the buildings we record. Doing so, of course, has implications for the way in which we record. Furthermore, if we achieve sufficient resolution in relative dating, we may be able to embark upon a detailed analysis of the changing use of space within the structure over the period of its use. But one way or another, these all represent technical advances – they are the carriages of the train. It is the questions we ask that will make it rattle and sing through the fields of knowledge and research. I have outlined some thoughts about the nature of buildings as bearers of social meaning because that is where my own interest lies. There are other approaches and equally useful ways of looking at them – as economic indicators, as aesthetic achievements, as feats of engineering and human ingenuity. I look forward to replies to this paper which present further case studies to illustrate such approaches. Finally, I hope that it will be clear that in my view, it matters little at which end of the train one begins in any particular investigation – what is crucial is that the whole process is engaged with and that investigation and explanation are never decoupled.

3 Recording for research and for conservation
by *Bob Meeson*

This paper reviews the use that is made and can be made of established approaches to the investigation of small traditional buildings in two very different arenas. Firstly, far from being a worked-out seam, vernacular architecture has only recently begun to yield its full potential as a subject worthy of detailed research. A full understanding of small buildings calls upon a range of historical and archaeological interpretative skills; as analytical processes are refined the full potential of the information that they can impart is only now becoming apparent. From a purely academic standpoint, as more rigorous analysis has demonstrated how much more may be learnt through detailed recording, many buildings that have been examined before might now be due for reappraisal. Secondly, the growing appreciation of the latent resource of small traditional buildings has practical applications for their conservation. If the special character and significance of small historic buildings can be more fully understood through detailed analysis, this has implications, both for the level of information required to plan works before they start, and to ensure that information is not lost when they do. Through practical building conservation with adequate understanding both of the general background and of the particular subject, the continuing tide of attrition of vernacular architecture may be reduced to a trickle. Such considerations condition the shape of this paper.

Few people doubt the *value* of buildings like Wells or Lichfield Cathedrals; their architectural and historical significance, their usefulness and interest to both the immediate and wider community have long been understood. But the smaller buildings lying in the shadows of their spires are equally important elements of our cultural heritage, as are those that line the streets of the medieval 'new towns' outside the closes. Beyond these again, in small towns and villages and scattered across the open countryside, are the mills and manor houses, cottages and cow sheds which make up the bulk of our traditional built environment. Vernacular buildings are integral to the character of the country because of their architectural variety, reflecting regional and local patterns of geology, economy and social history. Collectively, vernacular buildings are the antithesis of uniformity, employing a range of different materials, structures and plan-forms. Small buildings are also a record of the social evolution or working lives of the people who used them. Often their interiors offer richer rewards than outward signs suggest, containing historic fixtures and fittings, or unsuspected remnants of earlier structures. Every small building that contributes to this diverse cultural resource must at the same time continue to serve a useful function in order to survive, though that might simultaneously constitute a threat to its historic and architectural integrity.

Vernacular buildings can be seen both as an essential component of the architectural landscape and as a resource for scholars, and while there is clearly a coincidence of interests, equally there is a dichotomy between recording for research and recording for conservation. The primary objective of the scholar is to study buildings for their intrinsic academic interest and to enhance general understanding of the subject, whereas the contractor might undertake recording to aid the design process or resolve conservation issues, and that is why this paper falls into two parts.

The best independent research is based upon a distinctive group of buildings, either because they belong to a discrete geographical area, or because they conform to a particular structural type or period (Alcock, p 98–9). Through a process of comparative analysis of a large body of data, broad conclusions can be drawn concerning that particular group. Buildings recorded for planning purposes by individual contractors are too diverse to enable a select body of comparable data to be analysed sensibly. The contractor who decides to record only aisled hall houses will soon go out of business, but the independent scholar might fruitfully spend a decade comparing them. Even so, those with the freedom to indulge in research provide the essential comparators against which the characteristics and value of individual buildings can be measured.

Understanding small traditional buildings

First then, what are the established approaches to the study of vernacular architecture, and how are they changing? Since the late 1950s, the study of small traditional buildings has blossomed into a discrete area of research, employing methodologies derived from such related disciplines as local history, architectural history and archaeology. The growing body of information has proved useful to a wide range of specialists including geographers and local and economic historians, and also increasingly to householders and other owners, architects, surveyors and planners. The bibliographies published by the Vernacular Architecture Group now contain thousands of references to published books and articles on the subject; these range in scope from national, regional and local studies to papers on individual buildings. They cover such diverse aspects as plan-form, construction and materials, employing both the buildings and documentary sources as evidence. Though most such studies have been undertaken in a spirit of curiosity about the past, many must now be recognised for their practical role in conservation, as will be shown below.

In 1971 R W Brunskill set out to '. . . help the enthusiastic amateur . . . to add his own contribution to the national stock of knowledge.' (Brunskill 1971, 19). This and other initiatives provided the ground-rules for systematic 'extensive' surveys. The advantage of extensive surveys is that they provide a quick overview of the number and general characteristics of historic buildings in a given region, including the main construction materials, structures, plan-forms and functions.

A number of locally based studies conducted by university continuing education departments examined small buildings in more detail, leading to such excellent publications as *Vernacular houses of North Yorkshire and Cleveland* (Harrison and Hutton 1984). Others, like *Rural houses of North Avon and South Gloucestershire* (Hall 1983), grew out of personal initiatives. Meanwhile, the Royal Commission on the Historical Monuments of England (RCHME) produced such invaluable inventories as *Salisbury: the houses of the Close* (1993a), placing more intensive surveys of significant groups of houses in the public domain. *The medieval houses of Kent* and *The house within* (Pearson 1994a; Barnwell and Adams 1994) marked a move away from the compilation of comprehensive inventories towards more thematic surveys, incorporating more interpretation and thereby enlarging the scope of the work. Whether undertaken independently, or for professional bodies, each survey of this kind was a work of considerable labour, scholarship and value.

Most local and regional syntheses, whether in the independent or professional/public sector, depended for their successful completion upon the established approaches of architectural analysis and survey, backed up by documentary research. Agreed analytical techniques and terminologies have been refined for the communication of evidence and ideas about such aspects as plan-form, construction and materials. The establishment of common analytical techniques and vocabulary did much to facilitate the definition of local architectural character and the dissemination of that information, but some scholars looked in other directions for new perspectives. R J Lawrence (1983, 19–28) argued for social and cultural meanings and explanations to be explored. M Locock has argued that working with new theoretical frameworks might not present new information, but '. . . that new links are forged within existing data to create new narratives, and new analyses attempted in order to re-examine the conventional interpretations' (Locock 1994, 8). Nevertheless, the usual techniques of interpretation will continue to be at the heart of research in order to provide the raw material from which new theoretical analyses can be derived. As one of the principal exponents of theoret-

ical archaeology, Matthew Johnson (1993, ix) is amongst the first to accept that many new approaches can be reliably employed only when buildings are also understood through other disciplinary approaches. Thus, for example, formalised access analysis and considerations of the social use of space can only be employed for a given phase in the development of a house if its plan-form at that time has been established.

Whilst fully acknowledging the usefulness of alternative approaches to vernacular buildings, the continuing value of more conventional techniques of historic building analysis remains largely unquestioned. Perhaps it is right that this is so, as the established approaches have such a good track record; on the other hand, the full potential of conventional building recording and analysis has often not been realised. Too often, through force of circumstance, independent recorders have an opportunity to undertake only a basic level of survey and in consequence most historic building analysis has been based upon incomplete evidence.

For extensive surveys, the information collected upon any one building is necessarily limited, yet it has been possible to form a broadly reliable overview. However, such research carries the risk that new work will be interpreted against an established overview without first questioning its accuracy. The level of understanding obtained might vary according to the potential and accessibility of the evidence and the time and resources applied to its analysis and interpretation. There is a real danger when some of the relevant evidence has not been seen, and sometimes even when it has, that buildings will be misinterpreted. This is why, as new information comes to light, a general reappraisal may be called for. Sometimes that new information is based less upon knowledge of architecture than some understanding of the processes that took place inside the buildings, as has been demonstrated by John McCann's scholarly work on dovecotes (1998). While historians continually re-interpret the past from a finite body of documents, so new perspectives arise out of new thinking on historic buildings; there is no room for complacency in the analysis of the raw data, particularly as it is by nature a finite and vulnerable resource.

If the discipline is to remain healthy, vibrant and useful, the recording of small buildings will continue at all levels, from extensive survey to minutely detailed archaeological analysis of individual buildings. Recording will be undertaken alongside a continuing reassessment of the contemporary orthodoxies against which they are interpreted. Passing reference to the medieval unitary house plan will serve to illustrate the point. The conventional interpretation of such a plan includes the open hall at the centre, an upper-end wing, and a lower end, often referred to as the service end. Across England and Wales the majority of medieval houses of this plan-form are believed to have employed the spaces in the accepted manner – hall, solar, buttery and pantry, but in reality it was probably much more complex, there being no automatic correlation of form and function. By invariably associating the upper end with comfortable domesticity and the lower end with buttery and pantry, individual buildings can be mis-interpreted; significant regional variations and possibly chronological changes may be overlooked, particularly in early buildings. It is not only the 'new' theoretical approaches that can be applied to unravel the various uses to which these spaces were put, for conventional building analysis also has that potential. The traditional interpretation of plan-forms has been superseded at such late-13th- and early-14th-century buildings as Chilton Manor and Nurstead Court (Kent), where it has been 'inferred that no in-line ends in timber aisled buildings were designed to have upper chambers' (Pearson 1994a, 46). To what extent, for how long, and in which areas 'non-standard' use was made of 'conventional' house-plans will not be better understood until more people make such critical use of the available evidence. The following examples will serve to illustrate the problem.

A variety of building types have been identified which housed both people and cattle, including Northumbrian bastles, West Yorkshire laithe-houses, and classic longhouses, such as those in Glamorgan (P Smith 1975, 43; RCAHMW 1988, 340–71). These building types have been generally associated with upland areas, and perhaps in consequence such plan-forms have been overlooked elsewhere. Through extensive survey, a number of buildings in Gloucestershire have been interpreted as longhouses, thereby expanding the boundaries of that plan-form (Hall 1983, 12–15). As summarised by Eric Mercer (1975, 34–44), longhouses are conventionally associated with such areas as Wales and the Pennines, so most recorders tend not to include this plan-form and function in their thinking when interpreting houses elsewhere. This conceptual problem occurred at Henfield Farm, Westerleigh (Glos), visited for the RCHME by J T Smith in 1968. To quote from his recording sheet, the house was ' built in several phases from the late 16th century onwards. The oldest part appears to be the hall, in which the moulded main joists have what may be a late-16th-century section. It is assumed that this part of the original house was entered by a cross-passage below which there was certainly a byre; whether there was a parlour at the upper end is uncertain, but perhaps not'. A subsequent visitor for the RCHME wrote on the same sheet, 'If the mortices in the beam to the north of the byre are for tethering posts then there is no way into the byre from the through passage and the building is not a longhouse . . .'. Whether it was a longhouse as conventionally defined was not the issue; the relevant question to ask was whether animals had been accommodated in the lower end of the building, for it is more useful to consider how the building worked than to categorise it with a name. Much of Linda Hall's work has been of a thoroughness some-

where between that represented by J T Smith's single visit and intensive recording. One of the precepts underlying her analyses of the use of space in such buildings is the presence of either a service wing or an integral service room at the *upper* end of the house, as at 17–21 Perrinpit Road, Frampton Cotterell. Whether all of her examples should be defined as longhouses remains debatable, but the volume of evidence that she has now collected for integral byres at the lower end puts her broad thesis beyond serious doubt.

Gloucestershire is close to Wales, as is Shropshire, where Madge Moran (1985) has interpreted a building at Padmore near Onibury as a former longhouse, the byre having been destroyed in antiquity; both could be interpreted as outliers of a recognisable upland longhouse region. However, if houses with in-line byres survive in Shropshire, why not also in adjoining Staffordshire, almost in the centre of England?

Several years ago Jeremy Milln surveyed Hill Top, at Longdon near Lichfield, and discovered that it was the only intact medieval aisled house in Staffordshire. At the time the usual constraints of kitchen units, fitted wardrobes and wallpaper prevented more than the conventional level of survey and analysis. Accordingly, the house was interpreted conventionally, the service rooms being placed in the bay beyond the cross-passage. In 1995 the building was severely damaged by fire, and the necessarily intrusive works that followed were subject to a painstaking archaeological watching brief. This went far beyond the normal level of analysis, partly as a means of informing the repairs, and partly to mitigate the loss of information in original fabric too damaged for retention. In addition to informing the works, doubt was cast upon the earlier understanding of the building (see Fig 3.1). It can now be suggested that the primary cross-wing had only a single long, low room, with a samson post at its centre, and that it was more probably an upper end service room rather than a parlour. This raises questions about the use of the lower end. Evidence recovered from the truss below the cross-passage showed that originally the nave of the lower end was floored over, but the aisles were not. The building had been aligned across the contours so that the floor of the lower end sloped away from the cross-passage; the replacement first floor is agricultural rather than domestic. Even this level of analysis did not provide incontrovertible evidence that the building originally included an integral byre, and nor are all unitary houses with integral byres necessarily longhouses by conventional definition. Proof in the form of a drainage channel might have been found beneath the lower end floor had this not been replaced with concrete some years earlier. Nevertheless, this invasive and intensive archaeological analysis has raised the possibility that the lower-end bay might have served an agricultural function, possibly even as a byre.

What was plausibly a non-domestic lower end at

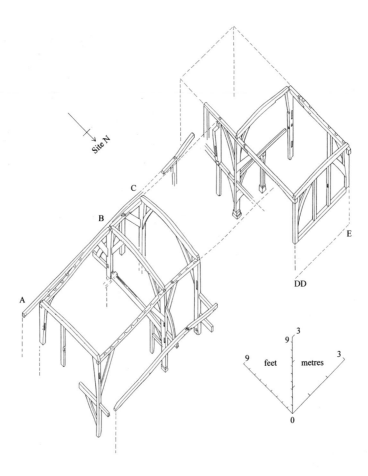

Figure 3.1   Hill Top, Longdon, Staffordshire. – a medieval aisled building with a non-domestic lower end?

Hill Top can now be considered alongside those examples cited by J T Smith (1992, 42–4, 98–9) in Hertfordshire, which is even further outside any of the conventionally accepted longhouse areas. This not only raises questions about the distribution of such dual-purpose dwellings; it also prompts concern that in at least a proportion of late-medieval buildings relevant evidence might have been missed or misinterpreted, thereby distorting our perception of their distribution.

Few small traditional houses have been subjected to the same level of analysis as Hill Top, and all too frequently, I suspect, the potential of archaeological recording has not been fully realised. Even so, whether rapidly appraising a building, recording in a conventional manner like Linda Hall, or researching with invasive archaeological rigour as at Hill Top, the conclusions drawn were the same: arguably, at some time each of the houses discussed had either a byre, or some other agricultural or trade function at the lower end. How different people react to these similar interpretations of the evidence is often conditioned by their own preconceptions, and debates upon the conclusions are in any case conditioned by the amount of analysis that may be possible from the secondary material generated, whatever the level of survey. There is, then, a continuing role for all levels of recording, ranging from a rapid assessment during a single site visit to a full

archaeological survey. The quality of each historic building report, however, will depend upon the level of information obtained, set against a wide background knowledge of the likely interpretations.

A comparison of Hill Top with another Staffordshire building will serve to illustrate two further general points. Surveyed prior to its sale in 1985, Brookside, a farmhouse at Horton, had five bays in line, of which only two were domestic; the other three accommodated cattle (see Fig 3.2). The building is now largely of stone construction, but originally it was timber-framed. Brookside is located in a moorland valley at almost twice the altitude (200m) of Hill Top so it might be argued that one is an upland house and the other lowland, but this is probably too simplistic. Other buildings can be found on lower ground, much closer to Hill Top, which accommodated both people and animals. Firstly, despite their relatively close proximity, one building is not necessarily the functional descendant of the other, for the transmission of given characteristics through time and from place to place was probably highly complex. Secondly, many English counties may contain atypical microcosms of form and function that would be difficult to identify without rigorous archaeological analysis.

During the recent recording of the much-altered Glebe Farm at Wilmcote (Warwicks), the conflicting evidence was so confusing that an archaeological ex-

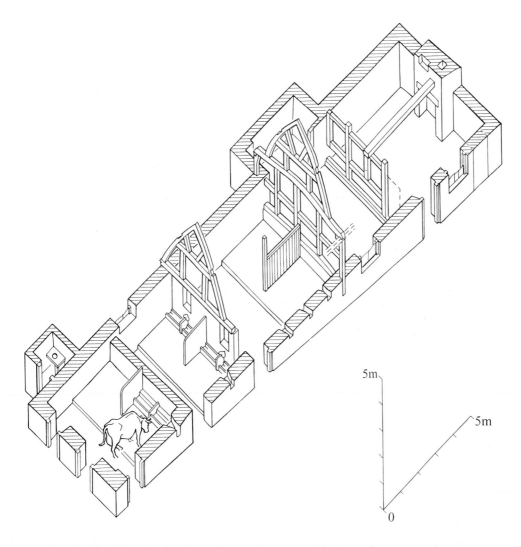

5m

5m

0

Figure 3.2   Brookside, Horton, Staffordshire. – house and byre under one roof

cavation and some limited opening up of the fabric were required to resolve some of the interpretative issues. The excavation proved the absence of a fourth bay at one end of the hall range, and the opening up of sufficient fabric to gain access to the upper roof of the two-bay cross-wing exposed smoke-blackened rafters, identifying it as a former attached kitchen. It may yet prove that the inaccessibility of the evidence, or failure to recognise it, has been responsible for the apparent lack of surviving kitchens in west midland houses. The case further illustrates how difficult conventional analysis and interpretation can be, even when most of the surviving evidence has been seen.

As in other disciplines, ideas change, and information accrued gradually over time may suddenly tip the scales in favour of a new insight. One successful challenge to an accepted orthodoxy revolutionised concepts of the development of the medieval unitary house. Many structures formerly categorised as Norman first-floor halls can now be interpreted instead as detached chamber-blocks; the ground-floor open halls that stood close-by having been demolished (Blair 1993; Impey 1993). Such scholarly revisions invalidate the notion that the overview will

be correct even if some of the collected evidence has been misinterpreted.

One orthodoxy that has gained ground in recent years implies a transition of building styles and techniques outward from south-eastern England. There are so many early buildings around London, in Kent and Essex, for example, and so much excellent work has been done upon them, that we are in danger of concluding that like ripples spreading from a pebble dropped in a pond, technological and cultural influences radiated from a single centre. The intention here is not to suggest that the economic impetus of the capital city should be overlooked, or deny any evidence of primacy. However, there is an imbalance between areas where a great deal of research has been done on numerous early buildings and those where attrition might have been greater or fewer specialists have worked upon what remains. This regional imbalance in the evidence was to some extent reflected at the Cressing conference in 1994 – now published – on *Regional variation in timber-framed building* (Stenning and Andrews 1998). One of the buildings described was Handsacre Hall, with a base cruck of 1306–15+20, apparently introduced into a formerly aisled hall of 1175–15+20 (*Vernacular*

Architect **21**, 1990, 38). The felling date of no later than about 1195 related to elements in the reconstructed spere truss, which included curved braces with mortice and tenon construction. The dates obtained were considered by some of the conference delegates to be too early for conventionally tenoned curved braces, especially at Handsacre, which is a long way from London.

The object of this anecdote is not to prompt a sterile competition about who has the oldest aisled structure; after all, the London waterfront excavations at Bull Wharf have provided a remarkable reconstruction of a 10th-century double-aisled building. Rather, the point is to suggest that it is time for a little positive discrimination, designed to test current orthodoxies constructively. For surely the evolution of building design and technology was significantly more complex than the ripples in a pond model. Perhaps this smacks unfashionably of a research agenda, but the information potential of the surviving corpus of medieval buildings can best be realised if we take positive steps to promote more research in areas that have received less attention hitherto, for occasionally they have the capacity to surprise. Take, for example, the near-forgotten Church of St Werburgh at Warburton in the Metropolitan Borough of Trafford. The listed building description reads 'Ancient structure mostly reconstructed in the second quarter of C17; north aisle late C16, chancel and vestry early C17...'. But how ancient is ancient? The radiocarbon date obtained from one of the arcade posts is 1250 ± 50 years uncalibrated (*ex inf* Alexandra Fairclough, who introduced me to the building). A date of construction somewhere between the mid-13th and early-14th century seems likely, and this is not disconcertingly early for the tenoned curved braces in this church; indeed it is conservative when compared with controversial Handsacre. But we simply do not know for how long or in what way aisled buildings had been constructed in north-western England, or what developing jointing technologies were employed in them. However, such extraordinary buildings as Baguley Hall (Greater Manchester), Smithills near Bolton, and the southern outlier of the type at Mancetter Manor (Warwickshire) suggest a thriving carpentry tradition in the north-west that has no counterparts in the south-east. It would not be a new idea to suggest that regionally distinctive carpentry traditions can be deduced, but rather it may be time to look at this question again with fresh eyes. The recent publication by Essex County Council contains much that is useful on this score but, as David Stenning has observed, 'it seems unlikely that we will ever be in a position to understand how many of these [structural variations] came to be created, and whether there really was a connection between similar-looking solutions many miles apart...' (Stenning and Andrews 1998, 142).

Though it is engaging and useful, the study of structural carpentry remains a minority pursuit, even within the Vernacular Architecture Group. Nevertheless, the analysis and comparison of structural carpentry will remain an important aspect of the study of traditional small buildings, not only as a tool for dating buildings typologically, but also for its intrinsic interest. The analysis of structural carpentry has played an important role in, for example, the debate about the origin of base-cruck buildings. J T Smith coined the term *base cruck* because of the cruck-like shape of the 'blades', but he made it clear that he believed the base cruck to be derived from the earlier aisled form of construction; it was employed primarily to avoid the visual and practical inconvenience of arcade posts across the centre of the open hall (Smith 1958, 111–49). Base-cruck buildings were included as a sub-category of cruck-framed buildings in Dr Alcock's first catalogue in 1973 and again in the enlarged catalogue published in 1981 (Alcock 1973; 1981). This is not to criticise the terminology coined by J T Smith, nor to argue against the inclusion of these buildings in the cruck catalogue, for when the catalogue was compiled it was thought relevant to place base crucks alongside full crucks. With the passage of time more evidence has emerged which supports J T Smith's explanation; for example, a number of base crucks have been recognised in Essex and Kent where no full crucks are known (Walker 1998, 8–9; Pearson 1994a, 54–7). In any case, as John Walker reminds us, the earliest tree-ring date that we have for a base-cruck building is older than the earliest date so far published for a full cruck. A base-cruck tithe barn at Siddington in Gloucestershire has an estimated felling date range of 1245–1247 (*Vernacular Architect* **23**, 1992, 44), whilst the earliest full cruck date obtained so far – from a house at Upton Magna in Shropshire – is of around 1269 (*Vernacular Architect* **26**, 1995, 70). Of course most researchers suspect that crucks are of more ancient origin than the earliest tree-ring date yet obtained from a surviving building. Nevertheless, as implied by the man who coined the term, base crucks might have derived from aisled halls, whether or not their design can also be shown to have been influenced by the full cruck tradition. Though it might often be the case, similar characteristics in different structural forms do not necessarily imply that they are typologically related, or that one is descended from the other. The application of tree-ring dating is now giving greater precision to these typologies, and, used in conjunction with documentary sources, it is becoming one of the primary tools for the refinement of typological dating (Roberts, p 115–21).

Despite the cautionary note on the origins of the base cruck, the systematic cataloguing of other building types and their principal structural characteristics would be a step towards achieving a more thorough understanding of such structures as aisled halls, crown-post roofs, Wealden houses or whatever, especially with a view to improving knowledge of the distribution of surviving examples and their likely dates of construction. Why, for example, are most surviving crown-post roofs found in south-east

England? Are the remaining examples in the mid-lands and the north scant survivals of many such buildings that were superseded by another carpentry tradition long before south-eastern builders abandoned them? Are they more commonly found in buildings of a particular social status, function or plan-form? Are the west midland crown posts the work of carpenters working outside their home territory? More systematic analysis of many different building types is long overdue, even in areas where a great deal has already been achieved. While Cecil Hewett (1980) established many of the ground rules for the typological analysis of carpentry, his masterful drawings were based mainly upon field sketches rather than intensive survey; far from final statements, they demonstrate the possibilities for continuing research.

Established recording techniques can now be supplemented by such new tools as tree-ring dating, and by new theoretical approaches to the evidence. However, putting aside the changing administrative background, two major trends are apparent. Firstly, the levels of recording that can be employed have widened, to range from extensive (non-intensive) surveys to the detailed and systematic archaeological analysis of all accessible building fabric. Secondly, the widening levels of survey and analysis now need to be compared with a mushrooming body of knowledge, making historic building interpretation ever more complex.

The potential of conventional recording and analysis is far from exhausted, and in present circumstances the principal resources for continued research lie in the academic and independent sectors (Pearson, p 10; Alcock, p 98). This is a heavy load to carry, for with it goes the responsibility of ensuring that the materials that we study survive as an academic resource, and to impart cultural identity to our descendants.

Building analysis and conservation

The full potential of vernacular architecture is only just being recognised. This is not simply a matter for scholars, for it is now more clear than ever that understanding and appreciation go hand in hand with good conservation practice; well-informed building conservation is indivisible from historic building analysis. Where the conservation officer is aware of its value, the general knowledge derived from research can help to inform conservation decisions to be made about particular buildings. Without such knowledge, how can a decision be made about repairs or alterations to any vernacular building, whose character is by definition particular to its region and time? As the first part of this paper emphasises, academic research tests theories and orthodoxies with a view to enhancing general understanding. However, a different approach is required in the analysis of particular buildings, or groups of buildings, for the purposes of conservation, for whilst the work might

coincidentally produce data that may be subsequently used for research, the objectives are entirely practical. Far from the common misconception that historic building analysis and recording is solely an esoteric pursuit, it can and should be employed to identify and validate historic fabric, to explain its value, and inform its conservation.

Historic buildings can provide the environment in which established communities thrive, offering a quality of life that cannot be replicated in most contemporary forms of redevelopment. The well-maintained commuter-belt cottages of 'middle England', where a threat sometimes comes from relatively affluent owners with the resources and misguided enthusiasm to make inappropriate changes to their homes, face different problems from many buildings in less prosperous areas, where neglect and decay may be the underlying cause of attrition. Urban Georgian and Victorian terraces offer a greater occupation density than either bland suburban estates or tower-block redevelopments, but general environmental decline can be a disincentive to maintenance and repair. Yet to conserve such smaller buildings is also to conserve unique communities and cultural identities. There are good social arguments for considering the value of the buildings that we already possess rather than assuming that what might replace them will necessarily be better. But the value of those buildings is contained as much within their separate parts as in their outer shells.

In some circumstances the replacement of individual buildings or groups of buildings is inevitable and appropriate, but too often in the past historic buildings have been lost because their intrinsic value and potential viability has not been generally recognised or appreciated. Such attrition of the building stock can be quantified on several levels – architectural, economic, and social – but the process is also an erosion of both cultural assets and useful information. It is in the nature of the work that the photographs, drawings and reports in the National Monuments Record – many of them derived from threatened building recording – catalogue so many sadly neglected buildings of historic significance, placed on record for good academic reasons immediately prior to their demise. Leafing through these records can be a depressing reminder of the wealth of historic architecture that has been lost and cannot be replicated.

Those of us who study small traditional buildings are more aware than most people of the processes that can cause irreversible change or decline. Whether historic building records are made by professional specialists, or by dedicated independent groups, they now have a major role to play in characterising the resource for both academic and practical purposes. This was not always so, for in Britain it has taken half a century to bury the post-war planning concept of a brave new world. In the town where I live – Tamworth (Staffs) – in 1954, 95 buildings had been listed for their historic or architectural importance; only seventeen years later 36 of them (38%)

had been demolished. In 1950, 25 listed buildings stood in Church Street but in 1975 only 13 of them remained, and perversely it was the best timber-framed structures that seemed singled out for destruction. In accordance with the mood of the time the (then) Chairman of the County Council wrote: 'Tamworth should be transformed into a spacious town of the twentieth century' (Aldous 1975, 58–63). It was both the despoiling of the physical environment and the disregard for the social consequences that encouraged me to take threatened building recording seriously for the first time.

Whilst some societies have shown tendencies to put their past behind them, others have found themselves in equilibrium with their history:

> In these stony old Tuscan towns, I get no sense of stepping back in time . . . Tuscans are of this time; they simply have had the good instinct to bring the past along with them. If our culture says 'burn your bridges behind you' . . . theirs says cross and recross. A fourteenth-century plague victim . . . could find her house and might even find it intact. Present and past just coexist, like it or not. (Mayes 1996, 159)

Post-war Britain lost confidence in its legacy of historic buildings and, coincidence or not, simultaneously lost much of its former sense of community. Yet it was out of a sense of the loss of the familiar fabric within which local communities coexisted that many people were driven to question the trend. Encouragingly, the rate of demolition of listed buildings has slowed to a trickle, as it is generally recognised that such losses are not only of buildings that might have had a viable and useful continuing lifespan, but also of cultural heritage. Nevertheless, although the pace of wholesale demolitions has declined, the historic character of buildings remains under threat as a result of a less obvious but equally insidious process. Partial demolitions and minor alterations – a sash window here, a lath and plaster ceiling there – sustain the attrition of our historic building stock. Through small and isolated events the erosion of historic architecture continues. Like demolitions, some such changes are inevitable, for no building is permanent. But many inappropriate alterations are still undertaken without first giving due consideration to their implications, because the historic character, significance, potential and architectural possibilities have not been recognised or understood. This less dramatic but equally damaging process is also eroding our connection with and understanding of the past, for the fabric of each historic building has its own particular validity and value. One of the new challenges is to help all those who find themselves responsible for the care and maintenance of listed or other historic buildings to understand and respect them, not simply out of sentiment for the past, but as a safeguard for our present sustainable environment. If there has been a fundamental shift in community awareness of sustainability and conservation, this is unlikely to be matched in practice without some appreciation of the practical applications and the mechanisms to achieve them. There is no guaranteed correlation between the ownership of historic buildings and the knowledge required for their proper conservation, and so the application of appropriate controls through the planning system will remain a crucial safeguard for the foreseeable future. Yet it is only recently that some local authorities have begun to take their role sufficiently seriously in this regard.

The publication in September 1994 of Planning Policy Guidance Note 15 (PPG 15) did not change the legislation; it merely advised on how local planning authorities could apply existing planning law. However, it marked a move towards better standards of control over works on historic buildings, and much emphasis was placed upon the need for any proposed works to be adequately informed. But how was this to be applied in practice? In which buildings and in what circumstances should a detailed survey be required before an application for listed building consent was determined? When should a watching brief during works be required, and what would be its purpose? These uncertainties and other reservations made some local planning authorities slow to adopt the recommended procedures (Baker, p 60). In an attempt to clarify the process the Association of Local Government Archaeological Officers (ALGAO) published advice to local authorities and applicants upon analysis and recording for the conservation and control of works to historic buildings (Baker and Meeson 1997). Recently more historic building assessments and evaluations have been supplied or required by developers and local authorities to inform the conservation process, but nationally the response remains thin and uneven.

Notwithstanding local politics and the varied sympathies and priorities of different planning committees, the definition of appropriate standards of recording and analysis to be employed in each historic building can be fraught with difficulty. A balance must always be struck between permitting works upon historic buildings without sufficient information on the one hand and applying unreasonable conditions on the other. For the conservation officer, the art lies in discriminating between those cases where little or no recording or analysis is necessary and those where a great deal may be crucial. Those who compile the written and illustrated reports which inform planning decisions about historic buildings also have a wider role to play, for they can educate owners and developers, promoting awareness, appreciation and good practice (Morriss, pp 69–70). Leading on from an adequate understanding of those characteristics that impart historical and architectural character to buildings, the design process can facilitate new uses in historic settings that will be appreciated and enjoyed by all who use them. Rather than a constraint, historic buildings can be an opportunity.

Although, over time, the assembled records may have research potential, recording for conservation has the primary objective of securing more appropriate works to historic buildings than would otherwise be possible. If in particular circumstances preconsent recording will not improve understanding of the building fabric, and thereby inform any decisions or proposed works, it is not justified. Given that, whenever possible historic buildings should be conserved, the first objective is to understand what makes them special, for each is only the sum of its parts. Since leaving a local planning authority to work as an historic building consultant, I have been even more convinced by practical experience that the most effective first step in the conservation process is the compilation of a straightforward catalogue of the elements of a building that contribute to its character as an historic building as part of the preliminary assessment. Most owners and their agents have yet to appreciate that the time to do this is not in response to proposals but in advance of the design work, and preferably there should be close liaison between the client or agent and the conservation officer. As well as providing some understanding of what makes the building historically and architecturally distinctive, an assessment should make clear which fabric warrants retention, and why. Armed with this information, everyone involved in the integrated processes of design, curation and control, and finally working upon the building, can have a clear understanding of the conservation objectives. In this context the advice set out in PPG 15 is entirely appropriate, and equally the English Heritage concept of a Conservation Plan for major works of architecture or historic areas can be extended to more modest buildings, as that which is understood and appreciated is more likely to be conserved.

One of the outstanding obstacles to a smooth transition from archaeological analysis to well-informed building conservation is the significant perceptual distinction between the appreciation of architectural style and the recognition of buildings as an archaeological resource. When decayed fabric is necessarily removed, or when enforcement action is taken against someone to replicate historic fabric that has been removed without consent, the aesthetic considerations may be satisfied, but the archaeological evidence has been irretrievably lost. In this way historic buildings are just as vulnerable to invasive changes as buried archaeological deposits. If we are to retain real buildings, and not just a pastiche, the primary objective should be to conserve the original fabric wherever possible (Clark, p 47–9). When invasive repairs or alterations are proposed, and when it is acknowledged that all or part of an historic building cannot be retained, a mitigation record might reasonably be agreed or required.

It is worth emphasising here that generally there is much to learn through practical experience about what should be recorded, how it should be done, with what purpose, and in what circumstances. It ought to go without saying that recording in mitigation should never be employed as an easy substitute for the retention of historic building fabric, though I

know of cases where it has. Equally, developers should not be required to carry out mitigation recording of fabric that will be retained, unless it is necessary to place threatened elements in context. If the unique decorations in a stately home require conservation or replication, analysis or sampling may be of paramount importance. Conversely, if works are proposed upon the fabric of a 19th-century cottage the sampling of 1960s wallpaper is unlikely to inform the process, and nor will it add much that is relevant to the sum total of our knowledge for the future. 'Proposals should be designed with a proper understanding of the level of recording appropriate to the case, and the techniques that can obtain it...' (Baker and Meeson 1997, 20). Experienced practitioners recognise that no amount of blind recording will help – recording must convey the results of analysis and thereby impart understanding, and it must be targeted to the need for information that is appropriate to each case. Appropriate analysis and recording is borne out of practical experience, intelligent observation and good communication.

Both the difficulties and the potential of targeted recording can be illustrated by a project at Darwin House – a conventional-looking mid 18th-century double-pile house, the Lichfield home of Charles Darwin's grandfather Erasmus (see Fig 3.3). Competent recording over two or three days by the York office of RCHME generated a report demonstrating that far from being of one build, the front portion of the house was constructed adjacent to a pre-existing building; the earlier structure was then demolished and replaced by the back range – a classic case of alternate reconstruction. Subsequent to the RCHME survey, some of the building was conserved, some of it was altered, and part of the interior was demolished; during those alterations a part-time watching brief brought out much new information. Putting aside the survival of the 14th-century cathedral close stone wall in one of the cellars, the reconstruction of the stairs, and an enlargement of the building achieved through the incorporation of the adjoining former medieval Vicars' Hall, the house can now be shown to have undergone numerous changes both in Darwin's time and afterwards. The original kitchen in the basement was replaced by one on the ground floor; old doorways have been blocked, new ones opened and subsequently sealed up; corridors have come and gone or been widened. 15th-century wall posts and roof timbers from the previous house were found between floorboards and the underlying ceilings, and part of a 17th-century wing was discovered, encapsulated within the later building. During the works an impressive arched alcove was discovered on the first floor, originally intended either for a sideboard in a saloon (the preferred interpretation), or for a bed. This alcove had been closed off to form a separate small room and forgotten until the recent alterations exposed the evidence.

That so much new information about the building was observed during the watching brief is certainly no criticism of the RCHME team who analysed what

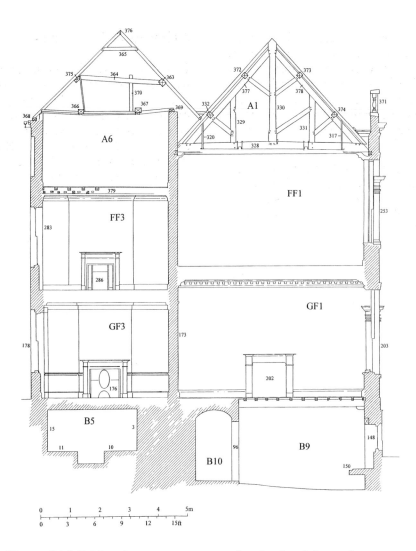

Figure 3.3   Darwin House, Lichfield – alternate reconstruction in the eighteenth century

evidence they could see over a few days and without intruding into the fabric of a listed building. Darwin House serves to illustrate that the best professional standards of analysis and recording achieved a fundamental understanding of the building sequence, but the building held yet more potential for a detailed appreciation of its historical development, serving the needs of the owners in the interpretation of the house to the public. This case is of particular interest in the context of PPG 15 because initially no requirement was placed upon the owners to arrange for a watching brief to take place during the works. The need for mitigation recording and an interpretative analysis was recognised and acted upon by the owners, perhaps reflecting a growing awareness in some circles of the potential benefits of archaeological analysis.

Darwin House illustrates that however useful they are, none of the usual types of historic building analysis and survey will necessarily produce a complete understanding prior to the commencement of works. Secondly, on a practical level, where works are proposed upon an historic building, a pre-planning consent evaluation will often not provide all of the information that ideally should be available

to those who make decisions about its future. In such circumstances a watching brief might serve not merely as the means of obtaining a mitigation record but more constructively, to inform the works upon the building as they proceed. A few enlightened local authorities are beginning to feel their way towards the best mechanisms for enabling the results of monitoring to inform works as they proceed without the delays that are consequent upon revised planning applications (Baker, p 55).

As we work our way towards better practice, there is a tendency for some professional agents to defend their own standards and methods. The need is not to determine who should achieve the appropriate level of understanding and act upon it, but to ensure that it is done. Following examples of good practice and appropriate curatorial control, conservation that is informed by a documented understanding of building archaeology and history may become the natural province of well-informed and appropriately experienced architects and other professionals, although many may continue to sub-contract this kind of work. Whatever specialist undertakes it, conventional historic building analysis and recording should be an indispensable part of the process that will inform decisions about the future of historic buildings; this applies as much to our often misunderstood and undervalued vernacular buildings as it does to our major monuments. Those whose drawn and written historic building analyses serve to educate and promote awareness of the cultural heritage will be the vanguards of informed historic building conservation, and it is part of their task:

> ... to assert the relevance of the past but, at the same time, to ensure that its tangible relics survive as the materials of historical study and as guarantors of historical identity for our descendants (Hunter 1981, 31).

Acknowledgements

Figure 3.1 is based upon a survey by the author for what has become the Department of Development Services of Staffordshire County Council; I am grateful for their consent to reproduce it here. Linda Hall and J T Smith are acknowledged for information on longhouses. Nat Alcock, Kate Hardcastle and Sarah Pearson are thanked for their valuable comments upon drafts of this paper.

Part II: Recording buildings: conservation

4 The role of understanding in building conservation *by Kate Clark*

This paper explores the role of recording in the conservation of small vernacular buildings. Others have shown how each small vernacular building is a document which provides a unique source of history; sadly that document continues to be shredded through a slow but insidious pattern of insensitive alteration. The techniques we use to record buildings can be used to prevent such damage.

Unfortunately, too often the recording and analysis of an historic building is done – if it is done at all – as a condition of statutory consent to demolish or damage it. The creation of a record is seen by some as an acceptable alternative to keeping all or part of the building. Yet small vernacular buildings are irreplaceable social documents, which may be important for many different reasons; they contribute to the special qualities and distinctiveness of the places where we live. Those of us who are able to read and articulate what is special about small vernacular buildings have a duty to use those skills in order to help pass those buildings on to future generations. Surely it is better to understand buildings to avoid damaging them, rather than because we damage them. This is not a new argument, but it is one which does not seem to have had the degree of acceptance amongst conservation professionals that it deserves. In this paper, I want to explore both the arguments for using building analysis in conservation, and also some of the possible reasons for resistance to using it.

Conservation and the idea of significance

There are many misconceptions regarding conservation. Most people see 'conservation' as synonymous with preventing change; others – perhaps more enlightened – see it primarily in terms of using historic techniques (such as lime mortar or traditional materials) to repair buildings. The first view is unrealistic; the latter view represents only one aspect of a very much wider issue. Instead, conservation might be defined as: *managing change in such a way as to ensure that what is significant is passed on to future generations.*

Conservation may involve maintenance, repair, or finding appropriate new uses for a building; it may involve creating something new which enhances a historic place, or it may be concerned with education and outreach. Successful conservation will involve working with people – most importantly the owners of historic places, but also local communities and indeed anyone who values a place. Conservation is not limited to buildings or monuments – there is a whole network of physical remains from the past, above and below the ground, under the sea, in landscapes and in urban areas, which together constitute the historic environment. In conservation, it is as difficult to draw hard and fast lines around sites and buildings as it is to set limits to the natural environment.

That which we wish to conserve can be distinguished from the rest of the physical remains of the past by the idea of significance. Significance – what matters – is central to conservation. Significance is, in effect, what we value. There are many different ways in which we value the remains of the past – they may be familiar, beautiful, rare, unusual, associated with someone special or a major historical event. All of these values contribute to the basic argument for conservation, which is that there is a public interest in the past, which justifies constraints on individual action. That public interest lies in significance – what we value.

One critical way in which the physical remains of the past are significant is as a document. Whilst this is not the only basis for conservation, it is certainly an important one. The concept of fabric as a document is, of course, the basis of archaeology, whether above or below the ground, of landscapes, buildings or buried remains. Buildings are unique historical documents, which can be used to chart people and how they lived, what they built, their thoughts, aspirations and ideas; buildings document the major social forces which have shaped history – events, changes, adaptation and reuse, technology, innovation and conservatism. Buildings demonstrate subtle social patterns which may never have been written down. The physical fabric of the past is a document in its own right, which complements the written word but as a source is distinct from it.

Reading buildings

The analysis of a building or site is the primary tool for reading fabric. As historians have a range of critical tools which they use to analyse documents, so archaeologists have a range of critical tools with which to read fabric. The tools of historic building analysis are documentary research, drawing and observation; they rely on a range of academic and specialist disciplines such as architectural history, construction history, architectural analysis of materials, dendrochronology, landscape history, archaeology and building sciences. The good building analyst can write, draw and analyse, and is comfortable with documents, fabric and formulae alike. Like a histo-

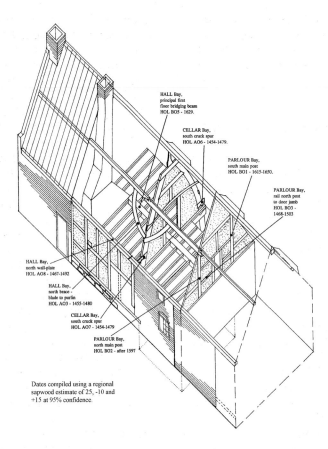

Figure 4.1   Lodge Farm, Hollington, Derbyshire. Analysis of the building and dendrochronology were used to inform conservation decisions about the future of this small cottage. (Drawn by Andy Wittrick, English Heritage. Dendrochronological dates courtesy of the University of Nottingham, 1994.)

rian, the building analyst knows not to take primary documents – in this case fabric – at face value, but instead to ask questions; to understand context and change; and of course to recognise that our own prejudices shape what we see and how we see it. It is a matter of training and considerable experience to be able to read a building well; to draw together all of the different strands of information into a coherent picture of a changing entity.

To return to conservation, it follows that if building analysis is one of the primary tools for reading the significance of a building, and significance is central to conservation, then there should be an important role for building analysis in conservation.

Every conservation decision involves assessing the impact of a proposed change on the special interest of the site. It is a matter of considering two things – the importance of the building, and the potential damage (or benefits) that the changes will bring. The skill of the conservation professional lies in negotiating the transition from past to future (Holland and Rawles 1993) which in turn involves reconciling significance and alteration. For a building, this might mean looking at how new materials could impact on existing ones, or how a new use might affect the significance of the plan. Obviously, the better the

understanding of what is important at the outset, the easier it is to understand the potential impact of changes, and to suggest practical ways of minimising that impact.

Prior understanding of a building is the best basis for conservation decisions (see Fig 4.1). It can show how the plan, the appearance, the materials and the style are important. Analysis can show which elements are recent and which are old, which can be attributed to the original builder and which belong to later phases. Analysis can help us to understand the building as a whole, and not just the obvious features. Far too often applications for consent are based on little or no information about the whole building, and in these circumstances it can be difficult to make responsible decisions.

Normally conservation officers will use their own expertise or knowledge of buildings to make assessments, and in many cases that knowledge will be enough to assess the impact of the proposals, and to establish whether or not those proposals put the special interest of buildings at risk. However, there will be circumstances where there is not enough information to make a decision. For example, it may be that the conservation officer does not know the building, the information provided by the applicant is poor, or a quick visual appraisal during a site visit is simply not enough to assess the impact of a major scheme of alteration. In such cases, a more detailed analysis of the building can be useful to a conservation decision.

Building analysis and conservation

If building analysis is a useful tool which assists decision-making then surely it should be a routine part of the process of building conservation. To what extent are such analyses used in the conservation process?

The primary mechanism for conservation is the planning system through which decisions about land use are regulated. The government publishes guidance on how planning legislation is to be interpreted, including guidance on archaeology and planning (PPG 16) and planning and the historic environment (including buildings) known as PPG 15. Both guidance notes are aimed at promoting the conservation of the historic environment within the land use planning system (see Baker, p 53).

Anybody who is interested in building recording might look with envy at the successes achieved by archaeologists using Planning Policy Guidance 16: Archaeology and Planning (PPG 16). This guidance document notes that it is reasonable for planning authorities to ask prospective developers to arrange for field evaluations to be carried out before planning decisions are made (para 21) – a principle that is now relatively well-established within the planning process (Darvill *et al* 1995).

The work is underpinned by Sites and Monuments Records, which can be used to alert planners and developers to the potential existence of significant archaeology, and to store the records of any evaluation work for future use. There is full national coverage for archaeological sites in Sites and Monuments Records (Baker 1999) and at a different level in the National Monuments Record, and there are extensive archives of archaeological material (Swain 1998). The archaeological profession has expanded in response, and there are now over 4000 archaeologists in Britain, about two thirds of whom are in local authorities or in the commercial sector (Aitchison 1999) and thus involved in archaeology and conservation.

The contrast with building conservation is sharp. PPG 15 provides equally clear guidance about the need for applicants to provide local authorities with information in paragraph 3.4, which notes:

> Applicants for listed building consent must be able to justify their proposals. They would need to show why works which would affect the character of a listed building are desirable or necessary. They should provide the local planning authority with full information, to enable them to assess the likely impact of their proposals on the special architectural or historic interest of the building and on its setting.

Despite this requirement (which is elaborated elsewhere in the PPG) very few buildings are evaluated prior to decisions on listed building or planning consent for alteration. There is no real equivalent to the private sector in archaeology – whilst there are conservation officers in most local authorities, there are few professional architectural historians or specialist building analysts in the private sector, although there are over 800 specialist building conservation firms (Cathedral Communications 1999). There are also discrepancies in the information base which underpins decision-making. Whilst the records of listed buildings are now computerised (but presently inaccessible to local planning authorities), the extent to which Sites and Monuments Records include buildings is variable, and apart from the National Monuments Record (which is by necessity selective) there are no consistent arrangements for storing reports on buildings (see Eavis, p 127).

It is possible that there is no need for such information, yet when asked, many conservation officers find that the lack of adequate information is a major problem in processing applications for listed building consent (Oxford Brookes, 1999). Many have never had an equivalent to the Sites and Monuments Record, and may not be aware therefore of the value of such sources. Those conservation officers who do make use of building analysis often find it difficult to find skilled specialists in the private sector, despite at least one full time post-graduate course dedicated to teaching building analysis and a number of other courses which include it in the curriculum.

Why is there a discrepancy between the two regimes? Why don't all conservation officers make explicit use of the requirements in PPG 15 in the same way that county archaeologists follow the equivalent advice in PPG 16 to ask for more information when considering applications for listed building consent? Why are the drawings that are supposed to inform work upon historic buildings so poor? Why are there so few heritage impact assessments or rapid appraisals of buildings? Where is the private sector in building recording?

More to the point, why were the arguments about the value of buildings archaeology to conservation not won years ago? The realisation that this was an essential part of good conservation had been recognised by Blore and Twopenny as early as 1847. But, as indicated by Pearson (p 7), little was achieved until the mid 1980s. Recording conditions for buildings receiving English Heritage grants were introduced only in 1985, and in the same year Rodwell published *Church Archaeology,* in which he attested to the value of building fabric as a source of history. The practical application of recording to conservation and to decision-making was then spelt out in the ICOMOS *Guide to Recording Historic Buildings* (1990). But in comparison with below-ground archaeology, all this is very recent. Skills in recording and analysing buildings are now a core competence for members of the Institute of Historic Building Conservation. Yet in practice, the majority of architects, engineers, conservation officers or inspectors involved in the conservation of buildings would still be unlikely to see the archaeological analysis of buildings as something which would – or indeed should – contribute substantively to the process of conservation.

This enduring situation puzzles building archaeologists. They had hoped that by reminding people of the requirements in PPG 15 (3.4) and providing greater clarity on procedures through documents such as ALGAO's guidance (Baker and Meeson, 1997), building recording would develop the same status as archaeological evaluations in the planning process, and the rest would follow. Yet by 1999, progress was slow. In April of that year, the merger between RCHME and English Heritage brought a body of skills in recording buildings much closer to the process of conservation. As a result of this merger, the role of recording in conservation is gaining a new potency.

Patterns of loss and damage in small vernacular buildings

One of the most significant reasons behind the difference between the treatment of archaeology and buildings in the planning system is the different perception of loss. It is easy to see – and to anticipate – threats to buried archaeology, especially in historic towns, where major new developments with massive foundations will result in the loss of archaeology. For buildings – which will usually remain standing but are simply altered in some way, it is far less easy to anticipate or understand loss. There is an assumption that alteration and continued use are invariably beneficial for buildings in the way that new development may not be for archaeology.

Small vernacular buildings can be used to illustrate general patterns of loss in buildings, and to indicate why those patterns might matter. Although they might not be architect-designed, or constructed for show or pretension, whether listed or not, small vernacular buildings are significant. Whether domestic, agricultural, or industrial, they define the character of our towns and countryside; they document ordinary lives, work, enterprise and leisure, and they contribute to the familiarity and distinctiveness of places.

Small vernacular buildings are not generally considered to be hugely at risk. In the first English Heritage 'Buildings at Risk' study (English Heritage 1992), domestic buildings were one of the lowest classes at risk, although industrial buildings scored rather higher. It has been assumed that where such buildings remain in use, often for the purpose for which they were designed (domestic accommodation), and are not demolished, they are not at risk. Yet if we look at those aspects of vernacular buildings which are most significant – including windows (see Fig 4.2), plan-form, roofs, patterns of construction, methods of heating (see Fig 4.3), form, function and context – a pattern of risk soon becomes apparent.

In Wotton under Edge, Gloucestershire, few weavers' cottages retain their original fenestration or characteristic large, top-floor windows. Few multi-pane casements survive, particularly on the back elevations of buildings where plastic windows are prevalent. Yet windows are often one of the keys to the status and function of buildings. New windows, doorways and rendering have totally altered the character of a row of cottages at Coalport in Shropshire (see Figs 4.4, 4.5).

Plan-forms are also at risk. Much of our knowledge of the development, status and function of medieval houses comes from our understanding of evolving plan-forms, and Alfrey (1994) showed how an equivalent understanding of industrial cottages adds a social dimension to industrialisation. Yet modern standards of space and hygiene make tiny, one and a half storey cottages extremely vulnerable. Realistically, some plan-forms were never going to survive. Barracks housing (Douet and Saunders 1998) accommodated single male workers, particularly in military establishments. There is little such demand today, as a result of which in the Telford area (Shropshire), only two ranges of migrant workers' barracks housing survived in the early 1990s – out of the many shown on early Ordnance Survey maps (see Fig 4.6).

Whole classes of buildings are at risk. Squatters' cottages represent a major social aspect of industrialisation. The movement of labour is illustrated in the gradual colonisation of former common lands by new groups of settlers away from the traditional agricultural areas. Such patterns are often not documented – the evidence lies in the buildings and spaces (Trinder 1981, 188–9). Squatters' cottages surviving in anything like their original form are very rare – an example at Lightmoor in Telford was listed precisely because other known examples had been demolished, altered out of all recognition, or moved.

Similarly, back-to-back houses were once relatively common, but few survive today. The row excavated at Newdale in Telford (Horton et al 1992) was, until the 1970s, a unique survival in the Coalbrookdale coalfield. Equally, purpose-built workers' houses, such as those in Carpenters Row, Ironbridge, built by the Coalbrookdale company (Muter 1979), are significant socio-historical documents. Although well appointed by 18th-century standards, small extensions to each in the 19th century show that the communal brewhouse was no longer acceptable, and people wanted individual kitchens. Today, the survival of a relatively intact row is highly unusual, but it is very difficult to conceive of a future for these buildings in modern domestic use.

Equally vulnerable, in an urban context, are the small buildings which lie behind the street frontage. Typically, burgage plots are being cleared to create parking (thus eroding an important clue to urban topography) and with them, the small workshops, stables, chainmaking workshops and brewhouses

Figure 4.2 (left)   Windows. Cumulative changes to vernacular buildings include the regular replacement of windows and joinery, thus eroding the character of whole areas over time.

Figure 4.3 (below)   Cottage at Little Dawley, Shropshire. This cottage included a rare surviving smoke hood. A record was made by David Higgins and members of the Ironbridge Gorge Museum Archaeology Unit in mitigation of a consent to demolish the building. The building was later reerected at Blists Hill Museum.

Figure 4.4 Cottages at Coalport, Shropshire, prior to conservation

Figure 4.5 Cottages at Coalport after conservation. Windows and doors have been replaced and considerable renewal has taken place.

Figure 4.6 Barracks at Lilleshall, Shropshire (the framing is painted). This is one of the few surviving barracks buildings in the Telford area.

which once occupied these spaces. Such buildings were an essential part of a domestic complex; they provide the social context to the houses on the street frontage, as well as documenting the mixture of work and by-employment or domestic manufacture which are so important to our understanding of the origins of industrialisation (eg Berg 1985). By-employment is poorly documented, yet few of the historians who write about this period have made use of the evidence on the ground; in losing these buildings, we are losing an important historical source.

Adaptive reuse can also erode character; particularly in the many agricultural buildings which have now been converted to domestic use, with the insertion of windows, partitions, dormer windows and the pressure for a domestic garden landscape to replace the cobbled courtyards of the farmyard.

The context of a building is vulnerable. Plot boundaries can illuminate construction and use, the relationship to other houses and to the street pattern will help place the building in the context of the development of the town. Yet plot boundaries are vulnerable to car parking requirements – visibility splays, turning circles, car bays, garages. Where such boundaries are the only way of documenting the origin of a community, and of distinguishing between, for example, the regular grid forms and layout of planned or speculative housing from the random scatter of plots created in a squatting landscape, then their survival matters. Once again, gradual erosion of a seemingly minor factor can soon lead to wholesale loss of character in an area.

It is ironic that conservation can be one of the most pernicious perpetrators in the erosion of character. There is a thriving market in recycled historic building materials – stone slates, stone, handmade roof tiles – resulting in the random loss of minor outhouses and stables for their materials. Conservation guidelines emphasise the importance of historic materials, and officers often ask that new build should be in traditional materials. The net result is that less well-known buildings, perhaps unlisted and outside conservation areas, are denuded of their historic materials. Even well-intentioned repairs have the potential to cause damage. In Wotton under Edge a group of almshouses dating to 1837 has been meticulously restored on the exterior (see Fig 4.7) with a public appeal and high standards of craftsmanship in the stone repairs, but inside, all is bare. Fixtures and fittings are gone; there are new plastered walls, new ceilings and concrete floors, altered stairs, new partitions and a new access (see Fig 4.8). What distinguished those buildings – small purpose-built accommodation for individual pensioners embodying Victorian ideals – has now been lost. In towns, conservation area enhancement schemes often include new paving, street layouts, kerbing and brickwork, or the replacement of old materials, often in a ubiquitous York stone, with little understanding of, or reference to, the original character. In our enthusiasm to do good by our centres,

Figure 4.7   Miss Ann Bearpacker Almshouses, Wotton under Edge, Gloucestershire, 1837. The exterior of the building has been carefully conserved. In comparison, see Fig 4.8, which shows that relatively little historic fabric survives in the interior.

Figure 4.8   Interior of almshouses, Wotton under Edge, Gloucestershire. The surviving staircase was about to be removed at the time this picture was taken.

we often eradicate the character which originally distinguished them.

Conservation issues, particularly for small vernacular buildings, are often seen in terms of individual problems and individual structures. However what might seem to be minor individual losses, can, when taken together, lead to a cumulative loss of character and diversity in a place. If this were ecology, we would be talking of extinction. The Black Country chainmaker's workshop is virtually extinct. Casement windows, smoke hoods and brewhouses are also on the verge of extinction. In the south-east, the unconverted listed agricultural building is rare, and the trend is moving steadily north and west. In other cases, the buildings themselves may survive, but what makes them special is gradually being lost. To continue the analogy with ecology, perhaps we are looking at the loss of habitat and diversity in the historic environment.

Reconciling interest and use

Of course many such losses are an inevitable corollary of changing social patterns and places. Critics would say that such losses are inevitable, as the long-term survival of such buildings depends upon keeping them in use, and that compromises will always have to be made if historic buildings are to meet modern requirements. A modern English family would not happily live in a Victorian back-to-back cottage or accept 17th-century hygiene arrangements, and therefore it is not reasonable to impose conservation requirements on the owners of historic buildings.

But building conservation is rarely a matter of simply *sacrificing* interest to use; it is a much more subtle art of *reconciling* interest and use. Not all of these losses can be prevented; but some can. For example, a historic barracks building could be sensitively converted to a single dwelling – even better, a more appropriate modern use (such as a Youth Hostel) might be found. In historic towns traffic restrictions may improve safety and do less damage than huge visibility splays.

Often the source of a conservation dilemma lies in wider issues such as policies on taxation (the imposition of VAT on maintenance, for example, does much to generate problems) or transport. Sometimes the solution lies in education – many building analysts say that the impact of their work is greatest on the owner of the building, who gains a new appreciation of what is important and why. Conservation is often a matter of finding creative solutions to problems; a matter of avoiding damage rather than preventing change. As ever, understanding must be the basis of this.

Loss and the case for analysing buildings

Yet how is this relevant to the question of building analysis? There is a critical link between understanding and loss. Damage to historic buildings of the sort set out here – the gradual erosion of character – is not usually deliberate; more often it is the result of ignorance, or the lack of the right information at the right time. The person making the decision may not know what survives in a building or why the street pattern is important. The information submitted by the applicant may be poor, and the local conservation officer may not have the resources to improve on it. Perhaps the list description is too old, or there is no conservation area appraisal to help set decisions in context. The architect who drew up the plans may not have had sufficient understanding of the importance of the window. The list of excuses goes on. For effective conservation decisions, access to appropriate information can help to buck the trend.

Once it is accepted that the built heritage is at risk unless we understand it properly, then perhaps the case for better information and thus the use of building analysis in conservation will be that much stronger. Possibly because we have not thought consistently and in the long term about what is happening to the fine texture and grain of the historic environment, we are not making informed conservation decisions. Perhaps more research into historic buildings and what is happening to them might highlight patterns of loss which arise from casual, ill-informed decisions, and help conservation officers and others to use and make a case for better information.

Perception of risk is perhaps the primary barrier to the better use of analysis in conservation. We don't always see small vernacular buildings as being under threat. Therefore, we don't always seek the information necessary to avoid such damage. There is a circular link between damage and information. Once we are aware of the risk to the resource, we are more likely to ask for what we need to know in order to prevent it.

Other barriers to the use of analysis in conservation

The perception of loss and risk is only one of the barriers to the use of analysis and recording in conservation; there are other barriers to their use in the conservation process. The people who most need to be convinced of the value of recording are not, in general, archaeologists; it is planners, surveyors, conservation architects, structural engineers and builders who are most likely to take the decisions which affect the historic environment. Such professions receive little, if any, training in these applications and need to be convinced that building analysis can help with conservation decisions.

Some of their resistance arises from poor experience of reports by building analysts. Such reports may be verbose and hard to read, the drawings illegible to an architect or engineer. The scope of the work may not be tailored to conservation decisions – there may be too much information, too little information, or the wrong information. In the context of a conservation programme, it is not enough to select a random 'level' at which to record a building; instead the work must be directed at the decisions which have to be made. These decisions may range from broad ones about appropriate use, to detailed ones about the choice of colour or joinery repairs. Either way, building analysts working in the conservation sector (rather than as academics or for their own interest) must be prepared to tailor their work and its presentation so as to inform the conservation process. This means producing everything from a 'quick and dirty' assessment, through to a fully detailed stone by stone analysis, depending not on their own criteria but on the requirements of the project. Too often building analysts focus only on their own areas of interest. It is still surprisingly common to see a report which ignores post-medieval changes to a building, yet it is those later changes which are most likely to be least well-understood and most vulnerable to loss.

Behind this lies a question of training; both conservation professionals and building analysts need to be trained in the application of such work to conservation. Conservation professionals need to know when and in what circumstances building analysis can be useful, and how to manage such work so that it fits into conservation programmes. Building analysts need to be trained in the application of their skills to conservation projects.

Another barrier to the better use of building analysis in conservation is what might be called 'the mitigation ghetto'. The myth persists amongst many conservation professionals that the most appropriate time to record a building is as a condition of consent; in other words, after key decisions about alteration, development or demolition have been made. Unfortunately, far too often it is only as the result of this recording that the significance of the building becomes apparent and the original decision is called into question.

To some extent, this myth persists because many of the documents which govern archaeological procedures – such as Management of Archaeological Projects (MAP 2), which explains the organisation of large-scale archaeological research projects – were designed with research rather than conservation in mind. Another source of this myth is the former RCHME role in recording threatened buildings, where the requirement of the Planning (Listed Buildings and Conservation Areas) Act 1990 to notify the Commission (and now English Heritage) of the demolition of a listed building, in order to give them an opportunity to make a record, has perhaps led to widespread confusion about the role of recording. In the minds of some local authorities, 'information needed to assess the impact of the proposals on the special interest of the building' and the 'record' made as a result of a decision to demolish part or all of a building are often seen to be separate. Because information and recording are not seen as related

issues, the potential of recording techniques to contribute to the better understanding of buildings *before* decisions are taken is often lost.

Thus, archaeologists and conservation officers alike can sometimes conspire for different reasons to place 'recording' firmly in the mitigation ghetto – perceiving it as something to be done as a condition of consent to record loss, rather than something which can make a positive contribution to an informed decision.

Behind this confusion is a genuine problem with terminology. There is no single word to describe the type of information needed to inform a conservation decision. *Recording* is often associated with preservation by record rather than something which informs conservation; *archaeology* is something invariably, albeit erroneously, associated with the excavation of below-ground remains; *buildings analysis* is much used, but suggests the activity is restricted to buildings and not the historic environment; *documentation* is used in America, but like recording seems slightly passive. *Survey* is a word which has too many meanings for too many different professions. The information requirements can also range from the broad overview of characterisation and conservation area appraisals, to the minute detail of architectural paint research or dendrochronology. A single term, which embraces the concept of research and analysis, as well as the variety of disciplines and professions involved, but which also makes a clear link to conservation, may be necessary before we can progress further.

The final – and to many minds the most important barrier – is the widespread perception that building analysis is a burden. The requirement to prepare an analysis of a building is seen as an additional cost for an already hard-pressed owner or developer. Of course there is a cost in analysing a building, but it is useful to put this into context. If undertaking an analysis at an early stage can reduce later costs for a developer, for example by reducing the risk that the project may be delayed or by reducing the use of conditions on a planning consent, the initial outlay may in the long term create a saving. Often the cost of analysis will represent a very small percentage of an overall conservation project – generally less than 5%. If, through analysis at the outset, the primary characteristics of the building and those aspects of its fabric that impart historic significance are properly understood, the processes of design and application for listed building consent will be immeasurably better-informed, quicker and cheaper.

A large percentage of applications for statutory consent are submitted by professional agents who claim expertise in dealing with historic buildings. Arguably, as part of the service that they offer, such agents should have skills in both rapid appraisal and the use of more complex historic building analysis. If this were so, building analysis would not be an additional cost to the developer, although in the short term such a requirement would generate training costs.

Some costs arise because work is not anticipated.

The potential constraints on development may only become apparent after money has been spent on engaging an architect to develop a scheme, only to find that further investment may be required to amend it when the historic building constraints are taken fully into account. Again, targeted building analysis at the outset can help to anticipate constraints, and thus inform the development of a scheme, avoiding the need for costly amendments.

The way forward

It is often argued that creating a record of a building is an acceptable alternative to retaining the building itself. This is certainly the basis for many 'recording conditions' imposed on statutory consents for demolition or alteration of buildings, and for the dreaded phrase 'preservation by record'. But is it enough to simply retain a record of small vernacular buildings?

A paper record is only ever a poor substitute for a building, which contains within its fabric a rich and complex document of social change. No record is ever complete, even the few – expensive – projects which have recorded and reconstructed buildings in loving detail, have not recovered everything. Nor is, in such circumstances, moving a building a wholly acceptable alternative. What is lost is the context, the relationship to the landscape, the archaeology in, below and around the building. Like an animal in a zoo, the building may be a curiosity and have contributed to science, but its survival in its own habitat is always preferable.

More importantly, what is lost when a building is demolished is part of a cherished local scene. The significance of small vernacular buildings does not simply lie in their potential for academic research. Small vernacular buildings are familiar, they contribute to the character of towns and countryside, they may be typical rather than special; some of them may not be beautiful in the traditional sense, but they have an aesthetic of their own. The history of people, of work, and of changing society, are written in them. Small vernacular buildings are unique social documents. A landscape devoid of them would be one which had lost much of its meaning. Equally, a landscape of small vernacular buildings which are essentially facades, behind which are new interiors, built of new materials which superficially represent old ones and around which new landscapes have been created, is one which has lost depth, meaning and potential. If small vernacular buildings matter to us and they contribute to the quality of life today, then they are worth passing on to future generations.

The papers in this volume have shown how the recording and analysis of small vernacular buildings is the key to reading the history locked inside them. This history is not just a dry academic matter, but something which can contribute to our understanding of the places around us and why they are important. It is part of – and contributes to – the quality of life. The process of articulating the significance of the remains of the past is absolutely vital to making the case for its conservation.

The battle for the value of recording vernacular buildings has been won – primarily through the excellent work of the former RCHME and the many volunteers and others who work in this field. The war itself will not be won until this work reaches its full potential by becoming part of mainstream conservation.

One reason for the marginalisation of recording is our reluctance to admit to the way in which buildings can be damaged. Perhaps because, quite reasonably, we are anxious not to depict conservation as a burden, we are reluctant to face up to the fact that historic buildings are under threat, often from those who own them, or more importantly, seek to develop them. Secondly, we continue to present recording in the narrow sense – something to be undertaken by volunteers or by the state for essentially academic purposes. We do not see it as a mainstream activity which should be informing the whole of the conservation process. Thirdly, those who do record buildings in the context of conservation projects may be applying techniques more suited to research than conservation, as a result of which the value of such work may not always be communicated to the architects, engineers, builders and even owners of the site.

The amalgamation between the RCHME and English Heritage has created a new opportunity to consider this issue afresh. Internal procedures on the use of buildings analysis in grant schemes are in place which will help to provide clarity on the better use of analysis in repair cases for buildings and landscapes. Emerging policy documents are likely to include more explicit statements about the use of information in conservation. The co-location of survey staff and regional teams in some areas is helping to bring conservation and recording closer together and the creation of a new Archaeology and Survey Department with skills in all aspects of understanding buildings means that there is an important critical mass of specialists in this area.

The emerging use of Conservation Plans is another practical initiative which is beginning to make better use of the understanding of a site in the conservation process. A Conservation Plan is a document which sets out the significance of a site, and how that significance can be retained in any future use, alteration, management or development. The Conservation Plan begins with an understanding of the site, whether a building or landscape, above or below the ground. Building analysis can make a direct contribution to that understanding although sometimes the level of work in the Conservation Plan may be more superficial. Techniques such as phasing, and aids such as gazetteers and typologies, which have long been used by buildings analysts, are now being applied on a much larger scale to the understanding of a whole range of buildings. Shorter, more quickly-achieved Conservation Statements draw on the rapid assessment techniques often used by buildings analysts, and provide another practical tool for linking the understanding of the building with practical recommendations for conservation (English Heritage 1999).

Conclusions

Understanding buildings should be the bedrock of building conservation. Every conservation decision is based on 'architectural and historic interest'. Unless that interest is clearly defined, then conservation is meaningless. In the conservation world, the pendulum has swung towards an emphasis on historic materials and techniques. Whilst this is to the good, it has to some extent been at the expense of the emphasis on understanding what is significant in buildings. Somehow we need to retrieve that balance, and to do it by placing analysis and interpretation back at the centre of the process.

It is not a matter of creating an extra burden. Rather, it should be very clear that understanding buildings genuinely helps us to care for the past, and if we don't do it, the small vernacular buildings which we value today will continue to be seriously at risk.

A historian would not condone the shredding of manuscripts or the loss of the British Library, and so the buildings analyst with a special knowledge of vernacular buildings should not condone their loss. For anyone who cares about vernacular buildings, using these skills to contribute to their conservation is a duty, not an option.

5 Information requirements for planning decisions
by David Baker

Introduction

This paper considers the *evidence* about small historic buildings that is required to inform the *processes* of repair and alteration, as regulated by planning law, and how they relate to each other. Evolving practice and professional or official publications have made the ground familiar to an increasing number of conservation practitioners, but it is not yet fully understood by everyone involved in the study or management of small historic buildings. These are matters that common sense suggests should be obvious and uncontentious, yet they remain controversial, largely due to differences of outlook amongst the range of interests engaged in conservation and research. By sharing these matters with all those concerned in recording historic buildings, not just those who are fortunate enough to work with them as a full-time occupation, it is hoped to help increase the constituency of support for introducing them more widely.

The conference at which the original version of this paper was delivered took place shortly after two of its contributors had completed a guidance note for the Association of Local Government Archaeological Officers (ALGAO) entitled *Analysis and Recording for the Control of Works to Historic Buildings* (Baker and Meeson 1997). The paper was coloured by the surprising degree of misunderstanding that had been encountered during preparation of the guidance, about the idea that targeted recording and analysis could be an integral part of the conservation process, in the same way that it is the long-accepted servant of research. Since that paper was published, the world has continued to change; during 2000 English Heritage undertook a rapid review of policies relating to the historic environment on behalf of the government. This was a strategic opportunity to ensure that all stages of the conservation process are properly informed. By the time this article has been published, it should be possible to judge how far the review has generated useful proposals for making progress on this issue, and how receptive the government has shown itself to their incorporation into its policies.

The paper begins with a summary of the context in which historic building recording may be appropriate as part of the process of cultural transmission of the historic environment, and a brief account of what is involved in the planning process as applied to the conservation of historic buildings. This is followed by a summary of information requirements at the various stages of the planning process, and how they might be met. The requirements are then compared, mostly unfavourably, with what actually seems to happen, and explanations are sought in attitudes to recording, on philosophical, practical and procedural levels. Suggestions for taking matters forward are largely aimed at increasing levels of awareness about how the efficient handling of information can improve both conservation and understanding, matters reiterated in sharper focus by a postscript on the case of historic churches, even though they are exempt from listed building controls.

Conserving the historic environment

It is worth beginning with a brief reminder of the wider context of the planning process and its requirements for information. Conserving the historic environment relates to past, present and future, but inevitably takes place in, and is seen from, the perspective of the present. The dual usefulness to society of the historic environment, firstly as part of its physical context, and secondly for the cultural significance of its various aspects, is emphasised in Table 5.1. This also reminds us how care and explanation depend upon knowledge and understanding, and that human curiosity is the driver for all but its most functional uses. Care and explanation need information, and information about the various aspects of the historic environment, extant and destroyed, is part of what is passed on for the benefit of future generations.

The planning process

The planning process facilitates uses for the historic environment, whether conserving or destructive: it is not a direct user itself. It is based upon the requirement that land-use changes falling within the legal definition of 'development' obtain permission from the local planning authority through a Council committee of elected lay members advised by professional officers. There is a general presumption in favour of permitting proposals that are consistent with policies in Local Plans formally adopted after proper public consultation. These Plans should provide a clear link to formal government guidance on various aspects of planning through its Planning Policy Guidance Notes (PPGs), and can embody policies derived from guidance issued by government advisers like English Heritage. The presumption in favour of permitting an application stands, unless proposals involve what are described as interests of acknowledged importance or other material considerations, in which case the issues are given special scrutiny so that any potentially adverse effects can

Table 5.1 The usefulness to society of the historic environment

Inherited from the past	Use in the present	Bequeath to the future
Identified as significant: • the 'received' heritage • a new class of historic survival • a new member of an already recognised class ↓		**Review received significance** in the light of current research and cultural/environmental outlook
Information acquired by survey and recording: • extensively to identify new examples • intensively to analyse known examples ↓	**Research**: • To advance knowledge generally • To inform conservation and repair → • To underpin other uses ↓	**Conserve** and **repair** elements chosen for survival
Stored information about extant and destroyed elements in record systems that • are **retrievable** • are **accessible** • have arrangements for **mediating information for non-academic/ technical uses**	To serve **current needs** for places, land and buildings To help provide **cultural and environmental identities** for people and communities **Education**: To inform people at all stages of life about their heritage and the issues it raises **Visiting and Tourism** To provide recreation, entertainment and information for people travelling in their localities and wider afield.	**Maintain integrity and accessibility of information systems**

be identified and assessed for their acceptability. These interests and considerations include all the elements of the historic environment recognised in statute and formal guidance, such as historic buildings of all sizes and types.

Some new-millennial tendencies may possibly affect the relatively clear-cut nature of this situation. Arrangements for so-called 'cabinet' government in local authorities may bring new sets of political pressures to bear upon some of the more contentious major planning applications, which often include issues affecting the built and buried heritage. There is also pressure for the planning system – somehow – to take into account matters strictly outside straightforward land-use considerations, relating to 'quality of life'. In some ways these extend concepts that are already part of conservation, such as historical associations, physical context and setting, but in so doing, they can easily get beyond the physical and tangible matters upon which people can usually at least agree to disagree. There is a risk here, of fudging a clear distinction between bringing social value into the equation when deciding whether to preserve or destroy, and opportunistically using the 'finite non-renewable inheritance' to make points about wider social or political matters largely unrelated to conservation or historical issues.

Nonetheless, it must be remembered that land-use planning is intended to achieve a good balance between economic development and environmental conservation. 'Balance' has a deceptively sound and sensible ring about it, but that may not always seem to be the best way of describing a pragmatic accommodation between conflicting forces of professional judgement, administrative convenience and political policy. There is however a potentially stabilising influence available in the recently emerged concept of 'sustainability', defined as the avoidance of actions whose impact upon the environment of today would prejudice the opportunities of future generations to benefit from its enjoyment.

In similar vein, there is also a need to be clear about the actual effect of listing historic buildings 'as of special architectural or historic interest'. It is not a guarantee of preservation come-what-may; it is a label, an earmarking for an interest of acknowledged importance, to ensure that it is given special treatment as a material consideration. The same applies to a lesser extent to those buildings recognised locally as making a positive contribution to the quality of townscape, landscape or local historical interest. In cases of conflict, the presumption in favour of preserving that interest can, but will not necessarily always, modify or override the presumption in favour of permitting proposals that are in accord with other policies. Similarly, earmarking to ensure that special consideration for certain proposals is not, as is often proclaimed, the same as 'pickling in aspic', a prevention of all change, though there are stringent criteria of acceptability for proposals that might affect the most important buildings.

Information requirements – what, when?

When dealing with any application for permission to carry out development work affecting historic buildings, for the planning process to work effectively, certain requirements must be met. The first is clarity about the nature of the special interests of acknowledged importance; the second is an assessment of any potential impacts upon them, and these should be measured against adopted policies, precedent and guidance. Planning officers need to know the significance of what is affected by a proposal, and how it is affected. This helps them to place values on both aspects and advise their planning committees whether, in all the circumstances, consent ought to be granted, and if so, with what safeguarding conditions.

The need to meet these requirements to provide satisfactory information has been built into the process with a view to avoiding potential difficulties. Appendix A of *Analysis and recording* gives the legislative background and government guidance as excerpts and refers also to the original documents cited. The most powerful of these is *Planning and the historic environment* – 1994 (PPG 15), the principal formal government guidance on planning and the historic built environment. This should be seen together with the earlier planning guidance – *Planning and archaeology* – 1990 (PPG 16). There is also the (former) Department of National Heritage's widely ignored *Guidance on local government reorganisation* (1995), which includes fundamentally important statements on the need for maintained information systems or 'resource inventories'. Of lesser weight legally (because it came from a quango), but of great value as a clear and comprehensive statement of procedure, is the paper by English Heritage on *Development in the historic environment* (1995).

These documents envisage a smooth flow of events in the handling of applications affecting listed and other important historic buildings, the vast majority being the small buildings considered in this volume; it already happens in enlightened and properly equipped planning authorities. The model for progress through the system goes through three broad stages. Firstly, an application is prepared and submitted, justifying the need for proposed works that would affect the character of a listed building, and providing full information about their likely impact on its special architectural or historic interest, if necessary after purpose-designed analytical recording work has been completed. Secondly, on the basis of

agreement about what is known and not known about the building, and whatever else may need to be known, and following consultations, planning officers assess the application and negotiate any desirable amendments in accordance with policies and the particular circumstances of the case. Assuming the applicant can live with these, consent is granted, usually with conditions. Thirdly, the consent is implemented and any conditions discharged. The conditions may include arrangements for further analysis and recording of structure and fabric after initial opening up, to feed into further decision-making at pre-arranged stages of the works, and arrangements for appropriate recording of material that is to be removed or altered.

These central three stages of the planning process sit at the core of a wider set of five, encompassing the proper management of historic buildings, all within the broad conservation process as outlined above. Each stage has its requirements for information as outlined in Table 5.2.

With the right information provided at the right time and awareness by all parties of needs and process, matters can proceed at a predictable pace. This is most effectively and economically achieved during the preparation of an application by adapting a sequential process of investigation to the particular circumstances of the individual case. The first step, *appraisal*, involves little more than rapidly considering the building, the proposed works and the available information to see whether or not all the information that is needed is already to hand. Any outstanding questions might then be answered through a more thorough *assessment* – a thorough review of all existing information and a careful inspection of the building itself, stopping short of undertaking new research. If that too proves insufficient, then a purpose-designed *evaluation* should be undertaken, including new analytical recording designed to answer specific questions that are directly related to the proposed works (Baker and Meeson 1997, 3–4). Failure to follow the appropriate version of this sequence can cause delays for lack of necessary information, or may lead to recording that is more extensive and expensive than is actually needed for the planning process.

All three steps in this sequence precede the determination of a planning application because they represent work that is part of its processing. There is little or no point in granting a consent for specific works with an attached condition requiring the recording work that ought to have been carried out beforehand in order to help decide whether that consent was actually appropriate. This is a familiar problem with archaeological matters, and it is easily done by a planning authority that may be well-meaning but fails to understand the role of information and the purpose of recording. However, this kind of muddled thinking should not be confused with more complex cases which require an incremental approach to investigation, both before determination, and afterwards where fabric has to be

Table 5.2   The planning process: information needs and recording requirements

Stage/task	Information needs	Recording required
1 Background and preliminaries		
1.1 Identify the significance of the historic building to all who have an interest in it.	A Statement of Significance covering 'historic' and 'community' values.	Some basic research and extensive (outline) analytical recording.
1.2 Identify need for works	A considered analysis of needs *preceding* the identification of specific alterations and extensions, repairs and maintenance.	A basic condition survey undertaken with an understanding of construction and materials, supplemented by more intensive (detailed) investigation as required.
2 Preparation for works and submission of application		
2.1 Design proposed works	A clear brief about the significance of the building, its condition and the needs that have been identified.	Supplement existing information as required with new extensive recording.
2.2 Identify impacts of proposed works on significance	A record of the directly affected parts/ fabric with sufficient detail and precision to provide a baseline for identifying proposed changes.	Supplement existing information as required with new specific analytical recording.
2.3 Prepare scheme documentation and submit formal application to LPA	Completed application forms; plans/ elevations/sections etc as required of existing and proposed situations; other documentation such as surveys, photographs, in order to communicate proposals and potential impacts clearly and fully for assessment and verification.	Informal consultations with LPA prior to submission may identify any gaps in recording work.
2.4 LPA registers application for processing and formal consultations	Registered application in multiple copies, for internal use and public consultation including neighbours, statutory amenity societies, etc.	(Sufficient recording to inform the application fully should have been completed by this stage)
3 Assessment and determination of application		
3.1 LPA assesses proposals and negotiates amendments	Assessments by professional staff and consultees whether impacts on the significance of the building have been identified and are acceptable in the light of policy, guidance and good practice. If impacts are not acceptable, to identify whether applicant's needs can be met by any modified or alternative scheme with reduced impacts.	Alternative proposals will need to be documented for the application and this may require further analytical recording to clarify impacts.
3.2 Identify and agree any post-consent analytical recording requirements	A scheme to be agreed before commencement of permitted works, based on an adequate existing analytical record, and identifying two main types of recording.	After initial opening-up works in order to determine strategy and details of repairs. In order to record significant historic fabric that will be destroyed by agreed works.
3.3 LPA determines application with conditions	Any conditions must be necessary, relevant, enforceable, precise and reasonable. Reasons for refusal must be clear and in accord with existing policies.	May include condition requiring analytical recording but must relate directly to the works. Lack of adequate information for assessing impacts upon special interest of a building can be a reason for refusal.

Table 5.2 (*cont.*)   The planning process: information needs and recording requirements

Stage/task	Information needs	Recording required
4 Implementation and verification of approved scheme		
4.1 Undertake works	Any information essential to doing the works properly.	Any post-consent recording required as a condition. In appropriate cases, preparation of 'as-built' drawings to show how what was done compares with what was proposed or permitted.
4.2 Monitor implementation of consent and conditions	Has post-consent recording been carried out to adequate standard?	Experienced monitoring required against brief and specification for recording work.
4.3 Complete and secure basic records of works in appropriate archives	Should include all outputs from all analytical recording conducted throughout project, ie records 'as existing' and 'as built'.	Deposit in accessible archives held as appropriate by owner/agent/LPA/SMR or equivalent or NMR.
5 Completing the conservation cycle: communication and review of significance		
5.1 Project results for academic, technical and popular use	Technical material for academic and conservation.	Arrangement for easy access and retrieval.
	Mediated material for education, tourism and visiting, community interest.	Preparation of material so easily available and useful for 'non-expert' uses.
5.2 Review significance of building	Information generated by project	Amend or supplement existing records

Applications vary widely in their complexity and information needs, and the model process outlined above should be adapted sensibly to the needs of each case.

This sequence does not include steps that have to be repeated due to inadequate provision of information, pauses and reversals of stages due to negotiations, or appeals against refusals of permission or conditions imposed on consents.

investigated progressively as it is opened up in order to determine the best solution for repairs or alterations.

To summarise, the essence of the information requirements, and the basis for deciding upon the appropriate extent of the recording work to meet them, is *fitness for purpose*, which is the ultimate test that they meet the planning criteria of being *reasonable and sufficient*. Hopefully, it will be clear by this stage of the paper that there are four broad categories of purpose:

- to obtain and communicate an adequate understanding of the works proposed and their impact
- to provide an adequate means of ensuring that proposed works are carried out as permitted
- to inform works in progress about matters that could not realistically be determined in advance of consent
- to mitigate the impact of works by recording fabric of value that it has been agreed will unavoidably be destroyed or altered.

What are the guidelines for translating all this into practice? *Analysis and recording* suggests that the extent, type and level of recording will be influenced by the likely impact of the proposed works on the building fabric and the site, and will also need to reflect the architectural quality, structural complexity and chronological development of the subject. Put more simply, the proposed works provide the scope for the recording requirements, but within the wider framework of an awareness of the nature of the whole building. It is that way round, from the works to the building, rather than allowing the whole building to dictate a recording strategy in the hope that part of what is done will actually coincide with the requirements of the works.

Thus, in the application for planning and/or listed building consent, although it is important to show the location and context of the works precisely and clearly on paper, there is no need to record unaffected parts of the building in the same detail that would be given to the affected parts. An effective substitute might be a properly minuted site inspection by the conservation officer, confirming agreement with the applicant as to the overall significance of the building. Even the list entry itself can sometimes provide an adequate context for the parts affected by the proposed works. Nevertheless, drawings of the affected parts of the building as existing must be at least precise enough to allow sets to be marked up with proposals and supplemented with method statements. They must provide an adequate basis for

58

controlling the works, ensuring that they are carried out as agreed, and acting as a record for the future of what was done on that occasion.

However interesting a fully researched analysis of the entire building might be, investigation and research *per se* are outside the primary purposes of land-use planning, and cannot be required as part of the planning process unless justified by the nature of the proposed works. When *Analysis and recording* was in preparation, some students of vernacular architecture complained that the piecemeal recording justified by the information requirements of the planning process was scarcely worth the effort because it stopped short of dealing with the whole building or tackling a major defined research issue. Of course there is nothing to stop anyone voluntarily carrying out more recording than is strictly justified, from a wish to understand the broader picture; it is likely to produce a result of greater academic value, and possibly of more value for the future management of the building. But that does not mean to say that the small episodes of recording, a timber truss here, and a stone wall face or a plastered ceiling there, lack intrinsic value and usefulness. They all contribute to the documentation of the building, the fundamental source of information that ought to be consulted every time significant works are contemplated. Buildings analysis and recording in the context of conservation should be accumulative rather than all-or-nothing, though what is accumulated needs context in order to rise above the 'rubbish collection' of which rescue field archaeologists have been accused at times for lack of defined research agendas.

Twixt cup and lip

If all this is so clear, one may well ask why there are any problems in relation to historic buildings about providing required information and using recording as a means of obtaining it. Surely it all ought to follow automatically. Yet recent pilot surveys of local authority practice commissioned by English Heritage confirm that to a considerable extent it does not happen, especially for small buildings, even though PPG 15 is over half a decade old (Kate Clark pers comm). Reasonable requirements for the submission of information with applications affecting historic buildings are not being properly satisfied.

Spelling this out in detail, Table 5.3 makes rather a depressing litany; it must be emphasised that much good practice exists, but the extent and persistence of the problems leaves no room for complacency. Many of the difficulties comes down to a lack of awareness and resources on the part of the main players in formulating and determining a planning application, together with a lack of incentive to remedy them.

Problems may be compounded because, in order to make up any information deficits, it is often necessary to try to reverse the progress of an application through the various stages between initial formulation and formal determination. This always sounds

negative, and can cause difficulties, including delays, frustration and antipathy towards the interests whose protection is being sought in that way. The process can be seen as a diversion from getting the envisioned result, and poses a threat of increasing costs.

Whatever the explanation, inadequacy of information and insensitivity to context are shortcomings with wider implications. They can make it more difficult to demonstrate the validity and viability of an overall process of repair, and therefore perhaps to attract necessary funding. They can cause opportunities to be missed for explaining to wider audiences why certain historic buildings ought to be cherished, a dangerous omission at a time when some seem to find it politically convenient to portray conservation as backward-looking and conservative.

Recording as obstacle or opportunity – problems of image and purpose

Why does this seem to be such a stubborn problem? There are several possible strands of explanation. A major leading factor is pressure of time and money. Lack of finance for recording work is sometimes argued as fundamental, but often in ignorance of actual costs (which need not be large), and usually as a smokescreen for having failed to take it into account properly, or at all, when fixing budgets and securing resources. Project management driven by the vision of outcomes may be the right approach to getting things done, but riding roughshod over process carries with it a high risk of unintended damage if it ignores the need to understand what is affected before deciding on the works to be carried out. Pressures to get results within pre-determined timetables and budgets often fail to recognise the sequential process needed to deliver the all-round 'best value' result. Analysis of historical construction may not only be essential for making the right repair decisions and getting predictable costs, but it can also add to the perceived interest of the building and be a useful investment for future maintenance and research. Encouragingly, primary repairs to major historic buildings and monuments and the work of the best architects and surveyors are increasingly being well-informed by a proper appreciation of process. But this still does not yet apply to many small-scale repair works and to alterations arising from current uses in historic buildings. Indeed, many such works are not designed or directed by appropriately qualified or experienced professionals.

For those who engage with building conservation only occasionally and while pursuing entirely separate objectives, and even for some professionals who are regularly involved with the process, the benefits of targeted recording requirements are still not widely understood. In preparing *Analysis and recording* a range of reactions was encountered, from planners, architects, and conservation officers. The

Table 5.3 Problems and shortfalls in the procurement and use of information

Task	Players	Problems & shortfalls
1 Basic recognition of significance and need for works		
1.1 Identify the significance of the historic building to all having an interest in it	Owner, ideally as part of acquisition	In only very few cases adequate records or statements go with the buildings or are easily accessible in a local public record system. Many list descriptions do not cover interiors or wider significance.
1.2 Identify need for works	Owner advised by Agent	Failure of purchasers to envisage future needs or understand the significance of the historic building which may constrain him/her. Exaggeration of failure of materials for lack of proper structural information or understanding of 'old' buildings. Dangers of wholesale 'restoration' rather than incremental maintenance and repair.
2 Preparation for works and submission of application		
2.1 Design proposed works	Agent with owner	Insufficiently clear brief from owner; changes of mind. The agent may not adequately understand historic buildings and / or the procedures of listed building control, or may seek to play down or ignore significance and potential impacts on it in what are perceived as the interests of the client.
2.2 Identify impacts of proposed works on significance	Agent with specialist advice; LPA preliminary consultation	If significance is not appreciated, impacts will not be recognised. Failure to document potential impacts through appropriate level of recording; recording not tailored sufficiently precisely to task in hand.
2.3 Prepare scheme documentation and submit formal application to LPA	Agent	Many applications omit existing situation or other essential information. Some agents fail to understand special needs of documenting historic buildings.
2.4 LPA registers application for processing and formal consultations	LPA, consultees	Applications appraised for acceptance by administrators rather than specialists may have information gaps that hinder processing but are difficult to fill within the limits of the time period started by the act of registration. Statutory consultees may be too busy, or have to choose the cases they have the time to consider properly, or there may be no credibly informed local society.
3 Assessment and determination of application		
3.1 LPA assesses proposals and negotiates amendments	Agent, LPA	Resources and will to negotiate (and sometimes ability to envisage less damaging alternatives) vary between LPAs according to quality of staff and casework pressures.
3.2 Identify and agree any post-consent analytical recording requirements	Agent, LPA	Specialist knowledge and willingness to work in with project is required in order to prepare brief for specifying appropriate scope and level of recording.
3.3 LPA determines application with conditions	LPA	Some LPAs' lack of awareness of value of documentation means necessary conditions are often not imposed. Some LPAs bizarrely make acquiring information needed for determination a condition attached to the consent. The elected members of the planning committee, in assessing recommendations made to them, or in adjudicating between competing interests, may not give adequate weight to the significance of the historic building.

Table 5.3 (*cont.*)   Problems and shortfalls in the procurement and use of information

Task	Players	Problems & shortfalls
4 Implementation and verification of approved scheme		
4.1 Undertake works	Specialist employed by Applicant or Agent	Clarity is needed on appropriate recording methods and on need to relate detailed work to overall building.
		Flexibility is needed in cases where exact recording to be defined after initial opening-up works.
4.2 Monitor implementation of consent and conditions	LPA	LPA often lacks resources / skills to monitor effectively, or applicant's agent fails to notify at agreed monitoring points.
Complete and secure basic records of works in appropriate archives	Applicant, Agent, LPA	Confusion between 'as proposed' and 'as built' records which can be different due to need for flexible approach to conserving old fabric.
		Lack of archives used to justify lack of any archiving action.
5 Completing the conservation cycle: communication and review of significance		
5.1 Project results for academic, technical and popular use	Applicant/LPA	Technical attitudes rarely envisage popular information outputs.
		Grant conditions often insufficiently sensitive to information publicising needs.
5.2 Review building's significance with any information from project	Applicant/LPA	A Statement or some kind of ordered archive needs to exist in the first place for any kind of review to take place.

less helpful included: 'What has recording got to do with me and my work?'; 'We have never been asked for this before so why should we start now? It will only slow down our clear-up rate'; 'Jolly good idea but of course there's no time and anyway management wouldn't wear it'.

One explanation for these attitudes may be that much of the development of recording to provide information for conservation purposes has tended to be associated with archaeological work, which is perceived as something more separate and different than it actually is. The reasons are complex, but foremost amongst them must be the contrast between the relict character of the buried or ruined heritage, the usefulness of which tends to be knowledge-based, and the practical usefulness of historic buildings as vehicles for continuing economic uses. The disciplines brought to management of the archaeological heritage tend to be academic and scientific, whilst for buildings in use they are more practical-architectural and judgementally aesthetic. Though there is scope for cross-fertilisation of ideas, techniques and attitudes on practical 'interface' matters such as the archaeology of upstanding buildings, there are also obstacles in the form of educationally reinforced professional divisions, separate legislation and aspects of administration diversely located at national, county and district levels. These have contributed to distinct mind-sets that can too easily reinforce differences rather than help identify the more obvious common factors, such as the scope for

contributing jointly to understanding a building in a place or solving wider historical problems.

Part of the difficulty seems to reside in perceptions of and attitudes towards 'recording'. These were unwittingly symbolised in the original invitation to the Oxford Conference, which was to speak about 'Recording for Planning Purposes'. A section of the original paper was devoted to arguing that the title ought to be 'Information Requirements for Planning Decisions'. The planning process produces an essentially 'yes-no' decision, even if sometimes hedged around with conditions, and its efficacy depends upon a well-defined and stable relationship between process and outcomes. Thus the aim was to refocus attention from the generalised means of data-gathering to the specific end of deciding what to do about a building. Talking about 'information requirements for planning decisions' helps connect means and ends, and stimulates the kinds of questions that help identify the need for analytical recording work.

In turn, that requires consideration of the appropriate approach and techniques. The revised title is more receptive to the idea that recording can take place at different intensities, depending upon the type of building and the nature of the proposed works. Different types of requirement for information mean different recording strategies, and failure to define objectives and specify suitable techniques may produce results that are more extensive or intensively detailed than needed, or are shown to have gaps when questions are defined or redefined after survey has been completed. Even worse, if the need for the effort and expenditure has not been communicated and understood, it may create resistance to the principle of recording, and a perception of it as 'punishment' (Kate Clark, pers comm).

The broader scope of 'information requirements' is a reminder that primary hands-on recording work should include other sources such as documentary or pictorial evidence, or even management records generated by previous campaigns of works. Also, 'planning decision', with its strong undertone of conflict resolution, stresses the need to address cases from the perspectives of all participants and as part of a wider conservation process. Owners and others are involved as well as building recorders and planning officers.

Standing back a little further, it is worth reflecting that the words 'record' and 'recording' carry deceptively dignified overtones of objectivity, analysis and reliability that can easily obfuscate precise objectives and techniques. An example is the never-lying camera, recording everything that comes through its lens. It may appear to provide an undifferentiated 'narrative' image rather than a selective analytical record, yet even that is heavily influenced by the choices of exposure, focal length and film processing that are made by the photographer. Another example with in-built uncertainties is recording in mitigation of impact, providing information as a substitute for conserving historical evidence. It assumes correctly that the bequest to the future combines upstanding historic buildings, and records of both extant buildings and of those that have been destroyed. Less safely, its misnomer in 'rescue' archaeology as 'preservation by record' encourages belief in an 'objective' record capable of answering as yet undefined future questions. Though records of what no longer exists physically are valuable and well-worth making, however well done they are certain to be inadequate to some extent for all purposes at all times. Research priorities evolve, bringing forward new questions whose needs for new data probably could not have been anticipated when the recording in mitigation was designed. For buildings, perhaps the closest conjunction of an allegedly 'objective' record, and a usable basis for future work, is in the form of rectified photography or photogrammetry, checked against the subject in situ, and intended as a baseline document for future management, research and explanation. Yet even this level of recording cannot reveal that which is hidden by later building fabric; unless selectively annotated, it neither analyses nor explains.

All record-making reflects purpose, but unless those purposes are clear and explicit, the results will not be consistent and reliable. Knowing why a record was made is an essential guide to what has been included and what may have been omitted. The intensive recording represented by a detailed drawing of a wall elevation incorporates conscious choices about the level of detail and types of features represented; their description should be part of the drawing. It is important to know that the extensive recording in the statutory lists of buildings of special architectural or historic interest has the purpose of identifying particular buildings; it explicitly does not provide a definitive description, particularly for interiors. Nevertheless, the fuller descriptions of the more recent lists were compiled systematically against a check-list; they assemble selective information about the more obvious dating and sequence of construction for the small buildings of an area, and can be extremely useful as long as their limitations are recognised.

Ways forward

Despite these difficulties there is a need to recognise that the recommended procedures provide the best means of ensuring informed conservation. The problem is how to apply universally and evenly what the best local authorities have already managed to put into place. The hard way is to reject applications out of hand if they do not incorporate the necessary information requirements, but that might be quite difficult to achieve in a customer-orientated age except for glaringly obvious cases. What could easily be represented in the adversarial context of a planning appeal as nit-picking bureaucracy might make people less friendly towards historic buildings for all the wrong negative reasons.

Information requirements have to be presented for what they basically are, as benefits to the project in hand, to an appreciation of the building owned, and to its long-term management. Documentation needs to become fully accepted as a sub-set of ownership and management. We need to encourage two sets of people.

The first set is owners. Ideally the list description would be automatically available at the time of purchase, because a copy had been filed with household administration papers (together with the standard health warning about it not being fully detailed and definitive). Those papers would include an accumulating dossier of information about past history, repairs and research that went with the house from owner to owner. This would at least create a reasonable expectation that owner and/or agent were aware of the significance of the building when contemplating alterations or major repairs.

The second set is local authorities. Formal guidance to them needs reinforcing, covering four main points, two about the provision of information, and two about its curation. The need for adequate information about potential environmental impacts of all kinds to be provided with planning applications should be reiterated, with supporting appendices clarifying the kinds of questions to ask and the types of information that might be expected in different situations. There should be a duty placed upon local planning authorities not to register applications found to contain information that is significantly insufficient for determination. Indications of categories and circumstances could also be given in an appendix to guidance. Support could come from a clear warning issued with listed building consent application forms that processing will be suspended if technical analysis of a registered application shows it to be significantly deficient. That requires dealing with the issue of statistics for cases determined within fixed deadlines, regarded by many councils as an overriding factor to the extent that it can adversely affect the quality of decisions. Is it too imaginative to suggest that positive performance indicators might include statistics on cases where the clock ticking towards the time limit for determination was stopped in clear and verifiable instances where information submitted was inadequate ?

Regarding the curation of information, it should be acceptable as a legitimate standard condition on a planning or listed building consent that the environmental information generated while preparing and implementing proposals ought to be deposited in appropriate formats in publicly maintained information systems. The legality of this would need to be confirmed, but it is certainly directly connected with the development, and arguably with future management, which the planning system exists to regulate or encourage. It might perhaps be included as part of a 'scheme of works' for necessary recording to be agreed before the commencement of development, using the analogy of procedures laid out in PPG 16.

PPG 16 provides a useful analogy because, for applications affecting sites of archaeological significance, there is a Sites and Monuments Record (SMR) to fall back upon, a source of combined expertise and information that should be able to provide a statement of the present state of knowledge fairly easily. But only 20% of SMRs include all listed buildings, and only 22% are consulted regularly about listed building consent applications (Baker, 1999). The principle represented by SMRs, that the investigation and management of historic items needs to be cumulatively documented, has not been applied with the same rigour to historic buildings, especially small ones. There is some evidence that those accustomed to dealing with architectural aesthetics find it hard to conceive of a practical archaeology of upstanding buildings. Many conservation officers maintain their own information systems, despite the heavy pressures of the day-to-day, yet we have no clear picture of their extent, structure or effectiveness such as is now being obtained for SMRs in the context of bids for Heritage Lottery Funding.

Using the analogy of SMRs raises wider issues of intelligibility. At present, most of these are essentially technical support systems, maintained by professionals, part of whose role is to retrieve and package information in response to enquiries. Direct access by external enquirers is difficult without knowledge of the system and how to use the types of material it contains. Much the same is true of general systems for storing the documentation generated by planning applications, which reflect the needs of the planning process, satisfying the demands of the law and in terms that suit often pressured professionals. Though these general systems may contain much material that is useful for the long-term management of a historic building, it will be hard to access, let alone identify whether it exists. Indeed, planning officers facing the scrutiny of 'Best Value' analysis would probably argue that an adequate system was one that catered for their needs alone. A broadening of the definition of 'value' to include other legitimate and relevant uses is required, so that either the main systems become more accessible through in-depth indexing and remote retrieval facilities, or an arrangement is made to transfer copies of relevant material to another purpose-designed system. Though some copyright issues might have to be resolved for certain kinds of documentation, better access could greatly improve information flows, certainly for conservation purposes, and in some cases for analytical research also.

Education and the future

The last word must be with education, providing 'new' ideas informally but clearly, and formal courses for various professionals and interest groups. Education is a powerful force, capable of changing attitudes, promoting new procedures and getting them generally accepted. The example of PPG 16 and the arrival of developer funding for archaeology is in principle encouraging, though no long-term solution has yet been found to the problem of dealing with the counter-productive side effects of commercially driven work upon the stability of research programmes and local services. Documenting smaller historic buildings in the planning process will be a whole new area of work for many planning officers and even for a few conservation officers; it is good, therefore, that it has been taken fully on board by the Institute of Historic Building Conservation. There are urgent training needs here, in conceptual, procedural and technical matters, for archaeologists, architects and other professional agents. There should be a duty on those who maintain local environmental information management systems (LEIMS – Baker 1999, 33) such as SMRs to make arrangements for ensuring that their information is accessible to all potential users. Information should be ordered in two main ways, for effective retrieval by direct expert research and conservation management users, and mediated (perhaps through external partnerships) for the needs of the other 98% of humanity through use by education, tourism, and local community interests. This assumes generally accepted protocols for controlling access to genuinely sensitive information that, in the wrong hands, might put, for example, the contents of a house at risk; accountability might be ensured through an appeal mechanism for aggrieved searchers.

That may sound a slightly negative note upon

which to conclude, but it does help to reinforce the point that the case for effective information management is based upon uses and users rather than on the facilitating systems, though these must of course be effective. Individual cases, longer-term programmes, and conservation strategy are best served by a continuing dialogue between uses as ends and systems as means. In applying that principle to information requirements for planning decisions, the lead must come from defining and meeting the needs of the ends whilst safeguarding other legitimate interests, whether based on security or the reasonable desire not to fund recording work going beyond a reasoned response to the needs of the case.

Postscript – historic churches

Most works upon historic churches are not covered by listed building controls due to 'ecclesiastical exemption'. Churches might also be regarded as too 'polite' architecturally and too specialised to come within the scope of small or vernacular buildings, but they embody unresolved problems of information management that are relevant to this discussion, and these too are being considered currently by the Church of England.

One specific need is for each church building to have a 'statement of significance' which briefly summarises why it is important, architecturally, historically, to its users, visitors, the locality and the nation. The content of such a statement would be selective rather than detailed and definitive, and a prompt for acquiring further information in specific circumstances; above all, it would be intelligible at the level of the interested layman (in both ecclesiastical and architectural senses). Writing such statements seems, at the moment, to be more difficult than might perhaps be expected, not least because their successful use depends upon ownership on the part of the church community (which may be small or have other priorities) deriving from participation in the process of creation. The task here for the recorder of buildings is to manage the available information (which may be uneven), to cut through the detail selectively to what is important in the big picture, and to involve primary users in a way that draws them in rather than turns them off.

Another aspect of selectivity is associated with works of repair to churches, usually arising from quinquennial inspections – a much more ordered approach to management than is usually met for smaller secular historic buildings. Many of these works are localised, and, except in cases such as where an engineering diagnosis of the reasons for structural failure is required, tend not to need much more information by way of providing a justification in support of obtaining the necessary consents. There is, however, the issue of proper documentation, securing adequate records of the existing situation and that created by the works of repair. This is important for classes of work such as stonework replacement and major repointing that might obscure constructional history. It usually does not happen for at least three reasons. Firstly, it is not an automatic procedure for many architects, especially those without experience of working on major buildings such as country houses or castles. Secondly, it is an added cost to works whose funding is likely to be a major financial challenge to the parish. Together, these two factors cause the need for documentation to be questioned on the grounds that 'the building will still be there afterwards', against the background of a misperception that recording is somehow detached from the process of repair.

The third reason, the lack of a maintained archive on the history of a church and its repairs, reinforces this detachment because there is no obvious place to put such information once obtained, such as will ensure its future usefulness. This comment is made despite the existence of legally required procedures in the Church of England for the maintenance of such records in the form of the Parish Log Book and other documentation, and in the knowledge that there are worthy exceptions with exemplary procedures for creating and maintaining records. This is an issue not only of building owners' consciousness of the need for recording but also the broader one of local environmental information management systems for historic buildings, in parallel with those that already exist for archaeology (SMRs). There is a need for the Church of England in conjunction with secular conservation interests to consider how dioceses and SMRs might jointly devise suitable record systems to serve the needs of all kinds of information users.

The creation of accessible depositories could greatly strengthen the case for properly incorporating information requirements into repair processes, where they can be regulated by faculty jurisdiction for stone medieval buildings, or by listed building consent for smaller vernacular buildings. For the latter, to bring this discussion back to the main theme, there are some obstacles to be overcome. These include suspicion of a take-over by the archaeological SMR interests, seen as inappropriate for and detached from building conservation, the immediate financial costs of making records and maintaining information systems despite the value of the long-term investment, and attitudes to records and recording, which are a matter for education.

Acknowledgements

The debts to Baker and Meeson 1997 will be clear, and therefore also to my co-author of that guidance, Bob Meeson. This paper has also greatly benefited from dialogue then and subsequently with Kate Clark.

6 The potential and limitations of the work of a professional consultant *by Richard K Morriss*

I have a small confession to make. I did not go to the Oxford Conference. It was not that I did not want to go, but I simply could not. Similarly, I have not gone to the recent annual conferences of the Institute of Field Archaeologists (IFA), or to those of the Association of Cathedral Archaeologists, or to virtually any other recent national or regional day school or seminar of note. The reasons for this apparent misanthropy are not due to a dislike of my archaeological colleagues. As a student and later, when working with large units with local authority backing, attending conferences was an enjoyable part of the calendar. Now, however, running a small consultancy of my own, money matters. That said, it is not so much the cost of the conference fees, but more the hidden costs of the time taken off to attend them and, of course, coping with clients' looming deadlines.

The work of the consultant

Like most in my position the priority has to be to ensure that, at the end of each month, we have finished enough work and taken in enough money to pay the wages, the taxes, and the bills. A day at a conference is a day without pay, and the time spent in travelling and attending is time not spent on finishing that vital 'can we have it by yesterday' report. In any given year there will be several conferences or seminars worth going to, some lasting more than just a day. To attend even a few could take up as much as a fortnight in total, with no obvious financial benefits. But the point of this introductory digression is not to gain sympathy for the hard-pressed archaeological freelancers and small consultancies. Instead, it is simply to emphasise the fact that ultimately, despite the vocational nature of the job for many of us, it is still a job – a profession that pays the bills.

As contractors, we neither choose the buildings that we wish to study, nor decide on the degree of analysis or recording necessary, nor set research agendas. We have to take the jobs we are offered, and carry them out according to the dictates of others. Like other similar consultancies, our portfolio is crammed with dozens of diverse buildings, from cottages to castles and from chapels to car factories. These have been studied according to the demands of different briefs, ranging from outline analysis to stone-by-stone recording. Few professional units can afford the luxury of specialising in any particular period or type of building; usually the only thing the projects have in common is that they have nothing in common. For the most part the professionals are simply undertaking works designed to meet the requirements that are placed upon our clients by local planning authorities or heritage bodies.

As a result the work of the professional is very different from that of the volunteer and the academic – and neither term is meant to be derogatory. Buildings archaeology, the oldest form of archaeology with a documented history dating back to the Italian Renaissance, was until twenty years or so ago, almost invariably an amateur pursuit – in the truest sense of the word – and such voluntary involvement remains vigorous and vital. The difference between the non-professional and professional buildings archaeologist today is not one of quality; there are many excellent amateurs and no doubt one or two less than excellent professionals. The real difference is that whilst the non-professional can usually pick and choose buildings of a particular type or region with no regard to a timescale or set brief, the professional cannot. Once a professional consultant has successfully tendered for and accepted a job, it has to be carried out to an agreed methodology, timetable and price. The work has to be undertaken as efficiently and speedily as possible without compromising academic – and sometimes moral – standards.

The number of professional independent historic buildings consultants – a term I choose carefully – is still small but slowly growing as planning authorities gradually but rather erratically take on board the various Planning Policy Guidance Notes (PPGs) now in print. In my practice, and I suspect in most, planning issues by far outnumber all other sources of job referrals. Private clients who commission us simply because they wish to know more about their buildings are few and far between, though heritage bodies such as the National Trust and English Heritage provide a fairly regular and very welcome source of income. Most of our work therefore is planning related and, in theory at least, our role as consultants employed by developers to understand the built heritage and thus inform planning decisions is dealt with in PPGs 15 and 16. By the end of any project, even a basic outline analysis, we will hopefully produce a considerable amount of new information on the particular building studied. That is, after all, what we are paid to do. The work should satisfy the planning authority and, barring any major unforeseen architectural or archaeological discovery, it should also help the client's proposals.

Whilst clients may not be too happy to spend money on the work, they will usually note that the historic building consultant's rates are only a fraction of the other professionals they employ – architects, structural engineers, quantity surveyors, etc. If the project is carried out to inform the planning decisions it should be produced before any such decisions are made and provide the necessary information. If it is required as a planning condition, to record during works, it will provide the necessary archival material. Everyone involved should be satisfied. Another small part of the built heritage will be professionally analysed, and the results disseminated to add to the growing corpus of historical data for posterity. So, is there room for improvement and are there any inherent problems in the system?

One of the most obvious facts is that, despite the work of the national heritage bodies, the IFA and the recently formed Institute of Historic Buildings Conservation, the implementation of the two relevant PPGs is still very patchy. In some areas, especially in parts of south-east England, the way in which these PPGs are implemented by the local planning authorities means that some consultancies have sufficient work within a fairly cohesive geographic area. Other consultancies, such as ours, have to roam further afield. This has the dubious advantage of allowing us to study at first hand the various ways in which different planning authorities deal with the archaeology of the built environment, whilst supposedly all singing from the same government hymn sheet. Looking at our projects map, and through discussions with colleagues in other areas, we can also identify those 'black holes' where the PPGs seem not to be taken seriously at all – and wonder how such local authorities manage to ignore them and still make adequately informed planning decisions on historic buildings.

Experience has shown that local authorities have, with a few exceptions, a fairly standard approach to the grander and more overtly important Grade I and II* buildings. Perhaps this is simply a matter of their perceived higher status, but it may also be influenced by the actual or potential involvement of national heritage bodies in such matters. Both English Heritage and Cadw have an interest in the type and scope of recording required and can advise on suitable briefs for such work. However, there is usually no such involvement when dealing with most vernacular buildings, listed or not, and it is with these more numerous buildings that there is a far greater range of approaches across the country.

Invariably, there is a brief for each job and, almost invariably, for each job we, the consultants, have had no involvement in the preparation of that brief. Instead we have to rely on the local authority to produce their individual brief. Some, naming no names, are succinct and well written; some, naming no names, are virtually incomprehensible. Unfortunately, too many are still little more than revamped briefs for archaeological excavation, complete with sections on context numbers, the site matrix and artefact conservation. Some briefs are quite obviously cobbled together using a selection of standard paragraphs and phrases from a template document

and the degree of care in ensuring that the correct paragraphs and phrases have been used can be suspect. Recently we had one brief regarding a mill complex in which the word 'agricultural' had been used mistakenly throughout instead of 'industrial'. Only very rarely, and usually only quite informally, have we been asked by a local authority to propose and design an appropriate response to a particular planning issue.

Our response to a brief is to produce a tender document, usually accompanied by a written scheme of investigation. Some local authorities will, quite rightly, vet the various tenders received by the client rather than always allowing the lowest bid to succeed. In order to tender for the work, with the hope of being successful, we have to virtually rewrite the brief, adding a few additional frills and furbelows, and present it, retyped and reset in our own house style, as part of our Written Scheme of Investigation (WSI). Although we may disagree with the brief, there is seldom any opportunity for discussion or modification. The work has to be done as closely as is practicable to its dictates, and this has to be reflected in the WSI and tender document.

Briefs usually require that suitably qualified and experienced practitioners undertake the necessary work, and an increasing proportion advise that project officers, at least, are Members or Associates of the IFA. By no means all also request that Members have the relevant area of competence. Nevertheless, it is implicit in any brief that the quality of the works produced will be up to the best standards possible – a fact that should be taken as read in any profession.

Normally the analysis is presented in a bound report, prefaced by the historical background and illustrated with reduced copies of the survey drawings and a selection of photographs. Such reports are easy to distribute and most local records offices and libraries readily accept them, as do the National Monuments Record (NMR) and other depositories. Curiously, most briefs do not indicate who is responsible for distributing the reports or how many should be produced. Should it be the clients, their architects or the archaeological contractors? Many clients prefer to withhold distribution whilst planning matters are under way and insist that they should hold all the copies for the time being. There appear to be no set procedures for checking that copies of the report end up where they are meant to go. On more than one occasion we have undertaken a project only to learn subsequently that an earlier report had been produced, but no one knew of it because the reports had not been lodged in an appropriate depository. Without some new initiative this problem is likely to grow (Eavis, p 126).

Less easy to dispose of are the other records produced as part of a contract – especially the survey drawings. Some briefs are quite specific about where the archive should be deposited and others are not. Some briefs simply ask that the finished inked drawings be deposited and others, again harking back to archaeological excavations, require site roughs and site notebooks to form part of the archive too – a rather odd notion, as these are normally inappropriate for building surveys, adding bulk but no substance.

It can be difficult enough to persuade some local archivists to accept even the inked survey drawings, though ideally it is surely better that records of local buildings be deposited in local records offices. This fact is not always reflected in recording briefs and it is clear that in many regions there has been little or no discussion between the planning authority and the local archives regarding the deposition of such records. Fortunately, the NMR will usually accept such archives. The photographic record can be another source of confusion; who keeps the prints and who keeps the negatives? Again one or two local archives have been reluctant to take large collections of prints of a specific building for cost reasons, but again the NMR can always assist in this matter. These are purely practical problems that could be resolved in advance through adequate briefs if there were more cooperation between the planning authorities or heritage bodies and the archivists who might logically be expected to take the results of the work. As far as I am aware, not many conservation officers have ever sat down with their local archivists to work out how to manage the large and increasing amount of archive necessarily produced by most historic building analyses, and the call for a national strategy relating to records, as advocated by Eavis (p 128) is to be welcomed.

Levels of record

Such practical problems are not as serious as the inconsistency of the levels of archaeological works set out in the briefs. Some demand surprisingly little or no recording, whilst others go beyond what seems to be required for the type and complexity of the building involved and the impact of the proposed works. This is easily demonstrated by our own caseload of the past few months. On two concurrent projects in neighbouring counties we were, in accordance with the respective briefs, on the one hand producing quite irrelevant detailed drawings of reused timber lintels in a Grade II building, whilst on the other, producing an interpretation of a Grade I building illustrated with hopelessly inaccurate architect's survey drawings. In two very similar farmstead analysis projects, mainly of Grade II buildings, one local authority insisted on outline survey drawings whilst another was quite happy with a good quality photographic record.

Ultimately the degree and extent of the archaeological work is still down to the individual conservation officers, their particular skills and experience, and perhaps as important, the influence they are allowed within the planning process. It is a great responsibility for the guardians of the built heritage – but to use, for the first and probably only time, dimly remembered schoolboy Latin – '*Quis custiodiet ipsos Custodes*' – 'Who will guard the guards?' It is not that conservation officers do not necessarily know about buildings, but not all are trained or experienced in the understanding of buildings, and there is a difference. Similarly, not all are aware of the capabilities of the historic building consultant.

In the face of an increasing number of planning proposals, a standard *pro forma* recording brief has become a safe, simple and quick method of fulfilling the planning authority's basic requirements under one or other of the relevant PPGs. Unfortunately, historic buildings are not as conveniently standard, either in their design, materials, condition, complexity or accessibility. Standard briefs have the potential to lead to too little or, far more commonly, too much detailed recording, well beyond what is really necessary to actually understand a building.

The bias towards too much recording is a continuation of the deep-rooted 'traditional' archaeological philosophy transposed from excavation methodology to building recording, and from PPG 16 to PPG 15. The necessarily detailed and comprehensive recording of the excavator was, particularly in the 1980s when archaeology was becoming more and more complex, seen to be equally relevant to the building archaeologist. This 'record-the-lot' methodology was secure, but necessarily expensive. Unfortunately it completely missed the point made through several centuries of building archaeology. Brunelleschi found the solution to finishing the dome of Sta Maria del Fiore in Florence in the archaeological study of the ruins of Rome. Even early in the 15th century he knew that to survey a building appropriately it is necessary to have at least a clearly defined purpose and basic understanding of it.

Any survey should surely reflect its purpose and objectives. Recording for recording's sake is unacceptable, both philosophically and professionally. There are of course situations in which a very detailed level of survey is appropriate, especially where that recording will be the definitive record of something that is to be altered or destroyed. However, amongst the most pointlessly expensive exercises that I have been involved with over the past twenty years or so are the complete stone-by-stone surveys of rubble-stone walls. What was (and sometimes, still is) the point? Rubble-stone can be deceptive, but any experienced building archaeologist should be able to pick out things like construction breaks, seasonal build breaks, beam or joist socket positions, changes in mortar, putlog holes, roof and floor scars, and levelling courses. These are the features that really matter in understanding a rubble-stone wall, so an outline drawing showing such features, accompanied by sufficiently detailed and, if possible, rectified and scaled photographs, are all that are usually needed – even for 'preservation by record'.

A second, and far more common example of over-recording in the field of vernacular buildings concerns the thousands of fairly standard designs of post-medieval timber-framed country cottages.

Figure 6.1   Late-17th-century Shropshire cottage with later cladding. A rapid and interpretative survey was considered of most use in understanding the structure.

Sometimes, where such buildings are listed and due to be developed, planning briefs citing PPG 15 will require a fully dimensioned and levelled 1:20 survey. These will, however, seldom if ever provide more significant information than 1:50 sketches drawn up using a rapid survey technique. Detailed surveys will necessarily have to take into account later accretions, surface finishes, existing windows and doorways and any lean or settlement that buildings have suffered. All these features are, of course, important parts of the history of buildings and could impact on decisions made about their future, but can usually be dealt with quite adequately in the text of archaeological reports.

With care, a rapid survey can produce far more useful *interpretative* drawings that show the origin and development of the timber frame – the kernel of the building. We normally use a system that takes the wall-plate as datum, and from it, assuming all horizontal timbers to have been intended to be horizontal, and all verticals vertical, develop a 'real-frame' drawing based on the true relationships of mortices, original apertures, etc. Not only is this, and other related methods, far more useful in understanding such buildings and thus informing planning decisions made about them, it is also very quick and, as a result, very cheap in comparison to the alternatives (see Figs 6.1, 6.2). Similarly rapid survey techniques can also be used for buildings of

other materials with equally informative results. The difference between two hundred and two thousand pounds or more in survey costs for an owner or developer can be vital. It is sometimes forgotten that, particularly in smaller buildings, we are often dealing with ordinary people's homes where money does matter, rather than stately homes, where for large budget schemes it might matter less.

Unfortunately, in most areas such surveys are seldom asked for in planning briefs and, at the moment, there is little or no opportunity for input by the professional consultants to request changes to such briefs, apart from through the unofficial contacts that we all have with certain of the more pragmatic planning officers. Equally, there is little or no opportunity to change a brief that is obviously flawed.

Recently we were asked to undertake a full stone-by-stone survey of some masonry to distinguish between the medieval and the 19th-century repair work. After visiting, to size up the job, and chatting with the real expert – the mason – we came to the conclusion that there was no medieval work at all, and that the differential weathering of the stones was due to their poor quality. This was backed up by a swift dip into the archives, which proved conclusively that the entire wall had been rebuilt from footings in the 19th century, and that the masons then had complained about the quality of the quarry

A5(E)

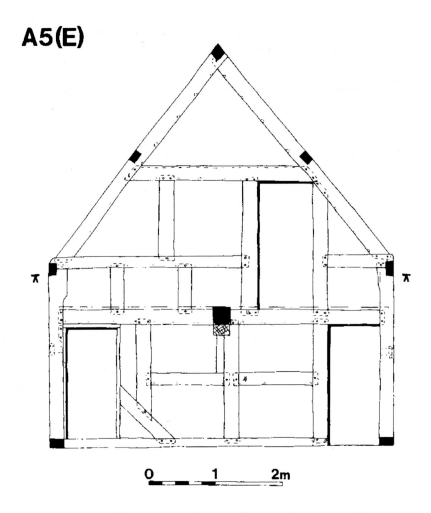

0   1   2m

Figure 6.2   Section through cottage illustrated in Fig 6.1. This outline 'assembly' survey was far cheaper and more informative than a fully detailed survey would have been.

from which the stones came. In this case no one could have been blamed for the decision to ask for a detailed record, but it does highlight the need for greater flexibility in the system, and the benefits of involving professional consultants in the process well in advance.

The timing of recording

Whilst common sense dictates that for many historic buildings the briefs for recording and analysis are often too rigid, another major problem with the process at present is that they are produced far too late in the project, often set after the planning proposals have already been virtually agreed. Indeed, sometimes a survey and analysis is required as a condition of a planning permission and it is obvious that the decisions have been made without the benefit of an historic building analysis. In thousands of buildings of undistinguished architectural or historic quality that is not, in itself, a problem, but even buildings that appear to be of no interest prove, on closer investigation, to be of far more value than first

thought. Where a brief for recording or analysis is set as a condition, the decisions about the building's importance might have been made purely on the advice of a planning officer and the available listing or SMR information.

PPG 16 (para 31) advises that if archaeological remains of national importance are discovered during a development, the Secretary of State for National Heritage has the power to schedule them, or to revoke a planning permission; the latter course is also open to planning authorities, although in view of the heavy compensation payments that might ensue from such action it has rarely been taken. For listed buildings, if there is any likelihood that works will reveal hidden features it is open to the planning authority to attach an appropriate condition to ensure retention or proper recording, but in my experience such conditions are rarely applied. Again a recent example from our own files can illustrate the point. We were asked to fulfil a brief set out for the photographic recording and local documentary research of a site that was due to be flattened to make way for a supermarket. It contained an early-19th-century inn and a large and, frankly, ugly, early-

20th-century shed latterly used as a garage. Although not listed, the conservation officer had flagged up the Belfast trusses of its roof and the tradition that it had been built as a drill hall during the First World War. As a result, the planning committee were persuaded to condition an outline record and analysis of the site, but only just before it was demolished – in fact, just a day or so before the bulldozers moved in. The documentary research was carried out retrospectively and nothing was found locally. However, some anomalies within the building led to questions being raised about its military origins and further research at the PRO in London luckily provided the answers. The building had actually been designed as a roller skating rink in 1909, but it had gone bankrupt within a year; nevertheless, it could have been the only one of that date left in the country. In this case, considering the indifferent architectural quality and poor condition of the building, the information would not have affected its fate, but as its original function was not discovered until it had been demolished, it shows the inherent problems of not ensuring that information is obtained well in advance and not as a condition of works.

These examples illustrate how important and worthwhile it is to know more about a site well before proposals are put forward or briefs are set, so as to inform planning decisions and conditions. Arguably, for many developments, the consultant's work would benefit from being divided into two sections – the second being dependent upon the first. For many vernacular buildings a short appraisal will be all that is required to inform not only the brief for any recording work, but also all the planning decisions. On more complicated or larger sites a more comprehensive assessment may be needed. This can be specified in an initial brief from the local authority, based on the results of the appraisal.

Interaction with planning authorities

As Baker has shown in the previous chapter, the information from the initial assessment should be sufficient to help mould the proposed development to respect as far as practicable or desirable the fabric of the building in question. The report should be prepared in advance of the discussions regarding the proposed works and the determination of the planning application. The document should be intelligible to the client, architects, structural engineers, quantity surveyors, conservation and planning officers. The costs of either appraisals or more detailed assessments are normally small, but the benefits to decision-making, both at the design stage and in the determination of planning applications, are generally out of all proportion to the money spent.

In some parts of the country this procedure is followed, albeit on a rather *ad hoc* basis. A few consultants, generally those whose work is confined to a small number of local authority areas, have sufficiently gained the confidence of the conservation officers to be able to more or less define their own standards and techniques. Sometimes they are invited to propose a recording brief and schedule and indicate how much this would cost. This approach has two advantages. Firstly, the busy curator does not have to spend time and resources defining what work must be done, and secondly, the work is more likely to be specifically tailored to the circumstances of the project by a contractor with appropriate experience of what may be required. This does not provide a one-way ticket to large and profitable contracts, as it remains open to the curator and the client to ensure that the recommended work does not go beyond what is necessary. In any case the consultant will generally be in a competitive tendering situation.

Despite the obvious advantages, this has led to very different techniques of recording and analysis being adopted in different parts of the country. For example, in East Sussex, although he has also undertaken numerous major and complex projects, David Martin has specialised in very rapid and cost-effective historic building assessments, generally achievable in a single working day. As a result, he has been consulted for a high proportion of listed building applications in the area where he works and has generated a formidable archive with much wider applications than merely informing planning decisions. In areas where planning authorities only tend to require a specialist input for large and complex projects the recording is more time-consuming and expensive, and the impression is reinforced that historic building analysis is unnecessarily burdensome. As a result, in these areas rapid assessments rarely enter the thinking of conservation officers, and local contractors tend to work only on large and complex schemes. The variety of standards and methods employed increases with the distinction between recording to inform conservation work and that to mitigate loss of fabric. Although attempts have been made to define what levels of analysis may be appropriate in given circumstances (cf Baker and Meeson 1997), these are no substitute for experience born out of regular application and liaison with colleagues, but as yet no forum has emerged for this specialised area of work.

The consultant as part of a project team

It may seem curious that not all larger developers include historic building consultants in the decision-making process, either at the design stage or in the discussions with the planning authority. However, the plain fact is that most do not understand the role of consultants and the potential benefits they can bring. It is still an uncomfortable fact of life that consultants are seen as an additional burden rather than as a benefit. When, particularly on large projects, I have been involved in buildings as a full member of the team, there has generally been a good interchange of ideas and better relations with the planning authorities. If a conservation officer is aware that a project team has an historic buildings consultant on board, and feels able to trust his or her advice, the advantages to both sides are quite significant. Although paid for by the developer, the consultant nevertheless has a foot in both camps and offers independent advice based on professional judgement. Were this not the case, his or her reputation, and ability to get work, would be badly damaged.

If the consultant is appointed to the project team at an early stage it is possible that he will have some involvement in formulating an archaeological strategy that is then put to the relevant planning authority for comment and, hopefully, approval. During the development works, the consultant can monitor the inevitable changes from the initial scheme and assess their consequences. Sometimes a memo or letter from the consultant to the planning authority is all that is needed to allow the scheme to progress without having each and every alteration taken through the 'due process' and causing inevitable delays. One project of this sort that we were involved with was on a Grade I mansion for the Ministry of Defence. After preliminary meetings and some early discussions with both the local planning authority and English Heritage, there was no other external involvement for the two years of the project other than the dissemination by memo of changes and archaeological responses to them, and the occasional phone call.

An advisory role

The benefits of historic building consultants on project teams is a useful point at which to veer away from possible improvements to planning procedures through greater use of the skills of historic building consultants, and on to more practical matters. Apart from making the clients and their teams aware of the archaeological constraints or costs of the schemes under discussion, consultants can also either offer advice or suggest places where it can be obtained, especially for those who have encountered few historic buildings. Advice can also aid other professionals. For example, apart from specialists, few structural engineers have experience of dealing with timber frames, but some historic building consultants can work out the original design of a timber-framed building, even when substantial portions have been removed. This can lead to the logical decision to replace missing members and restore original methods of support, rather than introducing incompatible and aesthetically unpleasing RSJs. Similarly, understanding the building can lead to significant design changes by the architect that more sensitively mirror the historic development of a building. Such improvements can sometimes be

achieved even after planning permission has been granted.

Still too often, unfortunately, the general perception is that the consultant is an added expense, and this will need to change if the maximum benefit is to be extracted from our own particular skills and experiences. Few developers, be they individual home owners or large corporations, are likely to be sufficiently interested in the detailed analysis and understanding of historic buildings to read the fine books available on the subject. They are even less likely to read the more specialist literature on buildings archaeology or the role of the historic building consultant. However, minds are concentrated during the planning process and it is perhaps in the leaflets produced by local planning authorities, and in preliminary discussions with planning officers, that the potential role of the consultants can be pointed out.

The site-specific nature of the work

So far this paper has concentrated mainly upon planning issues since, as already explained, these are a major concern for professional historic building consultants. From this it is clear that professionals face numerous constraints. We tend to deal mainly with buildings that are subject to change or demolition, because it is these projects that provide the funding for our work. As well as ensuring that the hundreds of thousands of other historic buildings not scheduled for major alterations are generally outside our professional remit, this also has another disadvantage. Ultimately, virtually all our research and recording is site specific. Our analytical skills are mainly used to untangle the archaeological and historical development of individual buildings, or groups of buildings, and our surveying skills are used to record them. Understanding the critical archaeological elements of buildings – their fabric, form and function – has to be based on observation, objectivity and open-mindedness. That understanding should be reliable and readily verifiable from the evidence.

Professional historic buildings consultants have the opportunity of studying, often in great detail, buildings and parts of buildings that are not normally accessible to the public. Yet, no matter how good or detailed a report we produce, it will only provide a greater understanding of one particular building or site. Its primary purpose is to assist in determining a planning issue, or help to inform decisions about the future conservation and use of the building, or to record something that will be lost. Some such work will also add something to our cumulative knowledge of the built environment. Seldom, however, is there any scope for this information to be placed into a broader context, or, indeed, to be widely disseminated. On most projects there is only limited time to compare the buildings involved with others of similar type or status, even in a perfunctory manner. Where such opportunities arise they are usually on higher status buildings such as churches, castles and great houses, for which there is already a good body of published research material available. Despite great strides in the past two decades, mainly on a voluntary basis, available published and relevant research on vernacular buildings is not easy to access, simply because of the huge numbers of buildings, their distinct local characteristics, and the diversity of journals.

Some planning briefs insist that time be spent on a short piece for a suitable local journal, but not all do. Very occasionally, there may even be funding to produce a proper article. Usually such papers have to be written for nothing, or a small honorarium, and even then the local journals have a financial struggle to print articles unless there is some direct grant aid. At best, the information produced by the professional consultant will serve as raw material for someone else's work in the future – and almost inevitably, that someone will not be a professional historic buildings consultant. At worst, the reports and drawings will lie undisturbed in a records office while the consultant moves on to the next project and starts all over again.

While the professional contractor is obliged to move on to the next funded project the volunteer and the academic may be able to extend the timetable for research. Accordingly, most of the broader research issues are beyond the reach of professional contractors unless they pursue research aims as an unpaid sideline. The opportunities for paid research on larger themes are extremely limited. Occasionally the historic building consultant can also work on more extensive surveys with a wider geographical scope, and local authorities can make use of such work for the compilation or enhancement of SMRs, in the preparation of local plans and conservation area documents, to name just a few applications.

The potential of non-intensive surveys

We are all aware of the inevitable limitations of the listing system. Despite the recent, and most comprehensive re-listing, the sheer numbers of buildings, the little time allowed to investigate, and the lack of space for descriptions, mean that the lists are only a very basic starting point for the appreciation of the significance of any building. Enhancement surveys, sometimes tied into the SMR, are extensive (non-intensive) surveys providing information about a lot more individual buildings, but not necessarily an academic overview. For example, in the early 1990s, the City of Hereford Archaeology Unit worked with its neighbours – the then Hereford & Worcester County Archaeology Service – on their Central Marches Towns study, providing information about historic buildings in individual towns and former towns in three counties as part of a larger and mainly archaeologically based study. Whilst the principle was good, only a day was spent on each town, so the

resultant information was really an improved listing with a fairly perfunctory overview for each settlement. Nevertheless, this was incorporated with good effect into the overall study.

On a smaller scale, this consultancy has worked with the West Midlands Joint Data Team on several parishes in Walsall and on the 'canal corridor' in Wolverhampton, providing information on all historic structures within the study areas. This work was mainly an information gathering exercise, improving listing information and the site details in the SMR for listed and other historic buildings. Even in such apparently unpromising survey areas there were some significant finds, including a 'lost' canal branch and lock chamber in Brownhills and an unlisted late-18th-century threshing barn in Little Bloxwich. The surveys also produced a descriptive gazetteer of virtually all the significant structures in these areas, from canal and railway bridges to the better examples of 20th-century architecture.

Historic building consultants have also been employed on slightly more intensive and integrated studies. An earlier pilot study in 1989 – the Hereford High Town study, funded by the local authority and English Heritage – included buildings as both archaeological and aesthetic resources, and added several buildings to the statutory list in the process. It attempted to formulate planning and development policies that respected the underlying archaeology, the built environment and the tenuous *genius loci* – the spirit of the place. By removing the rather costly input of the planning consultants who were also involved in that particular project, and the glossy production, and concentrating instead on the building sections in the report, this could form a useful model for relatively low-cost listing enhancements or for building databases. These in turn could help to inform Local Plan policies. None of this work could be developer funded, but the costs would not be great and would benefit local authorities. If the information was in an easily accessible, preferably published, form this would allow potential developers to obtain a basic understanding of the conservation issues in advance, and would perhaps save the council officers from having to repeatedly explain everything to them in preliminary meetings.

Conservation Plans

One relatively new development that is beginning to involve professionals in non-planning issues in a more intensive manner than SMR enhancements is the production of Conservation Plans, although the majority are related to larger and more significant grade I and II* buildings and monuments. Conservation Plans are generally required to support long-term funding packages from such sources as English Heritage and the National Lottery, although some are undertaken by a particular organisation simply because they are felt to be part of good long-term management strategy. Recently we have been involved in several Conservation Plans, such as at Powis Castle for the National Trust, on the Music Hall complex for Shrewsbury & Atcham Borough Council, and at Aston Hall for Birmingham City Museums & Art Gallery.

Vernacular buildings tend to feature in such plans only when they fall within a larger site such as a cathedral close. The main drawback with Conservation Plans to date is that some have become extremely over large and unmanageable, no longer remaining the succinct management documents that they were intended to be. There is a general awareness too that some sites do not require a fully detailed plan but merely a more simple 'statement'; this treatment could be extended to buildings and sites lower down the hierarchical heritage ladder.

Research projects

Although Conservation Plan work involves varying degrees of analysis and recording, from full-blown archaeological reports to simple overviews, broader studies such as SMR enhancements are not really cerebral processes; they are merely intelligence gathering exercises. They provide more information about individual local buildings but do not contribute a greater understanding of the general architectural heritage.

Such surveys are not really research projects, and it seems to be the fate of the professional buildings consultant to continue to study one building or group of buildings at a time, rather than to be able to contemplate broader themes. Although there are some paid research projects, these are not normally selected on the basis of regional or national research priorities and there is no understood system of selection, distribution or funding. The process is *ad hoc*, and it seems to be up to the contractors to make the suggestions. Whilst that is not a bad concept, there is potential for a more methodical way of determining priorities and allocating the necessary resources to appropriate contractors.

Nonetheless, there are still 'accidental' research themes that could be undertaken when funding is available. Some potential projects almost create their own agendas. For example, in the past five years or so this consultancy has been involved in archaeological work for the County Council on the surface remains of several of the mines in the Shropshire leadfield. This was in advance of consolidation works on the buildings, undertaken mostly by the County Council or, on one site, by a local mines trust, both using various in-house budgets and external grants. The leadfield is a fairly compact geographical area, literally on our doorstep, and there is an obvious thematic link between the various projects. Hopefully more mines in the area will be consolidated in the next few years, involving further surveys to inform the work.

At present, the results of the archaeological work on each individual mine are produced in our own in-house series of reports, of which no more than two-dozen or so copies are produced. The additional information is fed into the SMR, but the eventual location of the archive has yet to be determined. Accordingly, the results of the work are still site-centred and necessarily fragmented, despite their obvious research potential. A complete archaeological, architectural and historical survey of an entire leadfield would be both useful regionally and, on a national scale, provide contrasts and comparisons with other orefields in the United Kingdom. Such a study would not only make an ideal academic monograph; it would also explain significance, highlight potential, and place value upon the resource. Given the draconian cuts to their finances since the 1980s, the County Council is not in a position to commission and publish such a study, so funding would have to come from elsewhere.

Through a slightly different set of circumstances, the consultancy also found itself studying the two most intact claustral remains of the Gilbertines – the only medieval monastic order founded in England. Both Chicksands and Clattercote Priories, in Bedfordshire and Oxfordshire respectively, had been considerably altered since the Dissolution, but both offered substantial insights into the Order's architecture. Both projects were undertaken for planning purposes, one for the Ministry of Defence and one for a private client. Again, the results of both were published in our in-house series but no comparative study could be undertaken. As with the lead mines, a useful research programme could be based on the two sites. The amount of upstanding Gilbertine fabric is quite small, despite the large number of their houses, and the sites are mainly in mid- and eastern England. A thorough archaeological and architectural study of the buildings would enhance understanding of an entire Order for comparisons and contrasts with the others.

In both cases the research potential and academic benefits are obvious, but there is no agency that the professional can approach to obtain the necessary funds. Partly because of this, almost all 'blue skies' research and thematic studies have to be undertaken by the voluntary and academic sectors. In my home county of Shropshire there has been virtually no professional involvement in the overall understanding of the county's architectural heritage to date (though a much-awaited volume of the Victoria County History is due soon), yet Madge Moran, a locally-based independent specialist has produced excellent work on large groups of buildings in, for example, the towns of Much Wenlock and Whitchurch (1999). These are based on the work of many people of different experience and skill levels but under the direction of a part-time university tutor.

Conclusion

For the professional consultant, barring a huge influx of funding, the present situation is unlikely to change for some time. Does it matter? After all, providing that the necessary information is procured to inform each planning decision and, as a by-product, the reports are made available for others to use, professional consultants are at least performing a good service and getting paid for it. For some, the hands-on analysis and recording work is in any case more rewarding than pursuing more ethereal research, and for others, finding worthy and interesting areas of research is difficult. Nevertheless, it is sad that historic building consultants undertake such a small proportion of the thematic and contextual historic buildings research. For the time being this is mainly in the care of voluntary groups or individuals, and academics, though occasionally some professionals make spare time to follow their own research interests. Fortunately there are now very few professionals who still feel arrogant enough to dismiss 'mere amateurs'. It is unfortunate that the word 'amateur' has been sidelined for its derogatory connotations because its original meaning – doing something simply for the love of it – has become equated with the second rate. For centuries these 'amateurs' have been responsible for, and are still a vital part of, the survival and development of what we few fortunate professional practitioners now make our living from – even if we can't afford to go to conferences.

Overall the potential of the professional historic buildings consultant is slowly, but erratically, being recognised by both planning authorities and developers, though both are perhaps understandably reluctant to pay for their skills. For the one the work is a cost on the council tax that has to be justified to councillors and ratepayers; for the other it is perceived as an additional cost imposed upon them by the planning process. Consultants must continue to demonstrate to all sides that they are able, at a very reasonable (some might say too reasonable) cost, to help them and possibly even save them money.

Early involvement in the planning process, particularly at a preliminary assessment stage, can ensure the adoption of appropriate recording strategies that save money without diluting the necessary information or quality of archive. Properly timetabled involvement can also assist in the formulation of appropriate proposals for historic buildings. Continued involvement during projects can save developers and planning officers both time and effort, and reduce the number of delays to scheduled works, even when unexpected discoveries are made. Beyond such specific project-related issues, expanding the various forms of enhancement survey could add to the information available to the local authorities to inform local plans and planning decisions.

For the professional historic buildings consultant, the limitations at present are mainly those of funding, which will probably always be there, and the lack of a full appreciation of their role and abilities by both developers and planners, which, hopefully, will not.

7 Old buildings for the future: the work of an archaeological unit *by Robina McNeil and Michael Nevell*

Historical buildings do not belong to us only. They belonged to our forefathers and they will belong to our descendants unless we play them false. They are not in any sense our property to do as we like with them. We are only trustees for those that come after us.

William Morris

The Field Archaeology Centre is an umbrella organisation, housing two archaeological units at the University of Manchester. The Greater Manchester Archaeological Unit (GMAU) is the curatorial arm concerned with conservation and planning, whilst the University of Manchester Archaeological Unit (UMAU) is the teaching, commissioning and contracting arm. The division of the two teams prevents a conflict arising from the planning process, but the overarching role of the Field Archaeology Centre allows for a proper collaboration between the two units for the purposes of research, outreach, education and European initiatives.

The philosophy of the Field Archaeology Centre is underlined by three very simple principles – understanding, appreciation and preservation. All the archaeological work is guided by this philosophy. This rationale is the starting point under PPG 15, where information required for planning applications is obtained through investigations tailor-made to each building. This also contributes to wider research initiatives into, for instance, industrial building types or, for the purposes of this article, vernacular rural and urban forms, for which Manchester and its hinterlands are not well-known. Since C F Innocent found that 'there was hardly any information . . . available as to the design and construction of the smaller secular buildings . . .' (Innocent 1916, reprinted 1999) the study of vernacular architecture has developed beyond all recognition. Nevertheless, for the Manchester area and perhaps for north-west England as a whole, his comments are still largely true. The patchy state of our knowledge of vernacular buildings in the region is one of the principal reasons for their study today.

In Manchester we, like others, welcomed *Planning Policy Guidance Note 16: Archaeology and planning* (PPG 16), and *Planning and the historic environment* (PPG 15), for a number of reasons, but principally because government guidance forced consideration of the historic environment onto the agenda. The advice aims to ensure that 'below ground archaeology' and 'above ground archaeology', that is the built environment, are both considered in determining planning applications. Although imperfect and flawed in their application, they are the best means available at present, and if used judiciously can give the historic environment a platform and authority rarely achieved before.

A number of informative policy documents are available to guide both principles and practice (Baker and Meeson 1997; English Heritage 1995, 1998a; RCHME 1999). These tools, together with PPG 15 and PPG 16, can be used at two levels. At a pragmatic level they are planning tools and at a strategic level they serve as an authoritative voice, giving a framework and context for policy and best practice in buildings archaeology.

The Field Archaeology Centre is prepared to adopt, adapt and experiment with various national initiatives and so broaden the range of work. Buildings at Risk Surveys (English Heritage 1992, 1998c, 2000) and Conservation Plans (English Heritage 1998a, 1999) are particularly useful as they provide ways for looking at the importance of a building and the vulnerability of that importance, and enable condition or degree of risk to be measured. The judicious and pragmatic application of these allows for a greater understanding. Their main contribution is that they act as springboards for the resolution of archaeological heritage problems and form one of the mainstays for preservation. Ultimately our buildings, integral to our cultural heritage, make a significant contribution to local distinctiveness, sense of place and quality of life. Their reuse and preservation, and the wider implications of heritage-led conservation, are increasingly recognised as a valuable resource for urban regeneration and sustainable tourism.

The historic environment is now part of our cultural heritage. Inevitably, principles and practices are linked and frequently overlap to the benefit of the historic environment. The case studies below are used to illustrate our philosophy, which is to enhance understanding and, thereby, appreciation and protection of the historic environment.

Warburton: the value of regional surveys

The continuing archaeological survey of Warburton demonstrates how, despite constant development pressures, local research of a single rural township has contributed during the 1990s to the maintenance of the rural character of an agricultural community on the fringes of the Manchester conurbation. The township and ancient manor of Warburton, sandwiched between the rural market town of Lymm in the west and the dormitory town of Altrincham in the east, cover 1750 acres at the confluence of the rivers Mersey and Bollin on the

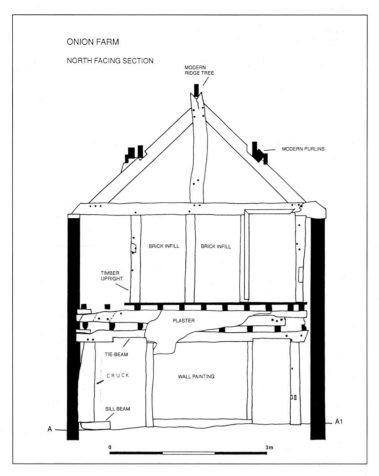

ONION FARM

NORTH FACING SECTION

MODERN RIDGE TREE

MODERN PURLINS

BRICK INFILL   BRICK INFILL

TIMBER UPRIGHT

PLASTER

TIE-BEAM

CRUCK   WALL PAINTING

SILL BEAM

A   A1

0   3m

Figure 7.1   Onion Farm, Warburton, showing timber framing, remains of cruck and position of wall painting. (Field Archaeology Centre)

Cheshire / Greater Manchester border. The archaeological units have been involved at Warburton since 1982, largely in response to development pressures.

During the 1980s the main archaeological threats were to the below ground archaeology, through pipelines and ploughing, but during the early 1990s the focus shifted towards the buildings of the township, as farmhouses and barns became redundant and were sold on for refurbishment and conversion respectively. Between 1990 and 1995 several barns were converted into dwellings, but the units only became involved on those sites with listed building status which could be encompassed within the orbit of PPG 16 and PPG 15. This involved two farm complexes, Onion Farm and The Bent (Hartwell 1989; Mayer 1992; Nevell 1995), only one of which, Onion Farm, eventually saw redevelopment (see Figs 7.1, 7.2). Planning conditions were imposed which required that archaeological work be undertaken prior to any alterations and renovations, and at Onion Farm the results of the building survey were used to change the final designs in order to safeguard unsuspected or well-preserved early architectural details. During restoration a cruck-framed, three-bay farmhouse was revealed with a mid-16th-century wall painting surviving on a timber-framed partition between the house body and the service area; this

feature was preserved with money from the local council, along with other surviving timber-framed elements.

The Warburton Archaeological Survey was established in 1996 in part as a response to increasing development pressures, with the intention of studying the landscape archaeology of the whole township. The project has four major research aims, but the one most relevant to the present discussion is the intention to study the archaeology of the buildings of the township as a single group. The modern township of Warburton contains approximately 150 buildings, about 120 of which have been assessed as pre-dating 1900 and being worthy of further research (Nevell 1999). The intention is to study half of this smaller group (around 60 buildings) over a period of five years from 1997 onwards. In addition to building up a statistically valid and detailed picture of the local vernacular traditions of one north-western lowland township, this research should provide the local council with detailed information on the importance of the buildings in the light of development pressures. To ensure evenness of the gathered data, the RCHME guidelines on building survey are used as the bedrock for all analysis and recording. Since 1996, 25 buildings have been studied. Five surveys (Birch Farm, Ditchfield Cottage, Moss Farm, War-

Figure 7.2   Onion Farm, Warburton. Late-16th-century wall painting with geese, rose and Elizabethan lady. (Field Archaeology Centre)

burton Mill and Wigsey Farm) were undertaken through conditions applied in the light of PPG 15, the remainder were carried out through the cooperation and permission of local owners and occupiers. The buildings include eleven farmhouses, six barns, five cottages, a mill, a cross-base, and the parish church.

The most interesting group recorded to date is the farmhouses. Amongst them are seven cruck-framed houses of two and three bays and one and half storeys. This is the earliest vernacular building tradition to survive in the north-west, common in the medieval period for both domestic and agricultural buildings. In 1981, 3054 cruck-framed buildings were recorded in England and Wales, of which 346 could be found in the north-west, 54 of them lying within Greater Manchester (Alcock 1981, 119–20). Since that date the number of cruck buildings identified within the county has risen to 72, although only 56 now survive, emphasising the need for well-informed curation (Burke & Nevell 1996: Nevell 1997). The examples from Warburton form the largest concentration of surviving cruck buildings in Greater Manchester and one of the largest in the north-west. However, these preliminary results suggest that cruck-framed construction was once very common, at least in parts of the north-west lowlands, and that the concentration in Warburton is perhaps deceptive, arising from the continuity of the rural community and the locally intensive survey work.

During the last four years the conservation officer and the planning department of Trafford MBC have employed the advice in PPG 15 not only to record in detail those listed buildings under threat but also to gain access to lesser buildings which were not listed, but nevertheless had some form of limited protection through the Conservation Areas Act. Buildings continue to be lost – most recently the corn mill – and development pressures continue, with applications for barn conversions and new housing next to disused farmhouses, but the survey has characterised the vernacular buildings of the township and given the local council another lever with which to maintain the rural aspects of the township.

Kersal Cell, Salford: winning over developers

Kersal Cell (see Fig 7.3), a grade II* listed building, demonstrates how the philosophy of understanding, appreciation and preservation can be applied over many years to a single historic building, despite a rapid series of changes of use. This timber-framed property stands some 90m east of the River Irwell, within the ancient township of Broughton in the city of Salford. The site takes its name from the monastic cell established here in the 12th century by the Cluniac priory of Lenton near Nottingham. The oldest part of the present house is the timber-framed south wing. Originally a cruck-built open hall, this was subsequently adapted, externally by the addition of frontal projecting wings and internally by floor and room divisions, to form a small country house typical of the lesser gentry of the 16th and

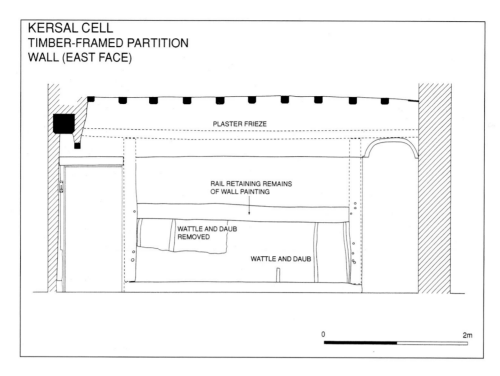

Figure 7.3   Kersal Cell, Salford, showing timber framing and position of wall painting on rail. (Field Archaeology Centre)

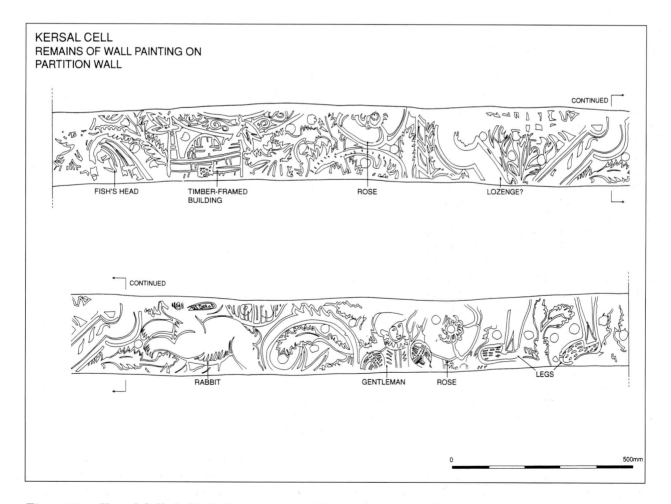

Figure 7.4   Kersal Cell, Salford. Wall painting. (Field Archaeology Centre)

Figure 7.5   Kersal Cell, Salford. Wall painting: detail of timber-framed building. (Field Archaeology Centre)

17th centuries. Plasterwork, panelling and wall paintings of this period still survive. Towards the middle of the 19th century the house was substantially enlarged by the addition of a brick-built north wing, partly demolished during its recent use as a country club (Arrowsmith and Hartwell 1989).

The building contains decorative plaster friezes at the west end of the hall and in the western upper chamber. The frieze in the hall depicts the head of a lion in the centre, flanked by an anthropomorphic face on either side. A pattern of foliage surrounds the heads, and representations of other creatures are interspersed amongst this. Unusually, all of the representations are water creatures, and include toads, fish, newts and dragonflies. The western upper-floor chamber contains the remains of two plaster friezes, both of which are heraldic. Decorative plaster is a common feature of yeomanry and gentry class houses of the 17th century, and it is likely that both friezes date from this period. The arms of the Byrom family, a chevron with three hedgehogs, with a crest and the initials EB above, can be related to the history of the house with confidence. In July 1692 Kersal Cell was bought from Thomas Kenyon by Edward Byrom, and the frieze was evidently set up to commemorate this change of ownership.

The main surviving painting, in the ground-floor parlour, is only a portion of a much larger interior scheme, dated to between 1595 and 1605 (see Fig 7.4). It depicts a series of roundels with foliage and flowers linked by strapwork, with an interlaced strapwork frieze. Despite its earlier date, it is stylistically not far removed from the nearby Scotson Fold fragment (see below). Another fragment, on the partition wall between the hall and parlour, includes a timber-framed building (see Fig 7.5), a male figure in Elizabethan costume, a rose and possibly a fish and a rabbit, for which a date between the mid-1580s and mid-1590s is likely (Arrowsmith and Hartwell 1989, 71–93; UMAU 1994).

The outcome of the Kersal Cell case was unusual. The original proposal was for public rooms on the ground floor and bedrooms above. Following discussions with GMAU and advice from Frank Kelsall, then buildings inspector for the north-west office of English Heritage, the developer adapted his plans. He realised the merits of an upside-down house with principal rooms at first-floor level, in which the subtleties and glories of the overmantel and mural could be displayed to dramatic effect, and the painting depicting a timber-framed building and Elizabethan male could be used as the centrepiece for the sitting room instead of being in a kitchen. In this way he was able to market Kersal Cell as a unique attraction. Interestingly, there has been speculation that the use of arms may have 'reflected a desire for upward social mobility at a class, if not individual level' (Arrowsmith and Hartwell 1989).

Figure 7.6   Scotson Fold, Radcliffe. Wall painting after initial conservation and after flood damage, but before re-conservation. (Field Archaeology Centre)

Scotson Fold, Radcliffe: the benefit of interdisciplinary studies

Scotson Fold, a grade II listed building, is a small timber-framed house of the early-17th century in Radcliffe, Greater Manchester. The presence of Radcliffe Tower, a 15th-century pele tower, for which James de Radcliffe obtained a license to crenellate in 1403 (Arrowsmith 1995), together with a fine medieval church and a tithe barn, indicate a settlement of some importance. But today Radcliffe is a relatively run-down town, with problems of urban decay and unemployment. The discovery of a wall painting in a former farmhouse on the western fringes of the town is surprising and unexpected in today's context of decline.

In 1994 the owners contacted the archaeological units as they had discovered a wall painting during renovation works and were undecided what to do with it. Although unsure what to expect, the county archaeologist went prepared with authoritative publications on wall paintings, including that by Reader (1941, 181–211), whose classification of Tudor domestic wall paintings is still relevant. On inspection, it soon became clear that the painting was a fine example of an early-17th-century work, presumed at the time to be contemporary with the construction of the house (see Fig 7.6). The isolated fragment showed part of a scheme of interlocking strapwork and floral decoration divided by imitation pilasters, executed in rich red, blue and green on a white ground, with outlining in black. It was provisionally dated to *c*1620. The discovery of this painting was particularly exciting as secular decoration of this quality and date is relatively rare, only four or five examples being known in Greater Manchester.

Following the initial inspection a programme was devised for conservation treatment which included research into the wall painting and the development of the house. The project now had the enthusiastic support of the owners and the backing of English Heritage, and attracted a grant from GMAU and Bury MBC. GMAU advised that the best approach was to employ appropriately qualified specialists. W John Smith carried out the research and Stephen Rickerby was appointed to undertake the conservation and analyse the pigments used (Rickerby 1995; W J Smith 1998). The conclusions of the two specialists were of great interest, providing a picture of high status and social pretension in the early years of the

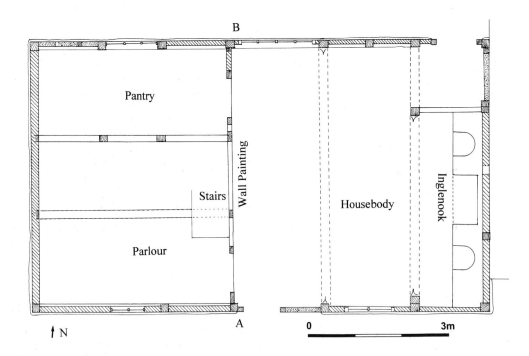

Figure 7.7   Scotson Fold, Radcliffe. Plan of 17th-century yeoman's house. (W John Smith)

17th century, each corroborating the findings of the other.

Scotson Fold is a neat timber-framed building with square and rectangular panels set on a sandstone plinth; except for the west gable it is structurally complete. It comprises two unequal bays, the largest containing the 5.5m long open hall, with an inglenook fireplace at the eastern end (see Fig 7.7). The smaller west bay, 4.3m long, was divided from the hall by a timber-framed partition, and contained the parlour and pantry with a full-height chamber above, originally reached by a staircase from the pantry. Smith has suggested that there was a change in the region from decorative panelling to simple open panels at the turn of the 17th century, and that the Fold was an early example of this (W J Smith 1998, 19).

From the available evidence it would appear that far-reaching changes occurred in the first half of the 17th century, including the creation of a full-height chamber over the hall. Before this date the Fold would have been unusual in preserving the tradition of an open hall in the region. There is little doubt that the inserted floor and the wall painting are contemporary (see Fig 7.8).

The wall painting is based on a typical Jacobean design of grouped strapwork panels divided by imitation pilasters on a white ground. They are unique as painted features, although similar examples are known in plaster relief in some West Yorkshire gentry houses (W J Smith 1998, 17). Although the palette is limited to three colours – red, blue and green – with outlining in black and the use of white highlights, the painting is striking for its exceptionally rich appearance. Considerable attention was

paid to such details as the rosettes at the centre of each panel. In addition there are floral and other designs of ovals, Greek crosses, stylised dianthus (gillyflower) and fleur-de-lys; the complete painting must have been splendid.

The multi-disciplinary approach and the use of specialists, with a clear set of research objectives adopted by the GMAU, has resulted in a much greater understanding and appreciation of the building than would have been possible if cost, as opposed to quality of result, had been the only consideration. All the indications are that Scotson Fold was a building of some status in the early years of the 17th century. The quality of the building materials and the excellence of construction matched the standards of decoration. The conversion of the house, by making the loft into an additional chamber, did not require a complete rebuild, although it involved fairly major engineering. Likewise the inglenook fireplace, virtually a room within a room and somewhat anachronistic by the early-17th century is, as W John Smith hints, possibly important in proclaiming the status of the family as one with lineage. The painting displays considerable skill – it cannot be said that the painter was an 'idle and lazy creature' (Rickerby 1995). Rickerby points out that the decoration was probably intended as a mark of social distinction, and cites a number of comparable local examples. These include an outstanding figurative scheme at Bramhall, and the less ambitious imitation panelling and antique work at Wythenshaw Hall, given social distinction by its specific association with the Tatton family, whose arms are incorporated into the decoration (Taylor 1991). More in keeping with the Scotson Fold example are the wall

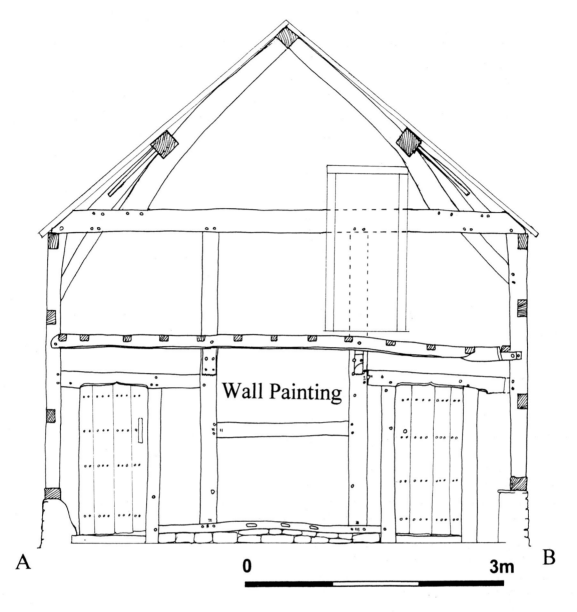

A   0   3m   B

Figure 7.8   Scotson Fold, Radcliffe. East facing section showing timber framing, inserted floor, and position of wall painting. (W John Smith)

paintings at Kersal Cell, and at Onion Farm, Warburton, the latter depicting two Elizabethan figures and two geese flanking a rose enclosed in a lozenge, all set against a foliage background (Hartwell 1989, 95–101; Nevell 1995).

Scotson Fold is a success story for a number of reasons, but mainly because its continuing conservation is based upon a well-informed appreciation of its quality and worth. Fortuitously, the initial conservation strategy included setting up a mechanism for future works, so when the wall painting was damaged by water from a burst tank a few years later the archaeological unit was able to carry out a rapid damage limitation exercise, which guided its conservation. Perhaps the real success is that the owners now open their doors on Heritage Open Days, thus enabling the wider public to share and appreciate the house.

Stockport: the role of recording in conservation and regeneration strategies

Recent work at Staircase House, on the north side of the Market Place in Stockport, represents an even higher degree of interaction between understanding, appreciation and protection. Stockport, 'upon one round hill hath this town . . . been built' (Arrowsmith 1997, 73, quoting William Webb), was granted its market charter in 1260. At its heart is the triangular medieval market place, with a church at its apex (see Fig 7.9). However, as in most of the lesser historic town cores of north-west England, no systematic record of the surviving buildings around the market place had been undertaken prior to the late 1990s, although at least in Stockport there were hints of substantial early survivals.

82

STOCKPORT OLD MARKET PLACE IN 1840.

Figure 7.9   Stockport Market Place in 1840, with Staircase House (A) and Meal House Brow (B) arrowed. (Stockport Local Heritage Library)

Figure 7.10 Staircase House, Stockport. 17th-century cage-newel staircase. Note the targets for rectified photography in the background. (Dennis Thompson)

Over the last 25 years Staircase House has been well-researched with analytical and photographic surveys being carried out by W John Smith (1977), the RCHME (1993b), and the two archaeological units at the University (Hartwell and Bryant 1985; UMAU 1995; McNeil *et al* 1998, 1999, 2000), together with dendrochronological surveys carried out by the Nottingham University Tree-Ring Dating Laboratory and the Sheffield Dendrochronological Laboratory. The surveys were originally undertaken as pure research into the form of a single urban building complex, but more recently they have developed as an integral part of Stockport's conservation and regeneration strategy. Understanding of the building has advanced considerably over the last quarter of a century, particularly during the 1990s.

Prior to the survey work of the 1990s, the property was recognised as a fine town house that had started as a cruck hall parallel to the market place. It had expanded to include a magnificent cage newel staircase (see Fig 7.10) from which the building takes its name (W J Smith 1977). To the rear are two large conjoined timber-framed ranges. In 1995 an arsonist set fire to the building, seriously damaging the cage newel

staircase and attractive 17th-century panelling in one of the rooms. Fortunately, English Heritage had recently funded an RCHME level 3 building survey, including a full set of drawings and rectified photography, which could be used to guide restoration and repair (UMAU 1995). Despite the previous wealth of information and knowledge, the Heritage Lottery Fund generously gave a further grant to reexamine the building. The discoveries made included the elaborate operations that had proved necessary in order to build on the site at all, and the relationship between the warehouse at the rear and the house itself. The analysis also highlighted the importance of three critical elements: the cage newel staircase, the courtyard, and the overall plan-form (see Fig 7.11). It is ironic that we owe our increased understanding of the building to an arsonist, who forced us to look at the relationships between the parts and the whole (McNeil *et al* 1998; 1999; 2000).

New information was provided on the relationship between the main phases of construction. During two periods, 1460 and 1618, considerable engineering works were involved, and on both occasions the problems were solved ingeniously. In 1460 sloping

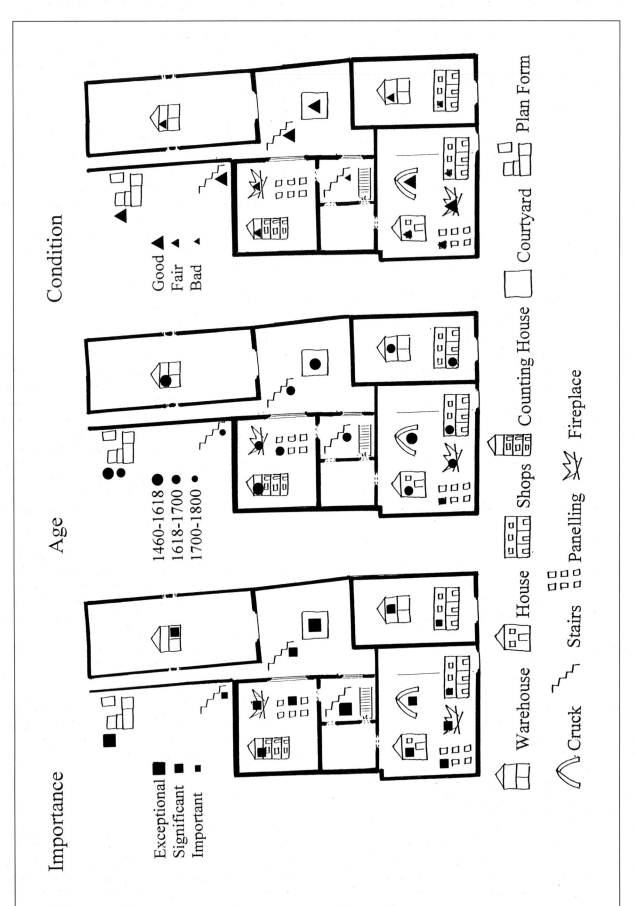

Figure 7.11 Staircase House, Stockport. Schematic plan overlaid by Importance, Age and Condition for principal elements. (Field Archaeology Centre)

ground and faulty bedrock made it difficult to raise a cruck building, so a massive buttressed stone raft was constructed to provide a level site. In 1618 the challenge was to create a cellar under the cruck hall while preventing the building from collapsing. The operation involved undermining the cruck hall, the excavation of slit trenches, and the construction of a cantilever wall to carry the weight of the building and allow the partial removal of the cruck blades. This in turn enabled the rest of the hillside to be dug out to construct a basement. At the same time the house was completely modernised and corner fireplaces were inserted – again an elaborate building operation.

The sophisticated civil engineering at Staircase House is an extremely interesting study of 'building construction without mechanisation', and what it achieved was fundamental to the use of the complex. Staircase House is now known to be much more than a fine town house. It is recognised as a rare survival of an intact merchant's town house with integrated warehousing, certainly datable to 1618 and probably to 1460, in which quality, flamboyance and expense are paramount. The house had a 15th-century cruck-framed open hall, with a timber-framed service, solar and staircase wing to the rear and, for the associated business, timber-framed and brick warehouses, shops, a stone counting house and a courtyard. This hierarchical arrangement of domestic and commercial rooms and spaces remained virtually unaltered for over 350 years, epitomising the success, wealth, power, status and social aspirations of the owners.

Because the courtyard was floored over in the 19th century, the articulation of the buildings was lost. The recent work has enabled a rediscovery of the functional and social relationship between town house and commercial empire. Stockport MBC has recognised this importance and, because of this, has determined that cultural uses should be found for the building as a local asset. A suitable reuse for Staircase House would be an interpretative display of its history as a merchant's town house with integrated warehousing.

The most recent work at Staircase House is based on partnership; the archaeological discoveries and understanding of the building would not have been possible without discourse between the partners, who included structural engineers, architects, geologists, dendrochronologists and building archaeologists. Stockport and the wider community have undoubtedly benefited from this pool of expertise.

The survey work undertaken in the 1990s at Staircase House made it clear that there was a high degree of continuity from the late-medieval period to the present day in the property divisions and building plots around the market place at Stockport, and implied that there was potential for the survival of early fabric elsewhere in the immediate vicinity. The knowledge thus gained has been used in subsequent redevelopment projects in this area, through the implementation of the advice in PPG 15 – the first time

such a coherent approach has been adopted in Greater Manchester. The first test case was Meal House Brow, a large building complex opposite Staircase House on the southern side of the market place. It encompassed two properties, ostensibly late Georgian and Victorian both inside and out.

One planning condition for Meal House Brow required that 'no development shall be undertaken until the implementation of an appropriate programme of building recording and analysis has been agreed in writing with the local planning authority, to be carried out by a specialist acceptable to the local planning authority and in accordance with an agreed written brief and specification.' The justification was that ' . . . [because] the building is of historic significance the specified records are required to inform works' (Baker and Meeson 1997, 17). The recommended survey was at RCHME level 2/3. In reality, here as elsewhere, a flexible approach was adopted, mixing various levels of analysis and recording to design a programme of works commensurate with the importance of the building and the scale of development.

The RCHME *Descriptive specification* is a most useful document, fulfilling many requirements, and used by GMAU to indicate the level of recording required, but as the RCHME recognises 'the guidelines . . . are not intended to be definitive. Circumstances will often arise when those involved with the conservation, management and understanding of an archaeological monument . . . will require records with the emphasis or content which may differ from those described here' (RCHME 1999, 1).

At Meal House Brow the survey work undertaken in accordance with PPG 15 revealed that this site incorporated three properties, one of which was divided by an alley, later subsumed into the fabric of the Georgian and Victorian buildings (Nevell 1998). These structures respected earlier building alignments and even incorporated fragments of 16th- and 17th-century buildings in situ. In addition, on the eastern side of Meal House Brow, there was a large portion of a two-storey stone revetment of late-medieval date. Although an extensive building survey was undertaken at the beginning of the redevelopment, the earlier fabric was only revealed during a watching brief undertaken while the building work was in progress. This methodological approach was taken directly from the experience gained in studying Staircase House.

Conclusion

The chief lesson learnt in Manchester over the last 20 years is that different buildings require different solutions, and the Field Archaeology Centre attempts to put this lesson into practice. The Centre has established itself as a centre of excellence for the resolution of archaeological and heritage problems. The keys to this are flexibility, diversity and, where appropriate, the facility to be unconstrained.

The mainstay of this is the skill and expertise of the staff. A multi-disciplinary approach and networking are other key considerations, and the FAC employs as appropriate the in-house team, consultants, specialists, partnerships, or a combination of these. The approach is varied; it may be straight, innovative or empirical, and not afraid to borrow, develop, adapt and experiment with methodologies which sometimes result in radical and far-reaching solutions, not all of which are successful. However, such approaches, at a minimum, raise and foster a level of understanding, the essential objective which underpins the work of the Field Archaeology Centre.

Research is a continuing process, whereby understanding informs appreciation and thereby protection. Although philosophy, policy and practice do not necessarily come together, and such aspirations are not always realisable or practicable, there is a growing recognition that the historic environment is a heritage asset. It is now believed that it can make a significant contribution to regeneration and sustainable tourism. In this context its protection is paramount.

Part III: Recording buildings: research and education

8 The traditional role of continuing education in the recording of buildings *by Barry Harrison*

Interest in recording vernacular buildings, on the part of professional architectural historians, goes back nearly a century, but it was not until after the Second World War that the systematic recording of smaller buildings, on a regional or local basis, began to take off. This new development was one aspect of a general shift in historical studies of all kinds, away from an elitist preoccupation with the politics, institutions and tastes of the rich and powerful and towards the everyday life and concerns of the common man. University academics were not to show much interest for many years to come, and the newly-formed extramural departments, which then had strong links with the Workers' Educational Association, took the lead in pioneering a range of community-based studies in response to local demands for archaeology, industrial archaeology, and local and regional history. Within such courses the recording and study of vernacular buildings began to find a place. The process was helped by the decline of interest in traditional 'working class' subjects, such as politics, economics and international affairs, in the relatively affluent late 1950s and early 1960s, and the need to find new constituencies of extramural students in suburban and rural locations where the demand was for intellectually stimulating leisure pursuits rather than 'education for social purpose'. By the mid-1960s various types of local studies were prominent in all extramural programmes, and beginning to dominate some.

Although few courses were offered specifically in vernacular architecture, the subject rapidly became a major component of local history classes, particularly after the publication of *The English Farmhouse and Cottage* (Barley 1961). This book placed housing studies firmly on the local history agenda, both by demonstrating the richness of documentary sources available – particularly probate inventories – and by showing that the study of vernacular architecture was a no less rewarding pursuit in the unfashionable provinces than it was in the Home Counties, hitherto the setting for most popular books on the subject.

The recording of small buildings however, lagged far behind documentary studies. Tutors who led extramural groups in producing local histories of exemplary academic rigour, including sophisticated documentary analyses of buildings, (Jennings 1967), did not themselves feel competent to record buildings, let alone induct their students into the art. Between the late 1950s and the mid 1970s, a few full-time extramural lecturers, such as Maurice Barley in the East Midlands and Bob Machin in Dorset, organised their classes into recording groups, as did a number of part-time lecturers such as Barbara

Hutton in Yorkshire and Madge Moran in Shropshire. However the number of courses was always small and they do not appear to have increased much in the last twenty-five years. Looking at recent university continuing education programmes, there is no marked increase in the number of courses upon vernacular architecture, and only a minority specifically mention practical recording work as part of the syllabus.

Continuing education is widely credited with a major role in developing the subject, perhaps because a number of the most distinguished pioneers had a deep interest in adult education at a time when it could still be regarded as a radical movement. Concrete evidence is however difficult to come by. A search for publications in which the recording of vernacular buildings by continuing education groups is acknowledged revealed only ten examples, four of them by groups led by the same tutor. In many other publications authors acknowledge the *documentary* research undertaken by students without any reference to recording, which, one can only suppose, was contributed by the tutor. Again, to judge by entries in the *Bibliography of Vernacular Architecture* (1972, 1979, 1992, 1999), publications by adult education departments are equally rare: only four by universities and two by the WEA. Of course the results of recording work may appear elsewhere – as articles in local society transactions for example – but it is nevertheless surprising to find the subject so infrequently dealt with directly by organisations which otherwise have a considerable published output in the local and regional history field. Indeed, of the few continuing education publications I have located, nearly half are cyclostyled documents, suggesting an enthusiastic tutor with a friendly typist rather than any firm departmental commitment to the subject.

Colleagues have been consulted informally in about a dozen university continuing education departments, and most insist that they have a real interest in the subject and promote numerous courses in which vernacular architecture figures prominently, although not always exclusively, and where students are 'encouraged' to undertake field recording of buildings. The absence of any national statistics for vernacular architecture courses makes it impossible to quantify, but recent course brochures I have seen show very few examples. Furthermore the majority seem to be short lecture series, one-day and occasional weekend schools rather than more sustained provision, and they rarely appear to involve students in hands-on recording.

Asked why this should be so, the most common responses are as follows:

1   There is a lot of vernacular architecture being taught, but it lies within the framework of courses in local history, landscape archaeology and architectural history
2   There is an inadequate supply of able and willing part-time lecturers for sustained work in the subject
3   The modularisation and accreditation of courses in the last few years, and their arrangement within part-time degree and certificate structures, has led to a reduction or even abandonment of the traditional non-vocational 'tutorial' class in which students often stayed together for several years at a stretch – the essential setting for long-term group recording projects
4   Many short, mostly unaccredited, courses are still offered, attracting large numbers of people, some of whom might be stimulated to become active recorders, and these students can be advised on how to set about it.

While such comments are valid, they seem to show a slightly apologetic and defensive attitude – a tacit admission perhaps that some university continuing education departments have not really built on the pioneering work of thirty years ago. This is surprising when one considers how overall recording activity has increased and how many people are now involved in it – not only 'professionals' in archaeology, planning and conservation, but also individual volunteers and local groups of enthusiasts. In addition, publications have increased dramatically, including many excellent introductions to the subject, and media interest is at an all-time high.

Vernacular architecture should have become a booming subject in continuing education; that there has been an hiatus suggests that there have been endemic problems that are difficult to resolve. Staffing is certainly one of them. Only a very small number of full-time continuing education lecturers have a research interest in the subject. This, I suspect, is due in no small measure to an understandable desire for academic recognition which only mainstream research can provide. Within the wider disciplines of history, archaeology and economic and social studies, only a handful of prominent scholars have yet recognised that the study of vernacular architecture can make any useful contribution to our understanding of past societies. In these days of research assessment exercises vernacular architecture is less likely to be seen as a priority area for research than it was in the past.

Much of the burden of continuing education in the subject has always been borne by part-time lecturers. Many have made tremendous contributions and they have introduced generations of adult students to both recording and documentary work. Such tutors have however always been hard to come by, in spite of the growth in the numbers of suitably qualified people. Extramural work has always been a labour of love, poorly remunerated for the time and effort expended, and it is hardly surprising if people

who are busy building careers should find a regular weekly teaching commitment, over a year or more, an unattractive proposition. Many part-time lecturers find the paperwork and deadlines associated with recently introduced assessment procedures irksome and sometimes ideologically difficult to accept. For example, of two tutors consulted who are teaching vernacular architecture in one department of continuing studies, one has withdrawn and the other is at odds with the demands of the department and might cease to lecture in this discipline in the near future.

There are of course problems with students as well as with tutors. Visits to vernacular buildings are extremely popular, but only a small proportion of students are usually willing to try recording (beyond holding one end of a tape measure). Even when it is possible to form a recording team, the finished work can take months to arrive. There is thus a strong temptation for the tutor to do the work, leaving students only the most elementary tasks to perform. Other problems include the failure of students (and often of tutors too) to adopt and adhere to standard formats in recording and reporting, and the even more serious failure to make proper arrangements for the deposition of completed work.

In spite of great public interest in vernacular buildings only a small minority of continuing education students have ever wanted to do much more than look at them and listen to someone else explaining the points of interest. Like other continuing education departments, that at Leeds has no difficulty in attracting full houses for short lecture series or day schools on the buildings of the immediate area. For Leeds the local area is the Pennine valleys and foothills; a disgruntled audience gave a very rough ride to a new part-time lecturer when he tried to focus on the eastern lowlands. Indeed student localism is a major problem in attracting new tutors who have a good general grasp of the subject but rarely have a detailed knowledge of the vernacular buildings of the immediate vicinity. Although there is a high level of public interest, the promotion of vernacular architecture has proved very difficult in urban centres. Possibilities still exist in smaller urban and rural communities where contacts with local societies, further education centres and sometimes Workers' Educational Association branches can still produce viable classes. It is in just such places, however, that the written work required for assessment has been most resisted by students and tutors alike.

If the above analysis of the direct contribution by continuing education groups to the recording of small traditional buildings seems pessimistic, their indirect achievements, in contrast, have been considerable.

One of the features of the last 30 years has been the emergence of independent recording groups in various parts of the country, many of which have affiliated to the Vernacular Architecture Group. Some of the older-established groups have recorded prodigiously; the Surrey, Sussex, Yorkshire and Somerset groups have each produced well over one thousand sets of drawings and reports, copies of which are securely lodged with the National Monuments Record and in local archives, and many of them have been published. Newer groups have been equally active in Durham and Northumberland, Suffolk, Essex, Gloucestershire and several other counties. Many areas are still without such coverage but some local archaeological and historical societies have small building recording sections that the enthusiast can join. It is difficult to estimate the role of continuing education departments in the promotion and fostering of such groups, but it has certainly been considerable in a number of cases. For example, the North-East Vernacular Architecture Group (NEVAG) has been closely associated with the Workers' Educational Association and the Continuing Education Department at Durham University from its inception. Founder members of the Group taught a series of continuing education courses in vernacular architecture, from which further members were recruited. The Yorkshire Vernacular Buildings Study Group began with a membership recruited almost entirely from Leeds University continuing education classes in local history, and continued for many years to add further members from the same source. As new members from outside the continuing education network joined – not least people whose interest had been stimulated by having their own houses recorded – the link with continuing education became less direct. Nevertheless, an annual residential recording weekend organised by the Leeds department sustained activity for over twenty years. The course was held in a different district of Yorkshire each year; it helped experienced members to widen their horizons and provided training for newcomers to the subject, many of whom subsequently joined the Group. Other groups may have different stories to tell, but continuing education departments, or at any rate continuing education lecturers have frequently been involved at some stage.

One role for continuing education in the future might be to use the still-common lecture series and day and weekend schools to recruit students to local recording groups or to attempt to establish such groups where none exist. Thus, for example, a new course sponsored by the Department for Continuing Education at Oxford aims to train recorders in surveying techniques, researching through maps and documents, and analysing historic buildings in the field. One of the major objectives of this initiative is to set up an Oxfordshire Buildings Record. There is, of course, a major problem here; university continuing studies departments are now funded by the Higher Education Funding Council who recognise only credit-bearing courses. The days when lecturers could support and service voluntary recording groups as part of their duties are rapidly passing. Even where it is still possible to run non-accredited courses, these have to be entirely self-supporting or even profit-making. The recruitment to a buildings

recording event such as the Yorkshire Group's annual weekend is of the order of only twenty to twenty-five people. Recruitment for short courses and field visits can be much higher, but they do little directly to add to the number of active recorders. The motivating force almost invariably lies outside the continuing education department.

Despite the problems, continuing education departments and tutors can help as facilitators, coordinating the activities of various groups and organisations that might not otherwise come together. For example, I taught a 20-credit local history course at Bedale, a small market town in North Yorkshire which, as it happened, was attended by four very active members of a local history society in the nearby village of Snape. Some months after the course finished I was asked by the Snape society to give a talk on the vernacular buildings of the area. Afterwards, I appealed to villagers to offer their houses for recording, which they did in considerable numbers. I then contacted the Yorkshire Vernacular Buildings Study Group, who agreed to hold a recording session in the village, jointly with members of the local society. Twelve buildings were recorded and the results presented at another village meeting, which in turn produced six more offers. A study of all these buildings can be seen in *Yorkshire Buildings* **27** (Spring 2000).

The point of this example is to suggest that there is still a role for continuing education tutors to play, apart from leading their students in direct recording. The events outlined above would not have happened without the contacts established through a class and, it is important to add, some voluntary input by the tutor. This is all in the 'great tradition' of extramural work; the same sort of thing is happening elsewhere, although such informal activity rarely finds its way into departmental annual reports.

It will not have escaped notice that this paper has shifted from continuing education towards a consideration of local voluntary groups; this is because they are closely linked, not only institutionally but also philosophically. Recording by continuing education groups or by groups working in that tradition has a particular flavour and numerous strengths. Standards of drawing may not always be quite as high as those of professionally trained people, but independent groups enjoy greater flexibility. Professionals are often concerned with particular buildings rather than with general characteristics of vernacular buildings within a given area; normally the buildings that they study are chosen for them on the basis of need, rather than for their intrinsic interest (Morriss, above, p 64). Local groups can choose buildings to record rather than the buildings choosing them. They may not always make the best use of opportunities, preferring to record some types or periods of buildings – particularly the very old ones – to others. However, some groups make the effort to record a typical cross-section of vernacular buildings in their areas and even take on areas where no work

Ground floor plan

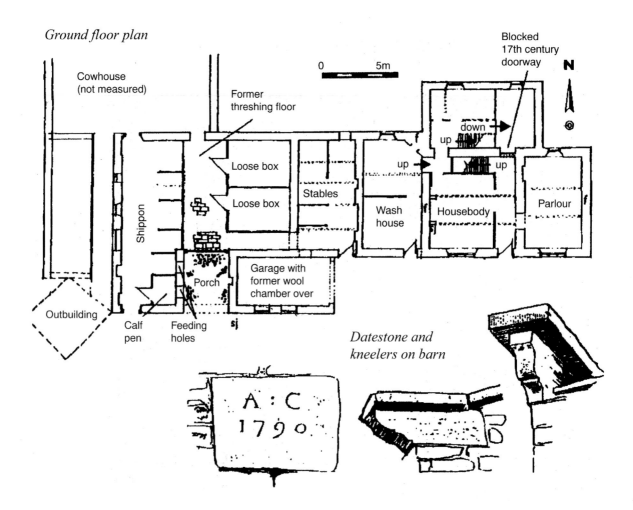

Figure 8.1   Ranelands Farm, Hebden, North Yorkshire: plan. (Drawn by Malcolm Birdsall)

has previously been done, in order to better understand the vernacular of an entire county or region. For example, the Yorkshire group has recently targeted Holderness in East Yorkshire, an area far distant from where most members live and one which, it has always been assumed, is a 'vernacular desert' containing nothing earlier than the 18th century. Another strength of local groups is the importance attached to historical research, both in respect of individual buildings and of whole villages and districts. The splendid publications of the Somerset Vernacular Building Research Group (eg 1982, 1996), who both record and research all the buildings in selected villages in different parts of the county, are a model of local historical as well as of architectural research. A typical example of the type of drawings that can be achieved is shown in Figs 8.1 and 8.2, and such records are generally accompanied by short written descriptions.

Another strength lies in the fact that local groups are able to develop close relationships with local societies and householders, which the professionals may not have time to cultivate to the same extent. In some ways it even helps not to be connected to a local

authority, national park or other public body. In general, householders like to share their enthusiasm for their own houses with others who have no axe to grind, and sometimes end up joining the group. The technical reports of professional recorders may appear to have little relevance to the residents; however, when local people record local buildings they retain a sense of ownership of their findings, and their work imparts appreciation and recognition of value to their historic environment.

There is a danger that local groups will concern themselves only with collecting building surveys in the way that some people collect postage stamps, paying little attention to wider historical and theoretical issues and to new developments in the subject. This is where continuing education departments can make a great contribution by organising events, providing a forum in which members of recording groups and individual recorders can keep abreast of new developments.

Although the character of external studies is changing, there are continuing opportunities for the study of small traditional buildings to be introduced in a variety of ways. For example, the Certificate of

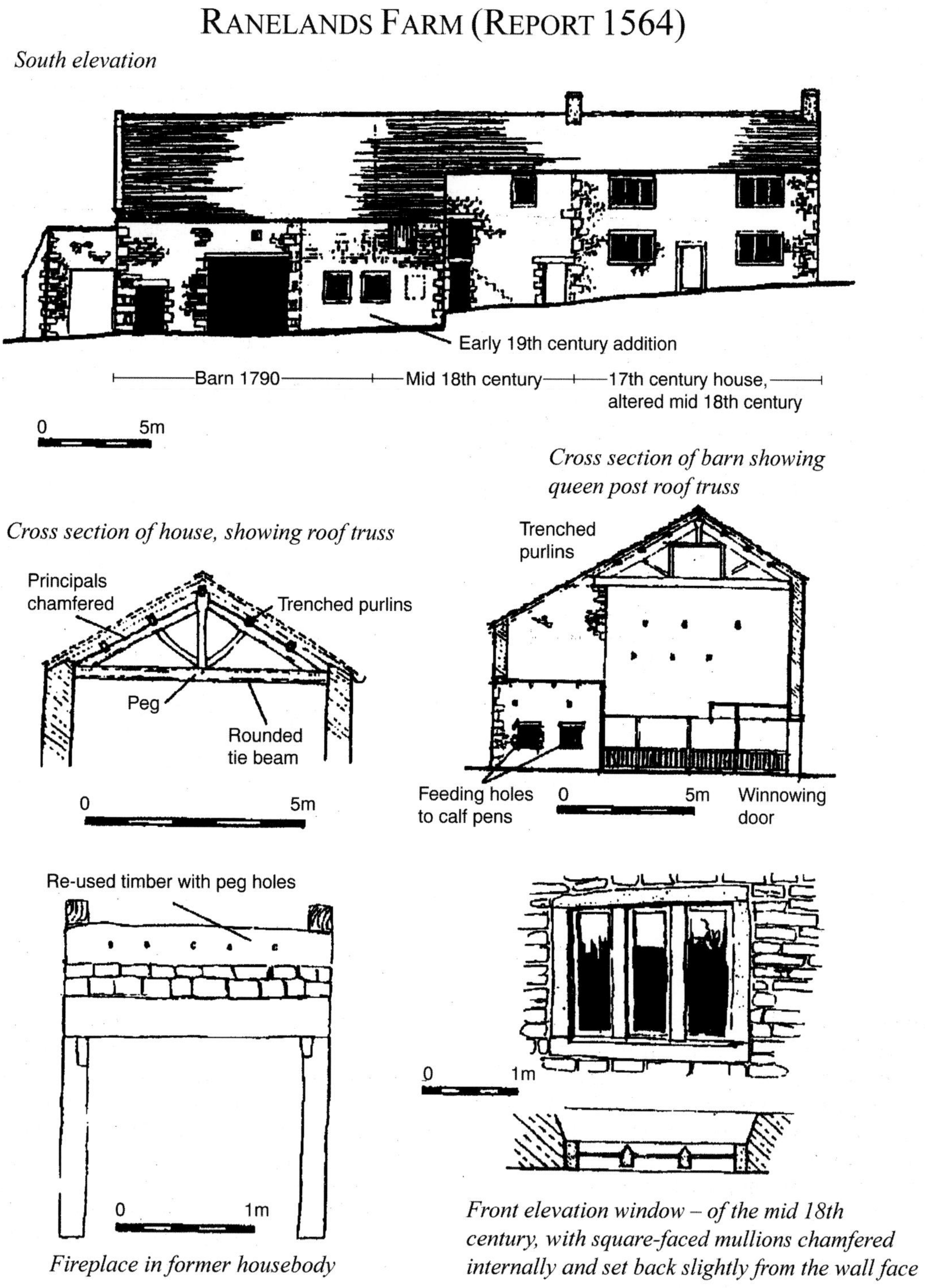

RANELANDS FARM (REPORT 1564)

South elevation

Early 19th century addition

|——Barn 1790——|——Mid 18th century——|——17th century house,——|
altered mid 18th century

0   5m

Cross section of house, showing roof truss

Cross section of barn showing queen post roof truss

Principals chamfered

Trenched purlins

Peg

Rounded tie beam

0   5m

Trenched purlins

Feeding holes to calf pens

0   5m

Winnowing door

Re-used timber with peg holes

0   1m

Fireplace in former housebody

0   1m

Front elevation window – of the mid 18th century, with square-faced mullions chamfered internally and set back slightly from the wall face

Figure 8.2   Ranelands Farm, Hebden, North Yorkshire: front elevation, sections and details. (Drawn by Malcolm Birdsall for the Yorkshire Vernacular Buildings Study Group)

Higher Education in British Vernacular Architecture offered by the School of Continuing Studies at Birmingham University is open to a wide variety of entrants; it accepts both professional and independent students and has quickly gained an established reputation. At the time of writing, the Department for Continuing Education at Oxford is preparing a course of study in vernacular architecture. In a sep-

arate initiative by the same department, the Technology Assisted Lifelong Learning Centre has included a unit on vernacular buildings for its undergraduate diploma in local history; this course of study is accessed via the Internet. As professional applications for historic building analysis increase, the demand is growing for a variety of courses in this area. The School of Archaeological Studies at

94

Leicester now incorporate the archaeology of standing buildings in their postgraduate certificate courses, and in their MA in Archaeology and Heritage by Distance Learning. The brochure promoting the latter course proposes the use of the World Wide Web to deliver information to students around the world; 'Course materials will be supplied in printed form, but it is hoped that students will . . . have access to computers . . . for the exchange of information . . . and to receive current and up-to-date material from their tutors.'

The content and level of study will vary according to the objectives of each course and the type of students attracted. Some courses will be more likely than others to offer or promote 'hands-on' experience in the analysis of historic buildings, but each of them might encourage personal involvement in the study of vernacular architecture. At the very least each course will increase awareness of the cultural value and academic potential of the largest and most varied group of historic buildings. Past experience has shown what a valuable contribution continuing studies can make, both directly, and in the promotion of local groups. While professional historic building consultants continue to be driven by the demands of their clients, local independent recording groups and individuals have the best opportunities for expanding our general understanding of the resource. As past experience has shown, many of these enthusiasts have flourished in the continuing studies sector, but often the personal commitment of their tutors to on-going local support has been crucial to their success.

Acknowledgements

Mr Malcolm Birdsall and the Yorkshire Vernacular Buildings Study Group are thanked for providing the illustrations to this paper.

9 New directions in continuing education
by David Clark

Barry Harrison has ably set out the history of vernacular building recording in continuing education, and raised some important issues for the future. He has shown that the growth in interest in vernacular buildings has only with difficulty been converted into actual recording activity, and has set out a role for continuing education departments in supporting the local groups which are a major force in building recording today. In this postscript, I would like to widen the analysis somewhat, and offer a broader view of opportunities for the education sector in this field.

The other papers at the Oxford Conference demonstrated why building recording is important. But they also showed that recording, in the sense of gathering together and making sense of a wide range of types of information in order to enhance our understanding of a structure and its setting, can offer many opportunities for people to get involved. In this academic sense, it is a truly interdisciplinary subject – historians of many specialisms, archaeologists, anthropologists, dendrochronologists – can all make a contribution. Those dealing with the more practical aspects – whether involved with the planning system through requirements such as PPG 15, working in the trades and professions involved with conserving and repairing standing structures, and even operators in the burgeoning architectural salvage industry – need to be aware of relevant research findings in order to do their work more effectively. It is also a subject in which amateurs following their own interests, whether local or national, can make significant contributions. The availability of Lottery funds has also been important in helping local groups to get initiatives going as part of the Millennium celebrations, but the new Local Heritage Initiative grants should provide longer-term support. The popularity of television programmes such as *The House Detectives* underlines the basic fact that we love our old buildings and engaging with them touches deeply felt links with the past which enrich the present for each one of us.

All this activity, while apparently disparate, offers the continuing education sector a range of opportunities and challenges. Each of the groups referred to has education needs, and in an ideal world all those involved in recording should contribute their findings and perspectives, and dip into that resource to enlighten and enhance their own understandings. Other bodies such as the Vernacular Architecture Group, whose object is 'the enhancement of public education in the study of lesser traditional buildings . . .', can also contribute in a proactive way.

The first area I would highlight is the need for the building and planning professionals to gain a deeper insight into the power which a multi-disciplinary study can give to those embarking on any form of building conservation. The Royal Institute of Chartered Surveyors has recognised this need and now has a two-year, part-time distance-learning course leading to a Postgraduate Diploma in Building Conservation at the College of Estate Management, Reading. In the traditional university continuing education sector, the relatively new Certificates in Higher Education in named subjects – generally two-year part-time courses at first-year undergraduate level offering 120 CATS points – allow vernacular architecture to be studied in some depth and would be ideally suited to those whose professional qualification did not cover the subject to the same extent. One of these, in British Vernacular Architecture, offered by the School of Continuing Studies at Birmingham University, has quickly gained an established reputation. The University of East Anglia at Norwich offers a broader Certificate in Architectural History, Recording and Conservation, which has a number of modules on vernacular buildings, while in 2000, Oxford University's Department for Continuing Education has launched a Vernacular Architecture Certificate course, which includes practical building recording.

The continuing education sector is also responding by offering courses in a variety of different formats, in order to widen participation in life-long learning opportunities. As well as traditional evening classes, some universities offer vernacular architecture through linked day-schools, with residential fieldwork programmes, using the resources available at the open-air museums such as Avoncroft, Chiltern, St Fagan's and the Weald and Downland at Singleton. Others are experimenting with course meetings exclusively at weekends, to enable students from a geographically wider area than usual to attend. There is as yet no specific vernacular architecture course on offer via the internet, but this will surely happen in the near future. Oxford's Technology Assisted Lifelong Learning Centre offers a module on vernacular architecture in its internet-delivered diploma course in Local History, and the School of Archaeological Studies at Leicester incorporates the archaeology of standing buildings in their MA in Archaeology and Heritage, which promotes the use of electronic mail for the exchange of information between tutors and students.

While university continuing education departments must endeavour to create attractive courses and market them to potential students, their catchment areas (until distance-learning courses are developed) will be relatively local. This can be a major asset in developing awareness of distinctive local building traditions. But there is also a need for a wider awareness of the importance that proper recording can play in enhancing our knowledge of standing buildings. The Council for British Archaeology does this to some extent by acting as a channel for university departments to place their offerings before its members. The VAG, through its journal, newsletter and conferences, provides mechanisms to allow those already involved in running courses for professionals to be fully aware of the latest developments and thinking in the field. All concerned should take a proactive stance in 'selling' the benefits of building recording.

The work of local groups, as has been noted, is crucial to the better understanding of the vernacular heritage. In some counties, the grass-roots interest is channelled into local history societies, many of whom seem reluctant to acknowledge the contribution that vernacular architecture studies and building recording can make to the understanding of the way their community operated in the past. We need to change this perception, and ensure that the documentary work of these groups feeds into the structural analysis of the standing buildings. Departments of continuing education not only have a role, but also a responsibility, to bring together documentary and material studies, since one without the other only gives part of the picture. Many of the courses now on offer show how to do this. The pressures on universities to offer accredited courses may be seen as a threat to the traditional support offered to local groups, but it also presents an opportunity for them to unite these two aspects of building recording and to offer to serious students broader-based courses in the understanding of the local environment. Such integrated and academically oriented courses could be supported by historical and architectural ones without accreditation offered by other organisations such as the WEA, who have a long and distinguished record in this field.

Looking at the wider picture, vernacular buildings in many areas of the country remain under-researched. As Harrison has pointed out, this is often because people have been persuaded that their area lacks interest. But only through careful investigation and publication can distinctive local characteristics be brought out, appreciated and conserved. In individual cases, the *House Detectives* have shown how a fascinating building history can lie behind even the most unprepossessing exterior. Now that the 20th century has entered the realm of 'history', and the 1901 census will soon be in the public domain, there is the potential for many more people to get interested in the origin and previous occupants of their own house and those of the locality. The demand for short courses on researching house histories is high: for the past three years those in Oxford have been oversubscribed, yet Oxfordshire has not been the subject of a comprehensive architectural study. Given that the development of the subject is greatest where individuals have taken forward their own interests, the departments for continuing education can address these issues head on and, with creative thinking, make them relevant to their poten-

tial students. Courses such as the two-year Certificates can address the issues in some depth: what are the key features of the buildings of the county or wider area; what is common, and what is rare? If dates can be determined, which features are early, which late? The development of a research framework for a local area would benefit greatly from the experience of others, and the national bodies referred to above could help here, as many of their members will have already done this for their own 'patches'.

Finally, there is the issue of what happens to all the work which is done in recording and documenting the history of buildings. Individuals working independently rarely develop the confidence to publish their findings, and such work will seldom outlive its author. Groups can often achieve the critical mass necessary for publication, especially with Lottery funding, but this literature is seldom made available beyond the local community, and hardly takes its rightful place in the national repository of knowledge available to future generations. This is where university departments could play a part. Tutors could identify student work of some significance and encourage and guide the author towards publication, or at least deposition in the NMR or a county archive. Specific courses on preparing material for publication could also be offered. Confidence thereby gained could lead to further work and broader conclusions, and the more widely these could be made available the better.

In conclusion, therefore, it seems to me that departments of continuing education, in conjunction with national bodies such as the CBA and the Vernacular Architecture Group, have a tremendous opportunity to address some of the key issues facing the study of traditional buildings today. The traditional programmes of the higher education sector have made a major contribution to the subject, but we must build on these by continual reassessment of what we are offering. Creative thinking in the design and presentation of courses, together with the use of new technology where appropriate, could help to tap the enormous potential market for such courses.

Building recording courses

The following organisations offer courses in building recording; some offer recording as part of a broader course, others may offer a number of separate sessions on different aspects. Single days or weekends are not included, but the organisations mentioned may also run these from time to time. The details of all these courses may vary from year to year, and examples are given.

Universities and colleges

School of Professional and Continuing Education, University of Birmingham, Selly Oak, Birmingham B29 6LL. Tel 0121 414 5606

Buckinghamshire Chilterns University College, John North Hall, Marlow Hill, High Wycombe, Buckinghamshire HP11 1SX. Tel 01494 450049. Email: kdoughty@qedconted.u-net.com

Centre for Continuing Education, University of East Anglia, Norwich NR4 7TJ. Tel 01603 593266

The Centre for Continuing and Professional Education, Keele University, FREEPOST (ST 1666), Newcastle, Staffs ST5 5BR. Tel 01782 583436

Department of Adult Education, University of Leicester, 128 Regent Road, Leicester LE1 7PA. Tel 0116 252 5905

Department for Continuing Education, University of Oxford, 1 Wellington Square, Oxford OX1 2JA. Tel 01865 270360. Email: ppcert@conted.ox.ac.uk

Oxford Brookes University, Gipsy Lane Campus, Headington, Oxford OX3 0BP. Tel 01865 741111

College of Estate Management, University of Reading, Whiteknights, Reading, Berks. RG6 6AW. Tel 01189 861101. Email: info@cem.ac.uk or j.f.gleeson@cem.ac.uk. Website: www.cem.ac.uk (RICS Postgraduate Diploma in Building Conservation)

Other bodies

Council for British Archaeology, Bowes Morrell House, 111 Walmgate, York YO1 9WA. Tel 01904 671417. Email: archaeology@csi.com. Website: http://www.britarc.ac.uk. The CBA keep a database of courses including those with a building recording component.

Chiltern Open Air Museum, Newland Park, Gorelands Lane, Chalfont St Giles, Bucks HP8 4AD. Tel 01494 875542. Email: coam@tesco.net

Weald and Downland Open Air Museum, Singleton, Chichester, Sussex PO18 0EU. Tel 01243 811363. Email: wealddown@mistral.co.uk. Website: www.wealddown.co.uk

10 The independent recording of traditional buildings *by N W Alcock*

In her introduction to this volume Sarah Pearson pins her hopes for future progress on those who work in the independent sector (p 10) – setting them a daunting objective. This paper illustrates how much independent recorders might achieve, but also considers whether they can lead the way towards a better understanding of traditional buildings.

The independent recorder today

Before considering the potential of their work it is necessary to ask who are today's independent recorders? Most of the voluntary independent historic building analysts discussed in this paper fall into three groups. A very few are from the academic world. An equally small number, while employed professionally to deal with buildings, have extended their research in their spare time. The great majority are undertaking voluntary part-time recording which has no direct connection with their professions.

Those academics who have taken small buildings as their speciality have generally been working within a broader discipline, sometimes architecture or conservation, but primarily archaeology; they are professionally required to undertake research and to publish, but the specific areas and agendas are theirs to choose. If personal experience is any guide, they will have little time themselves for recording. They do, however, provide opportunities for their students to investigate vernacular buildings; these are generating MA and sometimes PhD theses, adding to those produced in the past by students of, for example, R W Brunskill at the Manchester School of Architecture. Whether such students can be considered 'independent' is a question of semantics, but their best work gains a strong intellectual framework through the interaction of supervisor and student. As a result, such theses can be of real value, as Grenville shows. However, knowledge of their content and significance is often hard to come by as very few have been published. Notable exceptions include, for example, Wood-Jones' 1958 PhD thesis on the Banbury region for the Manchester University School of Architecture (Wood-Jones 1963). Knowledge derived through doctoral research might also generate published articles (see, for example, Green 1998). Student course work can also usefully be found in publications edited by others, as exemplified by a series of publications emanating from the School of Architecture at Canterbury College of Art (Wade 1986). Nevertheless, because of their inaccessibility, most such works have not been included in the *Bibliography of Vernacular Architecture* (Pattison & Alcock 1992).

The second group comprises those working independently at the same time as they are employed professionally, as not everyone who works voluntarily is solely a private scholar. This group includes individuals who, in the past, have made such fundamental contributions as J T Smith's groundbreaking classification of timber-framing (Smith 1965) and Cecil Hewett's establishment of the significance of carpentry joints in vernacular buildings (Hewett 1969). In any generation, such talented innovators and synthesisers are rare, and now increasingly they are being squeezed out by the increasing pressure of work that is placed upon them. The authors of other papers in this volume, whilst here presenting their experiences of targeted and contracted recording for such purposes as informing planning decisions, have also made important independent or voluntary contributions to our understanding of small buildings. See, for example, the work of Bob Meeson who, while employed as a local authority archaeologist, produced a series of articles widening our perception of small buildings in Staffordshire (eg Meeson 1996). Jane Grenville, as an academic working on vernacular buildings could equally be presenting the independent view (Grenville 1997). David Martin (a speaker at the conference though not represented in this volume) worked on a shoestring budget for many years with his wife Barbara to build up a picture of small houses in Sussex (Rape of Hastings Architectural Survey 1987–91), but is now undertaking contract recording in the same region. While in North Yorkshire, Barry Harrison, joint author with Barbara Hutton of one of the few book-length studies of regional architecture, based this in part on the fieldwork of the continuing education students that he directed (Harrison and Hutton 1984). Thus the borderline between professional and independent historic building recording and analysis has been flexible, with frequent movement between the two areas. Unfortunately, those recording professionally find that pressing commitments make standing back to consider the wider context of their work an unaffordable luxury (Morriss p 73).

The third and final group – individuals who record buildings voluntarily in their spare time – carry out the great bulk of independent recording. As well as those working entirely on their own, some of their projects are coordinated as continuing education classwork (Harrison p 91) and others are organised within the various regional building study groups, several of which have originated in evening classes. Their efforts cover a wide spectrum. Some groups have produced closely focused studies concentrating on one village, such as those by SSAVBRG (Somerset and South Avon Vernacular Buildings Research Group, later Somerset Vernacular Buildings Research Group) which has successfully recorded *and* published seven studies in the last fourteen years (eg SSAVBRG 1982; SVBRG 1996). The activities of other regional groups are more diffuse; they arrange access to buildings, carry out some group recording, make expertise available, and provide a vehicle for publication. The Essex Historic Buildings Group illustrates this approach and to date has produced ten volumes of *Historic Buildings in Essex*. These studies include a number of articles of more than local significance, including that which analyses building accounts of 1440–2 for two new timber-framed houses (Ryan 1993). The Wiltshire Buildings Record has coordinated independent work in that county, particularly collecting the records for individual buildings. Pam Slocombe has shown how this randomly gathered information can be put to effective use in her three surveys of Wiltshire buildings, covering post-medieval and medieval houses, and farm buildings (Slocombe 1988, 1989, 1992). The Domestic Buildings Research Group (Surrey) has recorded immense numbers of buildings, making significant contributions to our understanding of building development and generating valuable local studies (eg Harding 1976), but it has not so far inspired the production of the major regional overview that should be possible from the assembled data. Groups of this type provide support for recording, but their agenda remains that of individual recorders. They are drawn, as I was, to understand particular buildings or groups of buildings of very local significance, only later perhaps widening out to understand their regional or national context.

Strengths and problems

Voluntary recording by individuals has clear strengths but also corresponding limitations. *Skills* and *Experience* are the most variable aspects of an independent recorder's resources. One can, as I did, start recording knowing nothing at all about traditional buildings, and assemble a corpus of information about the houses of a locality. More often, by the time people are recording independently they will have gained an overview of the general pattern of vernacular building; even so, it can be easy to overlook the obvious. My first recording of timber-framed buildings was in Bedfordshire (Alcock 1969) and the publication included a drawing of a typical frame (see Fig 10.1). I simply did not realise that the purlin shown, a 'clasped purlin', was distinguishable from other types, since it was the universal form in the houses that I had surveyed.[1] The various glossaries that have now been produced (eg Alcock *et al* 1996) *should* put problems like this into the past, but in reality the fine details of local techniques still remain to be identified and recognised either as the idiosyncrasies of individual craftsmen or as part of the local tradition. One of the

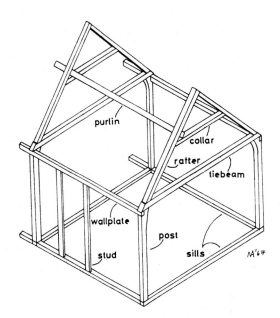

Figure 10.1 Typical framing of a north Bedfordshire house, showing an unrecognised clasped purlin. (Alcock 1969)

best ways I, like many others, gained experience and learned to recognise distinctive vernacular styles, was through the spring conferences of the Vernacular Architecture Group, which are run by people who know the buildings of their locality extremely well. My very first, in 1961, exposed a naïve young student, who had only seen Devon cob houses, to timber framing in the form of the heavily disguised aisled halls of the Halifax region. A better way to confirm the fascination of vernacular architecture cannot be imagined, particularly as these conferences provide both contrast and context for groups and individuals who might otherwise work in isolation.

Independent recorders may have distinctive strengths in the form of apparently irrelevant skills, which can enhance the understanding of buildings. Experience in family or local history aids research into the social background of houses and their wider context. Financial expertise should help elucidate the significance of building costs and accounts, though this important topic still needs to find its guru. It was Cecil Hewett's personal knowledge and practice of carpentry that led him to his appreciation of joints in timber-framed buildings. Skill in statistics should be valuable in quantifying blocks of information; certainly understanding the pitfalls of numerical data provides a caution about taking tree-ring dates at face value without appreciating the implications of the information (Walker & Walker 1998). My own modest knowledge of computers and programming, at a time when they were less familiar than now, underpinned the production of the catalogues of cruck buildings (Alcock 1973, 1981). What has now become a substantial database of more than 4000 records started out in the primitive form of 80-column computer cards.

One particular strength of the independent recorder can be in gaining access. Some householders have reservations about allowing 'officials' to examine their homes. Yet some of those who do not want their neighbours to see how they live have less objection to admitting a stranger who might enlighten them as to the history of their house. Occasionally local recorders are invited to visit a house which proves to be interesting enough to record in detail; it also helps when the owners of one house provide an introduction to the next. In retrospect, the number of houses where I have been refused access seems to be no more than a handful.

The most obvious problems for independent recorders relate broadly to 'resources'. Generally, the cost of photographic and surveying equipment may restrict the recording methods used, and the *expense* of travel is no doubt one of the reasons most independent work is locally oriented, but more important – I am sure – is that it is the unknown buildings of a particular locality (generally one's own) that entice the independent researcher. *Time* is not likely to be subject to the urgent deadlines of commissioned recording, but it may be limited by other commitments. Projects might be pursued over decades without any sense of urgency, ultimately never to be completed. However, the absence of deadlines makes it possible to pursue leads in documentation, seek decorative and structural parallels, and synthesise material in ways that would be far too time-consuming for targeted recording.

The agenda of the independent recorder

Elsewhere in this volume, the case for a clear recording agenda is cogently argued (Grenville p 12), and by implication it may be thought that most independent local recording lacks coherent objectives. This is a misleading view. Even though the local agenda may be implicit rather than explicit, it does exist and could be formulated as 'What are the specific characteristics of buildings in my locality?'. The traditions embodied in vernacular architecture are very localised, thus such 'local' research is an entirely legitimate pursuit. To discover these specific features and to compare them to the accepted regional and national trends are both realistic and valuable objectives; local surveys are particularly effective if the total stock of traditional buildings is examined, rather than just the highlights surveyed, which is generally all that targeted recording can achieve. Clearly this agenda is simple, but none the worse for that, especially as it also has implications and applications beyond its immediate horizon, particularly in conservation, by alerting owners to the significance of the individual features within their homes – the hidden panelling, the soot-blackened roof timbers, the lime-ash floors – which can too easily be destroyed or damaged during well-meant but uninformed renovation or alteration.

Does the independent recorder have any responsibility, other than in satisfying his own interest and intellectual curiosity and developing his knowledge and expertise? Surely the answer is *Yes*. He or she may see buildings or features that are subsequently destroyed or concealed and for which the recording may be the only evidence.[2] Equally, public knowledge of the character of a building may be invaluable in evaluating a listed building or planning application and preventing damaging alterations. This collective responsibility does not mean that all recording needs to be formally published. For some buildings, an appropriate action might be to deposit the information, perhaps in the county record office (as with the Wiltshire Buildings Record), so that the evidence on the building is accessible to others. Making such deposits is for many of us a counsel of perfection, but a few individuals and groups have achieved it, notably the late E H D Williams and his co-workers who have placed records of many individual buildings in the Somerset Record Office, and the Surrey Domestic Buildings Research Group who have made their very numerous records publicly accessible. A systematic policy of informing the local Sites and Monuments Record of these building records would build up information to support future conservation work.

Many independent recorders would very much like to see their work in print, but believe that this is impossibly difficult. In reality the problem lies mainly in the diffidence of the researcher. Perhaps the book does not need to be as long or as elaborate as is feared, for any publication should be selective. Not everything recorded needs to be included in an overview, in which the distinctive characteristics of the buildings studied should be identified and analysed if the work is to be of most use to readers. The experience of others who have published their findings can help resolve publication problems; membership of national or regional groups gives access to advice and assistance from those who have already succeeded in publishing their work.

Many routes to publication are now accessible. County archaeological journals, whose editors are generally very pleased to include articles on vernacular buildings, the journals of local groups, and free-standing publications like those of the Essex and Somerset groups, all provide the means of disseminating information. Until recently continuing studies departments have been delighted to see class work in print. As it is now relatively easy to achieve, private publication by the author or the recording group is a further option. Good quality camera-ready copy can be produced from word-processing programs and printing is not inordinately expensive. Local trusts can be approached for financial support. Some effort has to be put into marketing to ensure that costs are covered and information is adequately disseminated. Good examples of what can be achieved by this route include the Somerset Vernacular Buildings Group study of Shapwick analysing in detail or outline 43 houses in the village,

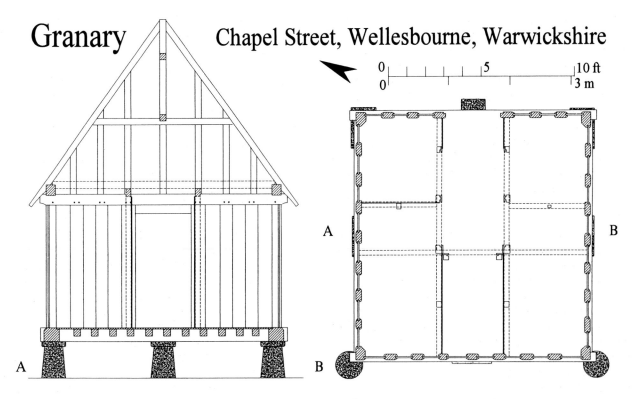

Granary Chapel Street, Wellesbourne, Warwickshire

0 | | | | | 5 | | | | 10 ft
0 | | | 3 m

A B

A B

Figure 10.2   Section and plan of the stud-and-panel granary in Wellesbourne, Warwickshire, tree-ring dated to 1639. (Alcock 1996a)

and Diana Chatwin's study of Rudgwick, Sussex with a gazetteer of almost 100 houses, of which 30 are described in detail (SVBRG 1996; Chatwin 1996).

Case studies

The strengths *and* weaknesses of independent scholarship can be illustrated from some case studies drawn from my own experience. Very much of this work has been chance-led: something interesting has come to light and has been followed up. The ability to seize such opportunities cannot be over-valued, and remains one of the great strengths of independent recording. Its reverse, however, may be the study of a random collection of buildings. With hindsight, these individually interesting buildings can turn out to be of wider significance; exploring the context of quite modest discoveries can reveal unexpected implications or raise important questions.

The Wellesbourne Granary

The invitation to look at a 'little building' in Wellesbourne, Warwickshire led to what proved to be unlike anything else known in the region. Granaries on staddle stones are now relatively uncommon survivals in farmyards, but this particular example was further distinguished by its extremely rare stud-and-panel external wall construction (see Fig 10.2). With difficulty and extensive enquiry from Vernacu-

lar Architecture Group members, four parallels were located, ranging in date and location from 1415 in Cambridgeshire (the closest in structure) to 1575 in Oxfordshire. Dan Miles kindly carried out tree-ring dating, producing the unexpected felling date of 1638/9, much later than the parallels indicated; he was also able to show that the internal partitions were original, rather than being a later alteration, as expected. Its publication in *Vernacular Architecture* has put on record an unusual building, but also raised a series of still unanswered questions (Alcock 1996a). Why was this type of walling used? Are the handful of known examples survivors of many more, or do they have specific links, say to the West Country where stud-and-panel is a normal form of partitioning? The study also highlighted the problem of searching for information at a national level. There *may* be many other examples of such granaries (although this seems doubtful),[3] but personal knowledge seems to be the only way of locating them. What is clear is that a rare structural type of national significance has been recognised.

Hall House, Sawbridge

The study of this Warwickshire house illustrates what can be achieved when time permits the correlation of detailed historical research with the architectural context (Alcock and Woodfield 1996). Sawbridge first came to my attention following an application for listed building consent that was referred to me by the CBA. Happily, my comments

Figure 10.3   Hall House, Sawbridge, Warwickshire, view from east

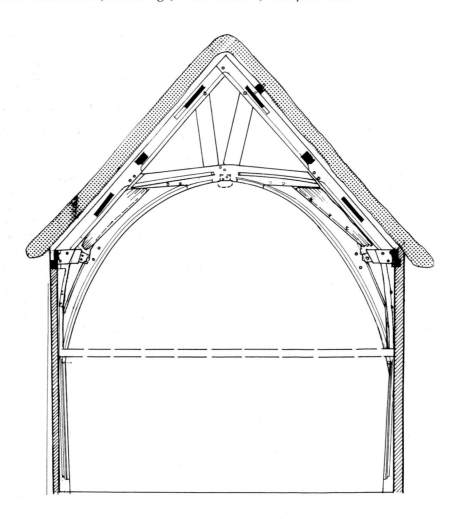

Figure 10.4   Hall House, Sawbridge, Warwickshire, section of hall truss. (Drawing by Paul Woodfield, from Alcock and Woodfield 1996)

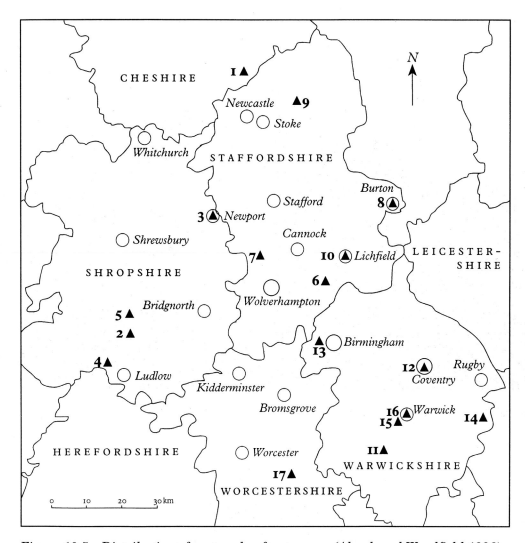

Figure 10.5   Distribution of post-and-rafter trusses. (Alcock and Woodfield 1996)

succeeded in deflecting a very damaging 'restoration' scheme proposed by an architect whose knowledge of timber buildings was obviously minimal and the house was later very competently restored. The example shows how a voluntary recorder can play a positive role in the formulation of planning decisions, leading ultimately to appropriate conservation. However, it also illustrates how diligent further research might place a building in its wider academic context – a facility that is not often open to the historic building consultant or contract recorder. The idea of making a detailed record with a view to publication emerged rather later than the formal planning consultation process. Paul Woodfield, who had also examined the building, carried out the detailed recording, while Nottingham University Tree-Ring Dating Laboratory dated the building as part of a regional research programme; the timbers had been felled in spring 1449. As well as sharing in the structural analysis, my part in the project was to investigate the historical background, which proved to offer surprising insights into 15th-century social history, of wider significance than the building immediately suggests.

The house comprises a two-bay open hall, service

bay and later cross-wing, having lost its original upper end bay in the 1920s, when it was used as labourers' cottages. Its carpentry detailing is exceptional, including a battlemented cornice to the wall plate; the hall open truss is of post-and-rafter form, functionally similar to a cruck truss, but of composite construction with a stub tiebeam (see Fig 10.4). This elegant truss form is rare, with a broad distribution in the West Midlands (see Fig 10.5); it is clearly of superior status, found for example in the Lord Leycester Hospital, Warwick, the former hall of Warwick's Guild of St George. Recognition of the structural parallels led to the key question: why did this modest village house use such a sophisticated structure, one most often associated with prestigious urban buildings?

Restated, this question raises one of the most fundamental and also most difficult problems for any building: who was responsible for the choice of plan and structural form, and why was the particular form chosen? The answer must lie in the interaction between the client and the craftsman, but both can make choices only from within the scope of their cultural experience, technical skills and resources. Here, the sophisticated features of the house indi-

104

cated that it must have been commissioned from an outside master carpenter, perhaps Coventry or Warwick based, rather than from a local man, who could construct an excellent plain cruck frame, as found in an adjacent cottage in Sawbridge, but would not have known how to work in this alien and sophisticated style, nor had the experience even to suggest it to his client.

Learning *why* this exceptional building stood in an undistinguished vernacular landscape proved a major task, with the appeal of a good detective novel. Documents had to be pursued in half-a-dozen repositories, including the College of Arms and the Church of England Record Office.[4] In 1850, Hall House was a block of six parish poor cottages, but in the 15th century it was the house of a one yardland freeholding (say 30 acres). The manor of Sawbridge belonged to Thorney Abbey, far distant in the fens, and they leased the 200 acre demesne to the owners of this freeholding, one John Andrewe in 1450. His family was rising in status, moving by 1496 to Charwelton, Northamptonshire and in due course becoming baronets and regular High Sheriffs of the county. As a result of their social prominence, they attracted the attention of the local antiquary, Augustine Vincent, who made extensive notes on the family, and transcripts of their documents (now in the College of Heralds). Thus, the house was built by a family on the make, which correlates with their choice of prestigious carpentry, patently associated with locally superior buildings. But, the story has one further twist to it. A deed of 1444, by which John's father, Richard Andrewe, transferred the family property to his son, carries an exceptionally sophisticated seal with the legend: *Sigillum Richardi Andrewe * Domini villae de Salbrigge* – a claim of lordship that would have seriously displeased Thorney Abbey, if they had seen it. In fact, they never would, because this is another piece of the family's social pretension, a forgery, probably of the late-15th century, used to give the family additional status. An armorial seal and a manorial lordship were just as vital to their claim to social position, as was their choice of a superior carpenter.

Stoneleigh

The most lengthy and substantial study I have completed was also chance-led, by my driving to work every day through the village of Stoneleigh, Warwickshire. It included a good variety of timber-framed houses, making it an obvious choice for a summer evening class on recording houses (I think in 1968). Two of the class members went on to help me write this up, identifying three structural types (Alcock *et al* 1973). This paper was very straightforward. From the examples recorded, three structural types were identified, for which tentative dates were suggested, and which were proposed as typical for timber-framing in Warwickshire, First were cruck houses of which six survived (see Fig 10.6). These

were succeeded in the early-16th century by houses using curved braces, mostly with big wall-panels; as the reconstruction of one example shows, they might have quite complex framing (see Fig 10.7). Finally came houses including square panels with short straight braces, attributed to the 17th century (see Fig 10.8). Fortunately, the surviving houses in this one village seem to be typical of the region and the dating we proposed then still appears to be broadly correct, even though the evidence for it was very sparse. Tree-ring dating has now established a range of dates for cruck buildings in Warwickshire of *c*1390 – *c*1510 (see below), and the other types broadly follow them in sequence, although overlap is clearly more significant than we thought in 1970.

This survey was quite similar to two parish studies already completed in Devon and Bedfordshire (Alcock 1962, 1969). However, it quickly appeared that Stoneleigh was also endowed with outstanding documentary evidence. I was indeed criticised for publishing this paper, which mentioned the evidence briefly without incorporating it. I can only say with hindsight that it was just as well that I did. The material was so voluminous that it took 20 years, until 1993, for the full study to appear, at book length, as *People at Home* (Alcock 1993). The emphasis was on lifestyles, using probate inventories, but in the process each of the buildings was reevaluated and examined in relation to the documentary sources. The evidence sufficiently demonstrated the very difficult problem of associating inventories with the houses to which they relate.

Sarah Pearson noted in a review that the buildings appeared as interesting additions to the descriptions based on probate inventories, but seemed slightly peripheral (Pearson 1994b). To some extent this is a fair comment – a similar book might perhaps have been written even if no buildings survived, and the book is structured around the inventories arranged by date. I had considered the reverse treatment, the types of buildings illustrated by their documents, but concluded that it would conceal the correlation of date and social standing. However, the ability to relate documents and specific houses much enhances our understanding of both. The recreation of half-a-dozen household interiors from carefully chosen inventories was very kindly attempted by Dr Pat Hughes, relating them to actual buildings. In reality some of the best inventories referred to lost houses. The 'medieval' lifestyle revealed in the 1556 inventory of Humphrey Hilles (see Fig 10.9) had to be mapped on to the cruck house illustrated in Fig 10.7: fortunately the early houses were very uniform in both dimensions and layout. It proved far more effective to visualise the distinctive lifestyles within their real physical environment, than in hypothetical structures. As an example, in one of the larger houses it became apparent from this correlation of the documents with the building that the brewhouse stood within the main structure, rather than being in an outhouse; the cheese chamber was above the brewhouse, a warm rather than a cool room. Thus,

Figure 10.6   Cruck house in Stoneleigh, Warwickshire (1 Birmingham Road)

Figure 10.7   Reconstruction of the framing of a house using curved braces in Stoneleigh, Warwickshire (11–12 Coventry Road). (Drawing by P Hughes from Alcock 1993)

11-12 Vicarage Road

2 School Lane Stretton upon Dunsmore

0 feet   10   20   30

Figure 10.8 Houses using straight braces: 11–12 Vicarage Road, Stoneleigh, and 2 School Lane, Stretton upon Dunsmore, Warwickshire (the latter dated 1662 on the gable tie beam)

Figure 10.9   Reconstruction by P Hughes of the 1556 probate inventory of Humphrey Hilles, using the house illustrated in Fig 10.7 as a base. (From Alcock 1993)

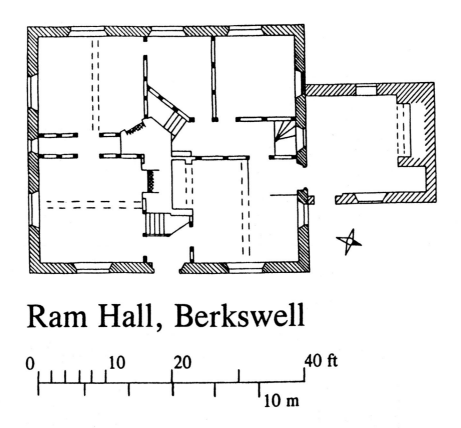

Ram Hall, Berkswell

0   10   20   40 ft

10 m

Figure 10.10   Ram Hall, Berkswell, Warwickshire, a house of c1685 with lobby-entry plan

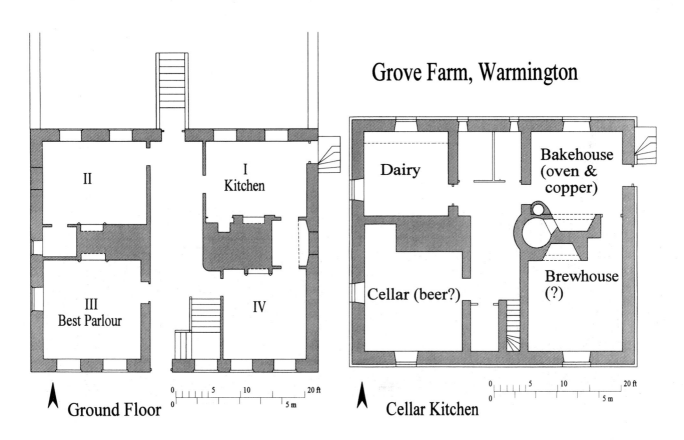

Figure 10.11   Plan of Grove Farm, Warmington, Warwickshire, a house of c1700 with a central stair-passage plan

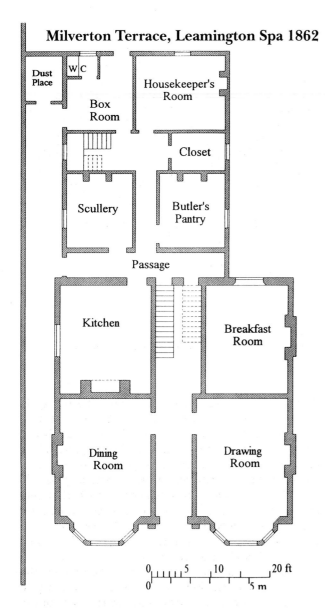

Milverton Terrace, Leamington Spa 1862

Dust Place

W C

Box Room

Housekeeper's Room

Closet

Scullery

Butler's Pantry

Passage

Kitchen

Breakfast Room

Dining Room

Drawing Room

0   5   10   20 ft

0   5 m

Figure 10.12   Proposed plan for a house in Milverton Terrace, Leamington Spa, of c1860, with a central stair-passage plan. (From Alcock 1996b)

the correlation of traditional buildings and their related documents is elucidating local agrarian practices.

The Georgian plan

Arising out of the work upon Stoneleigh, the opportunity for the independent researcher to pursue interesting ideas led me down another unexpected path. Berkswell, the next parish to Stoneleigh, contains several large brick-built double-pile farmhouses, a building type that had not appeared in the previous survey. Exploring the ramifications of this type led me well beyond the confines of typically vernacular buildings. The plan in Fig 10.10 (a house of c1685) shows that the lobby-entry plan in a double-pile house gives an awkward steep stair. This layout was

soon superseded by the central stair-passage plan as, for example, in Grove Farm, Warmington, Warwickshire of c1700 (see Fig 10.11). This plan-form has become very widely distributed, so much so that it is described as *the* Georgian plan, especially in North America, where it is also common. As well as noticing 18th- and 19th-century examples there, I realised that they also existed in my home town of Leamington Spa (see Fig 10.12). The Georgian farmhouse became the Victorian urban villa, built in its thousands in the London suburbs and in other town developments. Even though these houses stand well beyond what is normally regarded as the vernacular zone, they are certainly 'small', and they offer the same challenge to interpret their social context and patterns of occupation, their room use and its changes with time (Alcock 1996b).

Medieval peasant houses

My final example is significant in showing that an independent recorder can sometimes take a step further and undertake a substantial project with external funding (here from the Leverhulme Trust). It is also a rare example of a large-scale research project investigating traditional buildings.[5] The 'Cruck Project' has been mentioned above (Pearson, p 9), but this name is slightly misleading; its correct title is 'The Medieval Peasant House in the Midlands', though it just happens that most of the identifiable early peasant houses in this region are cruck-built; thus, the catalogue and distribution map of crucks gives a ready-made gazetteer of most of the relevant buildings (Alcock 1981). In all, 110 houses have been sampled and recorded, including some very interesting examples that were previously no more than names on the list of crucks. One such building is the Leopard Inn, Bishop's Tachbrook, Warwickshire, of c1410. Its ogee-braced open truss is remarkable, as is the composite closed truss (see Fig 10.13), while the two-bay hall contains traces of louvres in *both* bays, indicating that the hall was socially even though not physically subdivided into living and cooking space; this finding has important implications for the use of space in other medieval halls.

As well as the successful aspects of this project, it is also true that the study has been overtaken by one of the biggest problems for independent recorders – lack of time. Almost ten years after its formal completion, the results remain unpublished because the very bulk of this material has delayed completion of the project. Work on the analysis of the results is continuing, and we hope that just a little more patience will provide a worthwhile reward.

Other researchers have also successfully moved from following purely personal interests to work on a wider scale, particularly with tree-ring dating projects having county or regional themes (Cumbria by Nina Jennings, Hampshire by Edward Roberts and others, Shropshire by Madge Moran, Somerset by John Dallimore and others, and north Staffordshire

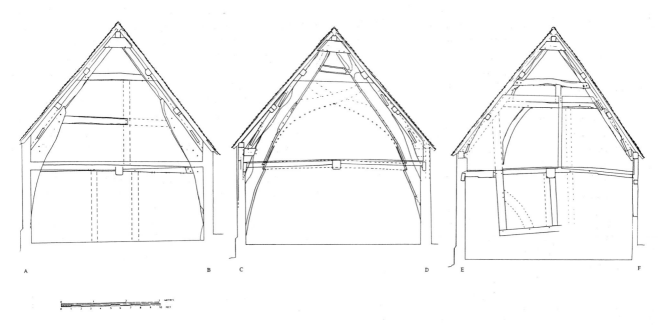

Figure 10.13   Sections of open and closed trusses in The Leopard, Bishop's Tachbrook, Warwickshire

by Faith Cleverdon). These parallel on a rather smaller scale the 'Cruck Project', and each has required immense efforts to raise funds from a string of supporters including owners, local councils, national research funding, and support from the former RCHME. So far most of these regional dating projects have been published only in the form of the annual tree-ring dating lists in *Vernacular Architecture*. A few dated buildings in north Staffordshire have been discussed (Cleverdon 1999), and several in the Whitchurch area of Shropshire have been more fully described (Moran 1999). I hope that all of these projects will be more successful than my own in achieving timely publication.

Conclusion

From what has been discussed, it should be apparent that independent recorders can make major contributions to the study of traditional buildings. They can achieve a great deal, although they generally work most effectively on a limited canvas, parish-based or perhaps county-based. They can provide 'added value' in searching out context and documentation, much enhancing the significance of a particular building. This type of research is generally too laborious to be undertaken, for example, as part of a targeted investigation in connection with a listed building consent condition. While often handicapped by lack of time to carry out large projects, or by lack of funds for tree-ring dating, they can with inspiration and effort surmount these difficulties.

Sarah Pearson's final question (p 10) was, 'where is the new Mercer for the new millennium?' From the viewpoint of this independent recorder, the response has to be to ask whether there will ever be a new Mercer. Does anyone now have the opportunity to look at as many varied buildings as Eric Mercer (1975) did for *English Vernacular Houses*? But also, in the more than 20 years since this book appeared we have learnt so much more on a regional and local scale that the grand view might be overwhelmed by details (something that was almost true even in 1975). It may be possible to hit a less daunting series of smaller targets, starting with a 'Medieval Mercer', not quite the wide-ranging *Medieval Housing* by Jane Grenville (1997), but focusing on medieval rural houses. This might be followed by a volume on the period of the 'Great Rebuilding', which is greatly in need of re-examining, particularly in the light of the theoretical approach to changing building traditions pioneered by Matthew Johnson (1993). Thirdly, the vernacular houses from 1700 onwards have hitherto lacked a champion to analyse their characteristics on a national scale; Alcock (1996b) attempts to make a start on this problem, on a small scale.

For the ideals of revealing the cultural background, the geographical pattern and the historical development of traditional buildings, it seems that we cannot depend on official bodies or individuals working professionally to provide the passion and insight needed for a new vision of traditional buildings. Thus, we must look to the independents following chance-led explorations to achieve these aims of interpretation and synthesis. They have a challenging agenda for the next 20 years.

Acknowledgements

I thank Lynn Courtenay, Bob Meeson and Sarah Pearson for helpful comments on earlier drafts of this paper.

Notes

1   This ignorance was perhaps excusable, as the clasped purlin was not distinguished in the pioneering work on roof types, Cordingley's *British historical roof-types*, which had appeared a few years earlier (Cordingley 1961).

2   Those concerned with conservation issues need to be aware that research-oriented and conservation-oriented recording do not necessarily produce the same result. In particular, the published description of a building may well not mention all the features worth preserving during repair or alteration. For example, the simple plans in Chatwin, 1996 are suitable for explaining the original plan, but do not reveal the architectural development in detail.

3   No more have been brought to my attention since the publication of this example.

4   The resources for local historians of the Church of England Record Office seem very little known but can be well worth exploring; in this case, its deeds for glebe property purchased with the assistance of Queen Anne's Bounty provided crucial evidence for the identification of Hall House.

5   The project was jointly directed by N W Alcock and R E Laxton and the assistants were R Howard and D Miles, employed as dendrochronologist and architectural recorder for three years part-time.

11   The potential of tree-ring dating
by Edward Roberts

Introduction

'Twenty-five years ago the provision of absolute tree-ring dates on a routine basis was not available to British archaeologists and historians' (English Heritage 1998b, 1). Yet by 1997 over 650 buildings in the British Isles had been dated by tree-ring dating, or dendrochronology (Pearson 1997, 25), and the number continues to grow. Sometimes, tree-ring dating has been carried out as part of well-funded and clearly-focused research: for example, the RCHME's project to tree-ring date 74 medieval buildings, or building phases, in Kent (Pearson 1994a, 148). But much work is commissioned on a more *ad hoc* basis: by amateur researchers drawing on limited funding from a variety of sources, by planning authorities in response to a planning application, or by house owners curious to learn the age of their properties.

To what use can and should this growing body of information be put? Probably the most significant attempt to grapple with this question is represented by the RCHME's work in Kent referred to above; but the advances in dendrochronology are so recent and the precision with which dates can be ascribed so breath-taking that its potential benefits are still largely unexplored. What follows is an attempt to chart some of this unexplored territory and to suggest some new and profitable ways of exploiting the evidence that may be of interest to historians, archaeologists, planners and students of vernacular architecture.

Dendrochronology

Dendrochronology is the most accurate and precise scientific method of dating buildings that has so far been developed. It is a technical discipline whose main principles can only be summarised here. As a tree grows, it puts on a new tree-ring every year, just under the bark. Trees grow, and put on tree-rings, at different rates according to the weather in any given year: a wider ring in a favourable year and a narrower ring in an unfavourable year. Thus, over a long period of time (say 60 years or more) there will be a corresponding sequence of tree-rings giving a unique pattern of wider and narrower rings. In effect, for any year in which a tree is felled, there will be a unique fingerprint.

The most common way of measuring this fingerprint involves taking radial cores from a number of timbers within a building. These cores should have a long sequence of tree-rings and, ideally, should retain the bark edge and final ring; that is, the last ring that was grown in the year in which the tree was felled. In the laboratory, each ring is measured to the nearest hundredth of a millimetre. So for each core there will be a series of measurements. This series is then matched against so-called master chronologies; these are tree-ring series that have already been dated. The longer the ring sequence, the more individual the pattern will be, and thus the better the chance of achieving a secure date. If the matching is statistically significant (measured as a t-value), then a felling date or date-range is ascribed to each core. Of course, a precise felling date is only achievable when the last-grown ring and bark edge is present. However, when this ring has been removed it may still be possible to ascribe a felling-date range provided the core contains some of the outer sapwood. The felling date-range is a period of approximately 32 – 35 years, depending on the location in which the tree was growing (Miles 1997).

It should be noted that, for a variety of reasons, tree-ring dating cannot always be successfully applied. For example, timbers may have too few rings to be datable, or they may be from an unsuitable tree species. Most historic roofs and timber-framed buildings were made from oak, which is the most suitable wood for tree-ring dating. However, elm and poplar were used occasionally and these trees are, at present, difficult to date. English Heritage is currently funding work on dating softwood that will be primarily relevant to post-medieval buildings (Pearson 1997, 26).

Finally, dendrochronology only gives us the date or date-range when the tree was felled. However, we know from numerous documentary sources that oak was used 'green', or freshly felled. This means that construction probably took place in the year of felling or within a year or two thereafter. Thus we now have a technique for dating a significant number of historic timber structures (English Heritage 1998b: Miles 1997).

Applications of dendrochronology: single buildings

Without tree-ring dating, most buildings can only be dated on typological or stylistic evidence. Some dates ascribed in this way have been broadly confirmed by dendrochronology but others have proved highly debatable and, in extreme cases, expert opinion has differed by a century or more. Such conclusions are, for many purposes, too broad to be of much use. For example, the ascription of a 14th-century date on typological grounds leaves unanswered the highly significant question of whether a building was constructed before or after the catastrophe of the Black Death. Dendrochronology can supply the answer. Indeed, at last many buildings that had no sure date and thus, in a sense, no history, can now be understood more fully in their archaeological and historical context. By the same token, this new information can contribute significantly to the debates of archaeologists and historians (Dyer 1997). This point will be illustrated firstly with regard to individual buildings and sites, drawing on examples from Hampshire.

(a) The barn at Home Farm, Breamore, Hampshire

This barn is situated at the Home Farm belonging to Breamore House, a large Elizabethan mansion. It is a fine aisled barn of seven bays and is some 85 feet long and 35 feet wide; a striking landscape feature

yet, without a building date, little more than that. Estimates of its date on purely typological grounds varied from 'mid-16th century' to 'late-17th century' and thus gave little scope for placing the building in its historical context (see Fig 11.1). Tree-ring dating was funded in connection with a grant for repairs and a precise felling-date of 1585 was given (Miles & Haddon-Reece 1996, 97). This result invited recourse to historical evidence that, in this case, was readily available in published sources (VCH *Hants* iv, 596–8; Hasler 1981 ii, 43–4).

The Breamore Estate was put together between 1582–84 by William Doddington, a Londoner, a minor government official, a land speculator and something of a man on the make. At first things went well for Doddington. He built the great house at Breamore soon after 1582 and the fine barn in, or soon after, 1585 – a barn which then would have been seen as a status symbol (Johnson 1993,129: Roberts & Gale 1995, 180). Alas, Doddington fell foul of a

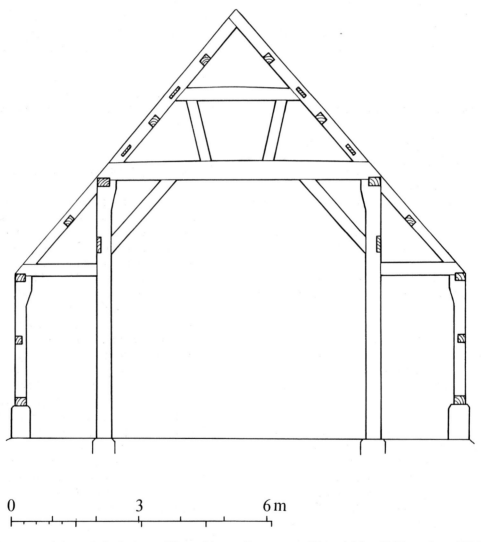

0   3   6 m

Figure 11.1   A cross section of the barn at Home Farm, Breamore, Hampshire (felling date 1585): the queen-strut roof and short, straight braces are typical of Hampshire carpentry from the mid-16th century until the late 17th century. Thus it would be difficult to ascribe a close approximate date to this roof on solely typological grounds.

local gentleman called Bulkeley, who pursued him relentlessly through the courts. Eventually, the strain of continual litigation drove him to suicide. In April 1600 he threw himself from St Sepulchre's steeple in London, leaving a note in which he blamed Bulkeley for his death. Thus a tree-ring date allows us to see the great barn at Breamore in a new and fuller light, as an aspect of Doddington's arrival as a country gentleman and ultimately as a part of the man's tragic life story.

Of course, research that is limited to one barn is likely to produce results of limited relevance. But, if the context of more barns were researched in this way, issues of more general interest could be addressed. For example, were such expensive rebuildings often associated with the arrival of a new owner with money and social ambitions? Or were they expressions of a landlord's wish to invest in his estate and to attract a suitable tenant, as seems to have been partly the case at Overton (Hants) in the 1490s and at Marwell (Hants) in the 1650s (Roberts & Gale 1995, 171–4; Roberts 1996)? Or were they more often merely part of the practical and inevitable cycle of decay and renewal? Dendrochronology, coupled with documentary research, offers the opportunity to answer these questions.

(b) Lodge Farm, Odiham, Hampshire

Lodge Farm comprises a well-preserved, timber-framed cross wing and elements of an open hall. It is situated in the former royal park of Odiham. Before it was dated by dendrochronology, there was uncertainty as to whether it had been built in the 14th or 15th century. A search through the late-medieval Crown documents relating to Odiham Park revealed numerous references to a building called 'The Lodge' (*logea*). Unfortunately, there were fairly long periods for which records had not survived and it was quite possible that Lodge Farm had been built during one of these periods. Moreover, there was no way of being sure that the building now called 'Lodge Farm' should be equated with the medieval park lodge (*logea*) of the documents. Admittedly, it was recorded that the *logea* was frequently subject to what was called '*reparatio*' but, unfortunately, this word can apply not only to rebuilding but also to minor repairs (Steane 1993, 76; Roberts 1995, 103). Consequently, without a precise tree-ring date, there seemed little hope of demonstrating which *reparatio,* if any, corresponded with the present structure.

Fortunately, dendrochronology was able to ascribe a precise felling date of winter 1368/9 to the cross wing and 1375 to the hall (Miles & Haddon-Reece 1994, 28). Returning to the documents a reference was found to *reparatio* at the park lodge in 1375 but, better still, the full accounts for building the cross wing in 1369 or 1370 were found. Any doubts that the surviving cross wing and the building referred to in the accounts might be one and the same were dispelled by Dan Miles's study of the quantities of timber, tiles and other materials, and the days taken in roofing, carpentry and other trades. These corresponded remarkably well with the dimensions of the standing cross wing (Miles 1995). In this case, the dating of an individual building did more than simply illuminate the building itself. It shed light on 14th-century building practices.

Moreover, the Crown documents showed that the park lodge had been built for William Prest, Edward III's yeoman of the buttery. Such a man would be of gentry status and thus we are given a rare indication of the social status of an early vernacular building. It is considerably smaller than the halls and cross wings that were built at a similar date for aristocrats, but larger than the rare peasant cottages that survive in Hampshire from the late-14th century. Its nearest equivalent in size and form are the 14th-century merchant houses that still survive in Odiham town. Thus we begin to form a picture of the houses then deemed appropriate to the various ranks of society.

Finally, houses which we today call 'medieval royal hunting lodges' were simply called the king's houses, or *domus regis,* by contemporaries. Lodge Farm was called a '*logea*' in the documents and thus indicates to us what contemporaries actually meant by this word (Roberts 1995, 91–103). Such a discovery would not have been possible without dendrochronology.

Building groups: national trends

Tree-ring dating can also be applied to building groups in order to elucidate periods of growth, decline and change in the building industry as a whole. But, taking a wider view, the building industry may be seen as a sensitive barometer of general economic activity (Machin 1994). This is not, of course, to suggest that the relationship between wealth and building activity is a simple one. Sometimes, for example, one generation accumulates for the next generation to spend. On other occasions, men have tried to invest their way out of recession. Moreover, tree-ring dating can only sample surviving buildings and these may not be representative of the original building stock (Currie 1988). Nonetheless it is likely that the relative frequency of tree-ring dates for any given period will relate to historic cycles of building activity.

So far, dendrochronological sampling has tended to focus on medieval housing and enough 14th- and 15th-century tree-ring dates have accumulated for some useful generalisations about the chronology of late-medieval building activity to be made. Sarah Pearson has analysed the results of tree-ring dates published in *Vernacular Architecture* (Pearson 1997, 34–7), charting their incidence along a timeline, and dividing the results into three categories: rural aristocratic and gentry house (195 examples), rural vernacular houses (193), and urban buildings in which social status is undifferentiated (106). These categories were inevitably based mainly on physical factors such as house size and building materials rather than on documentary evidence. She was, of course, well aware of the problems involved in drawing up such categories and in interpreting the results (eg Hall 1991). But it should be remembered that debate still rages on how to interpret the *documentary* evidence for economic trends and for the divisions between social strata in the late Middle Ages (eg Fryde 1996, ch. 1). The fact that the evidence from dendrochronology is likely to produce a similar debate in no way diminishes its importance.

Bearing in mind the difficulties of interpreting the dendrochronological evidence presented by Pearson, it is still possible to suggest how it could promote fruitful dialogue between economic historians and students of vernacular architecture. For example, her data reveals a surge of rural aristocratic building in the early-14th century that collapses during the century between 1334 and 1434. This result strikingly matches a hypothesis commonly held by economic historians, namely that landlords prospered in the early-14th century when a large population meant low wages and high demand for produce and rentable land. However, the Black Death in the mid-century ushered in a prolonged period of low population, lower demand for produce and rentable land and an upward pressure on wages. Landlords thus had less disposable wealth to spend on building. The evidence of dendrochronology suggests that the impulse and wherewithal for aristocrats to build did not re-emerge until well into the 15th century. This latter conclusion, however, fails to square with much that has been written by economic historians about a mid-15th-century recession (Hatcher 1996) but this does not detract from its interest.

Turning to urban buildings, the results so far obtained from dendrochronology imply that the catastrophe of the Black Death had a much weaker influence upon building activity in towns than in the country. This was certainly not because urban populations suffered less from the plague, but it may reflect a constant influx of rural peasantry attracted by the greater freedom that town life offered, as well as the chance to emulate Dick Whittington and make their fortune. Once more, as with aristocratic housing, there was a surge of new building after 1434 and, once more, this fails to match much that has been written about the urban economy in the mid-15th century.

Finally, rural vernacular houses, which were essentially the houses of the peasantry, present a profile of tree-ring dates that is significantly different from that of aristocratic house-building. Whereas aristocratic house-building declined steeply during and after the period of the Black Death, peasant house-building began to increase in the late-14th century, with a sharper increase in the period beginning 1434. This picture matches the view of many economic historians that the period following the Black Death, when labour was in demand and land in relatively plentiful supply, was a golden age for the peasantry.

Regional trends

National trends in building activity inevitably conceal regional differences that can only be explained by detailed local studies. Furthermore, it is more practicable to undertake parallel documentary research on a more restricted sample of buildings, especially where a researcher is familiar with local documentary sources. The combination of good documentation, building recording, and tree-ring dates can be fruitful, not only in establishing the economic and social status of builders, but also in illuminating the broader context in which building took place. Such an approach has been illustrated by a regional study of the chalklands of central Hampshire which reveals the way in which the houses of prosperous and poorer peasants were diverging in size in the late-15th century (Roberts 1996). For much of the 14th and 15th centuries, there was a great gulf between the houses of the aristocracy on the one hand and rural vernacular houses – in effect, peasant houses – on the other. The hall and chamber of the bishop of Winchester's rural manor house at East Meon (Hants), built in 1395–97, cover 296 sq m (Roberts 1993), whereas the average area of surviving rural vernacular houses from late-medieval Hampshire is approximately 65 sq m (Roberts 1996, 90). However, there is a fairly small group of much larger rural houses, generally called 'manor farms', whose average area is approximately 180 sq m (*loc. cit.*).

It is largely through dendrochronology that this group of houses of middling size has been better understood. A series of precise felling dates has shown that they began to be built around the year 1460, and that many were built in the decades around 1500 (see Fig 11.2). This was a period when the great ecclesiastical landlords, who held a significant proportion of central Hampshire, were beginning to lease out their manorial home farms on a permanent and long-term basis (Greatrex 1978, *passim*). This policy presented the ambitious peasant with an extraordinary opportunity to farm a much larger area than had previously been available to him, and many attained the status of yeoman or even country gentleman, becoming highly respected figures in their communities. This increase in status was often matched with a large new farmhouse, sometimes financed by the landlord.

This process is well illustrated at Court Farm, Overton (Hants), a manor farmhouse belonging to the bishops of Winchester that has been tree-ring dated to 1505 (Miles & Haddon-Reece 1994, 29). Recourse to the archives of the bishopric showed that a bailiff managed both house and farm until the late-15th century, the first lease being granted in 1488. In

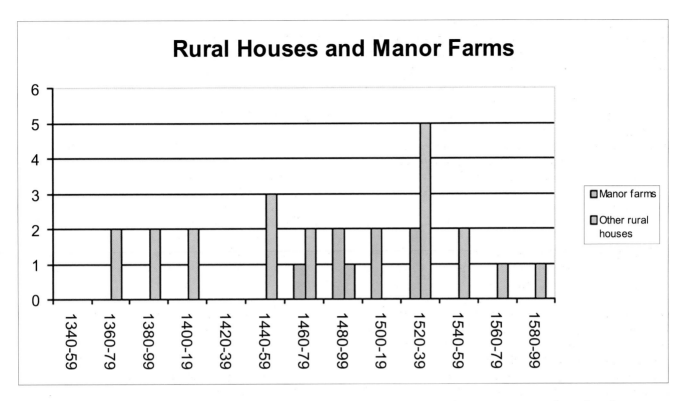

Rural Houses and Manor Farms

Manor farms

Other rural houses

1340-59 1360-79 1380-99 1400-19 1420-39 1440-59 1460-79 1480-99 1500-19 1520-39 1540-59 1560-79 1580-99

Figure 11.2 Rural vernacular houses and manor farmhouses in Hampshire 1340–1599: these dated examples illustrate an emergence and clustering of surviving manor farmhouses around the year 1500.

1496, a great barn was built for the new leaseholder, and building accounts for 1505–07 record the construction of the farmhouse, held by John Langton, who called himself a yeoman.

A parallel example is Littleton Manor Farm belonging to the Priors of St Swithun at Winchester. Here, John Smith, a yeoman, was given a short-term lease of seven years in 1457. It was not until 1480 that he was granted a 40-year lease that amounted to a vote of confidence in his reliability. It is significant that shortly afterwards, in 1485, a large farmhouse was built for him, and his memorial brass in the parish church calls him 'the farmer of this vill' (Miles & Haddon-Reece 1995, 63; Roberts 1996).

A final example is King's Somborne Farm, a large manorial farmhouse tree-ring dated to 1504 (Miles and Worthington 1999, 107). The landlords were the President and fellows of Magdalen College, Oxford, and their archives contain the building account for 1503/04. This recorded the cutting, trimming and carting of three score loads of timber to the site. It is reassuring to have a felling date so neatly confirmed! Essentially, then, dendrochronology has pointed the way to parallel documentation which has placed a group of houses in their historical context; a situation in which an opportunity arose for peasant farmers to lease areas of land vastly greater than anything the peasantry had held before. And with this land went the chance of a greater profit and a larger house.

Regional chronologies

Carpentry techniques

Historic carpentry techniques differed from region to region. Hence we need to develop regional rather than national criteria for dating timberwork in historic buildings. As we have seen, not all houses are suitable for dendrochronology and, in any case, it would be prohibitively expensive to try to date every historic building by this method. What can be done, however, is to sample a representative range of building types so that date ranges can be ascribed to the main carpentry features within a given area. In this way we will develop a much more precise framework for dating buildings on technical and stylistic criteria than was formerly possible. Take for example the crown-post roof, which is such a common feature of buildings in the south-eastern counties of England from the early-14th century until well into the 16th century (Gray 1990, 54). We were once at a loss to know why it was so rarely found in Hampshire's vernacular buildings. Were Hampshire's carpenters constructing crown-post roofs throughout this entire period, but only sparingly and in exceptional circumstances? Dendrochronology has answered this question. It is now clear that, in most of Hampshire, the crown-post roof occurred for only a short period, during which time it was by far the commonest roof-form. All the crown-post roofs

116

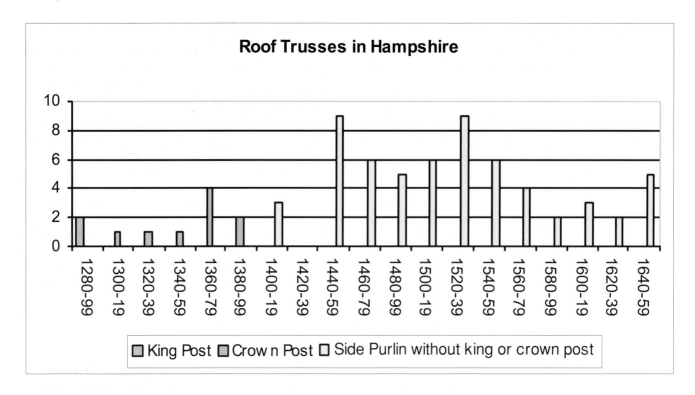

Figure 11.3 Roof trusses in dated box-framed houses in Hampshire 1280–1659: the crown-post roof emerges as a fairly short-lived phenomenon, thus explaining its relative rarity in the county.

that have so far been tree-ring dated in Hampshire fall between 1300 and 1393. Moreover, they account for nine of the twelve 14th-century roofs dated in Hampshire (see Fig 11.3). It would seem, then, that relatively few crown-post roofs have been found in the county simply because they were being constructed for a relatively short and early period; a period, that is, from which few vernacular buildings of any kind survive.

Clearly, it would be possible to make regional chronologies for other roof types: for example, it has become apparent that in Hampshire's vernacular buildings, the clasped purlin roof with queen struts predominates from the mid-15th until the late-17th century. Likewise it would be valuable to construct regional chronologies for carpentry joints, wall framing and other constructional features. The key point here is that, while dendrochronology will only give us a precise date for a small sample of buildings, it provides refined criteria by which to date many historic structures with more precision and confidence. Thus whole groups of buildings can now be placed in a more secure historical context.

Periods of transition

Tree-ring dating can tell us with some precision when crucial developments in house design and planning were occurring. It can also suggest the uncertainty of perceptions and the indecision that may have occurred during these periods of transition.

Plas Mawr, Conwy, North Wales

Documentary evidence shows that Robert Wynn, a courtier, built this great house *circa* 1580. Directly above Wynn's great chamber is an impressive roof carpentered with great care and no doubt expense. It is composed of a number of fine, arch-braced collar trusses with elaborate cusping between collars and roof apex (Turner 1997, 18–19, 35). Such roofs had traditionally been left exposed to the admiring gaze of those below. And yet this roof is entirely concealed by a plaster ceiling bearing the date 1580. Why should such a roof be constructed, only to be concealed?

Before tree-ring dating it was generally argued that, as the roof was clearly meant to be seen, it could not originally have been intended for Plas Mawr where it would immediately have been concealed by a plaster ceiling. It must have been taken from an earlier building and reused. In fact, while the plaster ceiling is dated 1580, dendrochronology showed that the felling date for the timbers of the decorative roof was 1578 (Miles & Haddon-Reece 1996, 108–09). Thus the period of time between felling the timbers for the roof and the making of the plaster ceiling was two years at most and probably rather less. So dendrochronology has given an unexpected result and created a new problem.

At present, the most plausible hypothesis would seem to be that there was a change of plan during construction. Robert Wynn originally intended to leave his great chamber open to the decorated wooden roof in what had long been the traditional manner. The carpenter was instructed and then began to make up the roof somewhere away from the site. Meanwhile, building progressed and it was decided to introduce a large stair-tower, which unfortunately protruded into one corner of the great chamber. This meant that the new roof could not be installed without partially destroying one of the trusses. It seems that Wynn decided to draw a veil over this inelegant botch by inserting a plaster ceiling.

If correct, what does this re-assessment tell us? It has been suggested that it was probably the lack of any full-time professional supervision over the building works that led to the planning error. While this is plausible, it is also possible to see this example as reflecting a period of indecision when preconceptions about exposed roof timbers in great houses were undergoing change. Whereas, during the 14th and 15th centuries, there would have been no doubt that a fine, exposed timber roof was a *sine qua non* for a great chamber, the introduction of decorative plaster ceilings into England in the mid-Tudor period (Jourdain 1924, 10) led to a period of transition.

The demise of the open hall in Hampshire

In Hampshire, dendrochronology has illuminated another period of transition and apparent indecision. The open hall had been an essential and accepted feature of houses at all social levels throughout the Middle Ages. On present evidence it seems that in Hampshire, and elsewhere in the south of England, preconceptions about the inevitability of this arrangement were beginning to break down by about 1480 (Pearson 1994a, 108). Although the aristocracy retained the open hall as a prestige feature, and existing houses often remained unmodernised until well into the 17th century, the construction of open halls in new-built, vernacular houses had gone out of fashion by about 1570 (see Fig 11.4). The period of transition, and perhaps uncertainty, between *c*1480 and *c*1570 can be illustrated with three examples.

The George Inn, Odiham, Hampshire

The George Inn at Odiham presents an early example, when floored-over halls with chimneys to carry away the smoke from the fire were novelties. Its hall range has been ascribed a felling date of winter 1486/87 (Miles & Haddon-Reece 1995, 63). The hall range has fine quality carpentry enriched with elaborate mouldings. It was also very up-to-date in being floored over, with a great chamber above the hall. The only heating is a timber chimney,

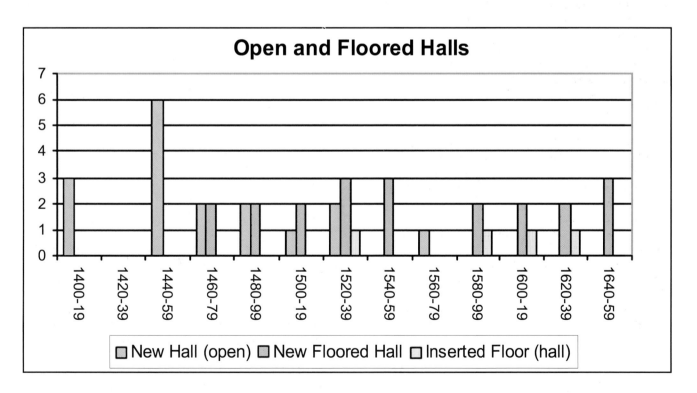

Figure 11.4   Dated open and floored halls in Hampshire (1400–1659): the occupants of open halls often deferred the insertion of a hall floor until well in to the 17th century. However, it was in 1566 (felling date) that the last dated open hall was built. For nearly a century before this date there was a period of transition in which either open or floored halls were built.

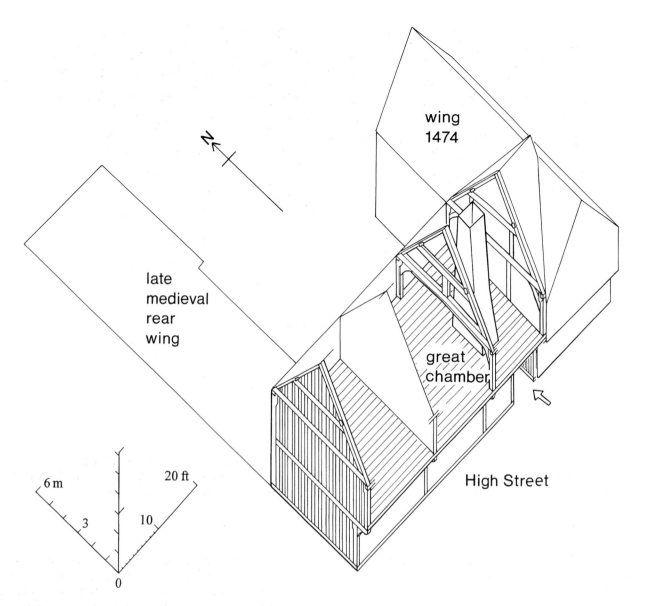

late
medieval
rear
wing

wing
1474

great
chamber

High Street

6 m

20 ft

3

10

0

Figure 11.5   The George Inn, Odiham, Hampshire: The hall range (felling date winter 1486/87) stands parallel to the High Street. Immediately above the two-bay hall is a two-bay great chamber divided by an open truss with an arch-braced tie beam. A timber chimney (felling date 1487) protrudes awkwardly through the floor of the further bay.

of relatively crude construction, which both obscures some of the fine mouldings in the hall and intrudes awkwardly into the great chamber above (see Fig 11.5). Before tree-ring dating, the obvious explanation seemed to be that this chimney of crude workmanship was inserted in an entirely separate building campaign, perhaps a considerable time after the hall was built.

Surprisingly, dendrochronology dated the timber chimney to 1487. Thus the fine hall and relatively crude chimney were part of the same building campaign. How can this apparent paradox be explained? Could the timbers of the chimney have come from a demolished building that had been constructed in 1487? This seems unlikely because the timbers from the chimney bear no empty mortices nor other indications of reuse. Could they, however, have been laid

on one side in a carpenter's workshop for many years only to be used when a timber chimney was required? While this is possible, it becomes more implausible as the supposed gap between the construction of hall and chimney lengthens. It would be uneconomic for a carpentry business to retain valuable timber for many years and an extraordinary coincidence for a carpenter to select precisely those timbers for the chimney, which many years before had been left over from the hall.

The most likely explanation seems to be one that parallels the situation at Plas Mawr. A master carpenter made up the timber frame for the hall range. In 1486/87, he could have had little experience of accommodating chimneys within halls and, as at Plas Mawr, there was probably no full-time professional supervision over the building works. So the problem

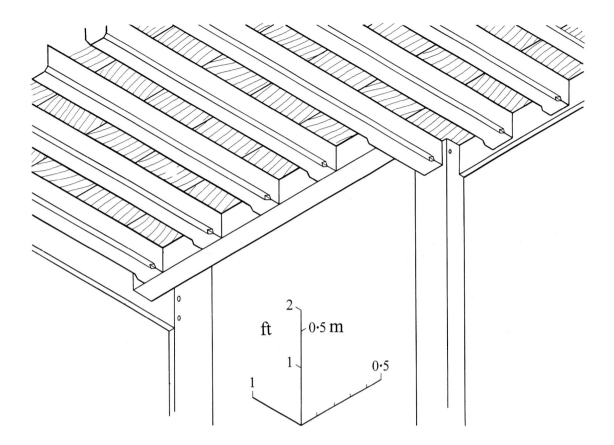

Figure 11.6   75 Winchester Street, Overton, Hampshire: the ceiling joists of the hall, showing a trimmer bridging across what had apparently been intended as a window in an open hall. Both the frame of the hall and the ceiling have been ascribed a felling date of 1544. (Drawing by Jonathan Snowdon).

of inserting a chimney in the hall was not properly addressed and apparently another and inferior craftsman was employed to set the timber chimney in a space that had not been created for it.

75 Winchester Street, Overton

Let us turn now to an example near the end of this period of transition, almost 60 years after the construction of the hall at The George Inn. By this time, floored halls were not uncommon and the construction of open halls was falling out of fashion. At 75 Winchester Street, Overton there is what appears to be a standard, late-medieval house with an open hall in the central bay. The two outer bays are floored with axial, unchamfered joists. The floor of the hall bay appears, on stylistic grounds, to be later and to be the work of a superior craftsman. It has a spine beam and transverse floor joists bearing narrow chamfers and quite refined diamond-shaped chamfer stops. This evidence led to the conclusion that the house had been built with an open hall, which had been floored over many years later (Roberts & Miles 1997, 20).

In fact, dendrochronology showed that the whole house, including the hall floor, was of the same date (1544) (Miles & Worthington 1997, 176). It would appear that the carpenter made up a house with a traditional open hall. At some stage it was decided that this was too old-fashioned and a hall floor was inserted, apparently by a superior carpenter with a more up-to-date notion of what a floor should be like. One difficulty he faced was that the inserted floor now cut across the tall window that had been designed for an open hall. A special trimmer had to be made to bridge the space across the window to support the transverse joists at this point (see Fig 11.6). Of course, lack of supervision can lead to errors in any period but it may be significant that the errors are clustered in precisely that period when men are coming to terms with innovations and when traditional preconceptions about house design are being questioned.

Old Manor, Ashley

A third example is hardly an error but illustrates a transitional, almost experimental, approach to the open hall. At the Old Manor, Ashley a detached kitchen similar to those recently discovered in Sussex, was built in 1521 or shortly afterwards

120

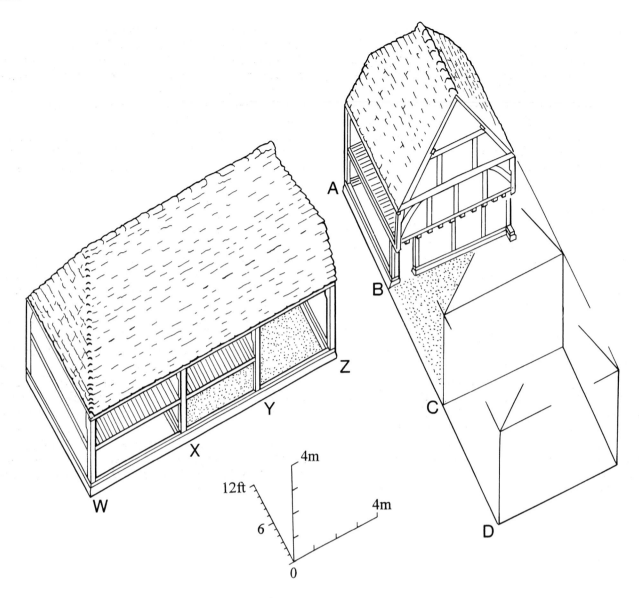

Figure 11.7   The Old Manor, Ashley, Hampshire: the building on the left (W-Z) is presumed to be a detached kitchen (felling date 1521 or soon after), serving the house on the right (felling date 1530). The hall of the house (bay B-C) has an internal jetty but unsooted rafters. A ceiling was inserted over the hall in 1605/06 (felling date).

(Martin & Martin 1997, 85). About a decade later, an associated hall house was built close by (felling date 1530) (Miles & Worthington 1997, 175). It was clearly intended as a hall house for the internal jetty, or dais canopy, still survives (see Fig 11.7). As in the previous example at Overton, the hall floor seemed stylistically later than the floors in the end bays and yet, strangely, the rafters over the hall were completely unsooted (Roberts 1997, 115). Had there been a change of mind so that the hall was floored over as soon as the house had been built?

Dendrochronology showed that the hall floor was, in fact, a much later insertion (felling date 1605/06) (Miles & Worthington 1997, 175). It would appear that the possession of a detached kitchen obviated the need for cooking in the hall, hence the absence of soot on the rafters. But does this mean that the occupants shivered in an unheated hall for over 70 years

or did they perhaps find a charcoal brazier sufficient for their needs? It is possible that a chimney was erected and yet the hall remained open and unfloored, although there is no evidence for this and the present chimney is structurally integral and thus coeval with the hall floor of 1605/06.

What does seem clear is that, having decided on an open hall just as that tradition was beginning to die out, they felt no urgency to convert to a floored hall as the householders at Overton had done in the previous example. Overton was a small town and perhaps more fashion-conscious than Ashley, which is a remote hamlet. But other examples both in Hampshire and Kent show that there was no rush to floor over existing halls for many years after they had ceased to be built from new (Pearson 1994a, 114–15).

Historians have had to rely heavily on William

Harrison's contemporary account of how and when the open hall gave way to the chimney (eg Platt 1994, 4–6; Williams 1995, 206). Dendrochronology promises new evidence, and the hope of finding answers to some related questions. When were floored halls first built in new houses? When were floors inserted in existing open halls? When did open halls in houses below aristocratic level cease to be constructed? And how did house-builders react to these changes in long-standing tradition?

Conclusion

It has been written of some historians and students of vernacular architecture that they are two groups of people studying the same themes but barely reading each other's publications (Dyer 1997, 1). In the past this was, to some extent, excusable. Before dendrochronology, vernacular buildings might be described as 'late medieval', or 'probably 14th century'. Such imprecision was fairly useless to the historian. Even when dating on typological grounds is relatively precise, it is still valuable to have confirmation by dendrochronology so that the date can be received with more confidence. With this increase in precision and confidence, students on both sides of the divide may be encouraged to read each other's work more often, and to collaborate more fully in exploiting fresh evidence.

In essence, there is now a strong case for team-work among those whose expertise lies in building survey and analysis, and historians whose expertise lies in the reading and interpretation of documents. The student of vernacular architecture will know which buildings and features are structurally significant. The historian will know which buildings are most likely to be well-documented. Together they should identify common ground and converging lines of enquiry. Only then will they be best placed to employ the skills of the dendrochronologist.

Acknowledgements

Much of the paper is based on a research project to date historic timber buildings in Hampshire organised by the Hampshire Buildings Survey Group. The project is principally funded by Hampshire County Council, with additional funding from district and borough councils within the county, private individuals and local amenity societies. Grateful thanks are due to all of them. The work of Dan Miles and Michael Worthington of the Oxford Dendrochonological Laboratory is also gratefully acknowledged. John Hare, Dan Miles, Liz Lewis and Peter Smith are thanked for their help in various ways during the preparation of this paper. Finally, my thanks to Sarah Pearson for her generous encouragement and advice throughout the process of preparation and writing.

Part IV: The records

12 The management of information *by Anna Eavis*

Introduction

More information about small buildings is being generated than ever before. It emanates from a complex landscape populated by professionals, academics and independent researchers. Many of them work within a number of contexts, producing reports for a variety of different purposes which range from development control to pure research. In the simplest terms, this body of information about buildings derives from work carried out by, or on behalf of, national agencies and local authorities, individuals in a private research capacity and postgraduate students. The value of the records they produce can only be exploited by ensuring their durability and accessibility. At the time of the *Recording Small Buildings* conference there was no national strategy for the preservation of this material or for the provision of access to it. The original paper argued that an information management strategy must be informed by reliable understanding about the scale of the task, taking account of the quantity of relevant material, its whereabouts and the suitability of the conditions under which it is stored. It also stressed that, if we are to address the challenge of providing information in any long-term and adequate sense we must think carefully about the audience and its requirements. Who needs the information? Who wants it? Who do we think could benefit from access to it?

Since the conference, various organisations have begun to address the relevant and extremely complex strategic, political, technical and logistical issues. The most significant initiative has been the establishment, under the aegis of the Council for British Archaeology (CBA), of the Heritage Information Resource Network (HEIRNET). In 1998 HEIRNET, whose membership extends to all the relevant national bodies, commissioned an audit to give an idea of the range of existing heritage information records and the likely scale of any future attempt to coordinate activities. The scope of the resulting report (Baker *et al* 1999) extends beyond small buildings, but its discussion and recommendations are extremely valuable and cover the relevant issues in far more depth than is possible here, in particular those opportunities offered by web technology. It is hoped that they will be published in due course.

This paper considers the range of relevant material, its whereabouts, accessibility and potential readership, and offers some thoughts on how to manage this substantial corpus of information. Although not written as representative of the view of the National Monuments Record (NMR), this paper is nevertheless informed by the NMR's considerable experience of information collation, curation and dissemination. The NMR, formerly the archive of the Royal Commission on the Historical Monuments of England (RCHME), is now the public archive of English Heritage,[1] maintaining and providing access to information on England's historic buildings and archaeology. Its collections, which contain approximately ten million items and comprise photographs, drawings and written reports, have been assembled over the last 90 years. They derive from a number of sources, including the RCHME's own photographers and survey teams. The NMR welcomes visitors to its public search rooms in Swindon and London and provides a research service for remote enquirers.

The information

The large number of building records in existence represent a vast potential resource for researchers. In reality, of course, they are difficult to track down. Only a small proportion are published and retrievable through the valuable bibliographies produced by the Vernacular Architecture Group (1972, 1979, 1992, 1999) and the CBA's *British and Irish archaeological bibliography* (BIAB 1992-ongoing). The national agencies (the Royal Commissions, English Heritage, Historic Scotland, Cadw) have ongoing publications programmes, which include synthetic accounts of particular building types. In 1994, for example, the RCHME published, in three volumes, the results of its five-year survey of the medieval houses of Kent (Pearson 1994a, Barnwell and Adams 1994, Pearson *et al* 1994). Other regional surveys have been funded by local authorities (eg Slocombe 1992), or produced by individuals, working alone but published with the help of a local institution (eg Hall 1983). Scholarly and local historical societies, however, continue to shoulder the burden of publishing accounts of individual small buildings.

Unpublished records

A serious problem, therefore, relates to the whereabouts and accessibility of unpublished records, which represent most of the relevant material. A substantial amount is generated by specialists working in a private research capacity, many of whom are affiliated to at least one scholarly society, and who pursue their own research agendas, whether with a topographical or with a typological theme. The quantity of information produced is at present unknown, although a sense of it can be gained from the number of records – well over 1000 – produced for the Rape of Hastings Architectural Survey, a voluntary recording project set up to study historic architecture in East Sussex. Of the many records produced by individuals in a private research capacity, some – like the Rape of Hastings Survey - are deposited in the relevant NMR,[2] county record office or local library, where they can be made available to researchers. Many independent recorders, however, are building up personal archives of their own work, not least because their reports represent 'work in progress'. Such records are difficult for other researchers to locate. They also bear risks of damage and decay that should not be underestimated. The death of an author can lead to loss, dispersal or destruction. Instances of the damage sustained by unpublished excavation archives through damp, fire and even rodents, are well known. The loss of parish registers through church fires eventually led to the statutory protection of parochial records. Building records are invaluable resources that have none of the safeguards set in place by professional archives to ensure durability and security, and there is no provision for public access.

The planning process (in particular the application of Planning Policy Guidance Note 15 in relation to listed building consent applications) generates reports and drawings at national and regional levels. The amount of material produced as a result of 28,000 annual LBC applications is probably far lower than it should be, but there is already a significant number of drawings, plans and reports, for which a management plan is long overdue. The records are often produced – in a professional capacity – by those independent researchers mentioned above. Copies are deposited with the client (this may be the developer, the local authority or English Heritage), the relevant conservation officer and the owner of the building. Although some may find their way into the relevant Sites and Monuments Record (SMR),[3] NMR or record office, the majority remain in the casework file, where archival conditions are generally poor and public access almost non-existent. In addition, these files may be subject to regular 'weeding', with some material being microfilmed or shredded after a few years. There are also risks of loss and destruction associated with the reorganisation or relocation of departments and the departure of staff.

The number of relevant postgraduate dissertations is increasing as more university archaeology departments embrace upstanding structures (eg York, which offers an MA in the archaeology of buildings). They are generally filed in the relevant university library, where archival conditions and public access facilities are usually adequate. In the absence of a comprehensive index to such unpublished material, however, it is difficult to locate them. A small proportion are published, but much good work remains unconsulted.

Digital records

The growing number of databases developed by national and regional agencies, consultants, academics and private researchers complicate the picture further. There are many in existence, functioning as casework management systems, as indexes to archives or as site-based inventories supporting statistical analysis and thematic enquiry. Elements of many buildings' records find their way into them. National agencies maintain databases for site or casework management purposes and for dissemination – English Heritage's List Management and Listed Buildings System are two such databases. The Listed Buildings System probably represents the largest corpus of buildings data in this country. It was created by the Royal Commission on the Historical Monuments of England (RCHME), in collaboration with English Heritage and the Department of National Heritage (now the Department of Culture, Media and Sport). The Listed Buildings System is a computerised version of the *Statutory List of Buildings of Special Architectural or Historic Interest* ('Listed Buildings'). It provides access to scanned images of the 360,000 list entries and enables queries on a wide range of themes (date, building type, roofing material, for example) as well as on specific buildings. Despite legitimate questions about the quality of some of the list entries (a problem which English Heritage is addressing in its ongoing listing programme) the database does at least provide an inventory which can be used as a basis for research. Many local authorities develop their own systems to track, facilitate and inform casework. This may be more common at county than at district level (it is certainly true that an increasing, if small, number of SMRs hold information about buildings). Record offices and local libraries are developing databases, relating if not specifically to buildings, then to material of local relevance. In universities where there is, generally speaking, good provision for access to computers, academics and students are working on ways of storing data which will enable thematic analysis.

There is no doubt that such digital records are potentially valuable to researchers. As with other unpublished material, however, the problem is knowing that these resources exist. If anything, with the exception of those systems specifically set up to facilitate public access, it is harder to get at information on other people's databases than it is to read a copy of a report. This is not only due to the incompatibility of formats; often it is difficult to make sense of data compiled for a different purpose than one's own. The creation of numerous data sets over long periods of time by a variety of different people, using various methods and standards, bodes ill for consistency and accuracy. It is worth noting that the experience of SMRs in this field shows that technology does not ensure compatibility, consistency or quality. Although compiled and maintained for the same basic purpose, these records, produced by around 80 separate SMRs over three decades are variable in all of these areas. Plans to create a national 'network' of SMR information systems are thus constrained by the challenge of minimising the disparities (Baker and Baker 1999).

Limitations of existing finding aids

There are no comprehensive national, regional or local indexes (whether in hard copy or database format) to unpublished building records, and no guide to where they might reside. Any researcher will probably have to consult several national and local repositories, navigating a range of service levels and cataloguing systems. It will be necessary to contact academics and conservation officers, who may or may not have sufficient time or inclination to help with such enquiries. Despite best efforts, a proportion of material will remain unknown and inaccessible in private collections or casework files. Research is, of course, partly about the joys and frustrations of such detective work and about learning through contact with others. Learned societies are critically important in establishing, nurturing and extending scholarly communities and there is no substitute for this sort of exchange of ideas and knowledge. However, in terms of improving the basic research tools, there is much to be done.

Current levels of accessibility depend, as we have seen, on the purpose of the recording activity. Reports produced as part of development control procedures, for example, are written for a specific and immediate aim. In one sense their receipt by client and conservation officer is the end of a process. In reality the best of them have a more enduring interest and relevance, which should extend beyond being kept on file to inform future casework. As Meeson implies, useful information on historic buildings is often buried within a mass of procedural papers with relevant drawings in the form of impermanent dyeline copies. The same is true of some reports produced by individuals in a private research capacity, of which only a limited proportion are published. Those engaged in this sort of study may be motivated by a particular personal interest, but the resulting drawing or report can have a wider significance to other researchers at a future date.

The audience

The potential users of building records form a broad group, with a variety of requirements which, although linked, are distinct, and can be broadly characterised as:

- conservation
- academic or specialist research
- formal education
- general/local interest

The conservation, academic and specialist requirements are reasonably well-understood and have been covered by a number of authors elsewhere in this volume. In general terms, current and comprehensive information on a given site is necessary for any kind of survey. For those engaged in the planning process, either as a conservation officer, English Heritage caseworker or historic buildings consultant, rapid access to comprehensive coverage is critical. There is also a need for information for comparative purposes, about a particular building type or regional characteristics of style and construction. This kind of thematic research may be undertaken at high speed for a PPG 15 report, but it is also essential for anyone – academic, independent, national agency – pursuing a research agenda. Certainly, the establishment of positive research agendas (as advocated by Kate Clark, Grenville and Meeson in this volume) depends partly on the assimilation and analysis of large chunks of data in ways which can demonstrate trends, patterns and – extremely important – gaps in existing knowledge. Thematic enquiries, of course, demand complex and detailed levels of database indexing, which have significant cost implications.

Beyond this relatively small, informed audience there is a wider pool of potential interest. In a world in which sustainability is an increasingly important issue, history and conservation have an important role to play in education. Local history study is now a compulsory part of the curriculum for 7–10 year olds. Pupils are required to investigate how an aspect of a local area has changed over a long period of time, or how the locality has been affected by a significant national or local event, or by the work of an individual. New for the 2000 curriculum is a greater emphasis on the local dimension of history for 11–14 year olds. Teachers are encouraged to examine the local dimension of the established national topics (Britain 1066–1500; 1500–1750; 1750–1900). The most commonly taken history exam at 14–16 is the Schools History Project, in which students have to undertake a local study using primary source material. Many schools begin local historical studies by working on their own school, its grounds, its local environment and the community of which it is a part. Records produced on vernacular architecture have a relevance but, although already used by some schools, are simply not accessible enough in a form which can be used to create stimulating educational source material. Local studies in schools are extremely valuable, especially where they are linked to the consideration of wider environmental issues. Effective conservation depends, in the long term, on education and schools have a crucial role in influencing whole communities.

Among the wider public there is evidence of a growing interest in the past, expressed through increased use and enjoyment of archives, web sites and television programmes. Each year around 18,000 people use the enquiry and research services of the NMR.[4] Apart from conservation professionals, academics, and commercial users, around 60% of enquirers represent a group of people loosely classified as the general public. They range in age from school pupils to pensioners. Some are the owners of listed buildings, others are affiliated with local history societies or local studies courses, yet others are engaged in formal research programmes. Many have no formal agenda. In general they are not interested in distinctions between archaeology and architectural history, or in the politics of conservation and planning. They have a common interest in questions of place, time and people.

In 1998 more than 617,000 people visited local archives, the majority of whom had an interest in constructing their own family trees or in local history (Boyns 1999). Both areas of study tend to be undervalued by professionals and specialist researchers, which is unfortunate, given that useful information is often unearthed. The current widespread interest in genealogy is evidence of the most basic human impulse for constructing history. People have a desire to place themselves within a specific historical context, to establish or build on a sense of identity by understanding more about their own stories. Once the family tree is completed and the documents assembled they often gravitate towards more tangible evidence of the past. Family history may begin with genealogy but it can come to life in landscapes and buildings, and particularly in the sort of buildings embraced by societies like the Vernacular Architecture Group, which are often closer to people's personal histories than is grand architecture. There is also a growing public interest in industrial buildings. It is a sad irony that the dismantling of major heavy industries in this country has created a constituency of ex-industrial workers who now have a place in a newly recognised area of 'heritage'. The North of England Open Air Museum at Beamish may have its detractors, but it has recreated the lives and the work of local people (some in the very recent past) and established the importance of their contribution to the region's history. Shortly after moving to the former offices of the Great Western Railway in Swindon the NMR had an open day attended by 400 ex-railway workers who wanted to hear about and share in the history of the building. Nurturing and encouraging this latent interest is important because it has an inherent educational value in itself, raises awareness about the importance of the built heritage and related conservation issues, and connects people with their local environment and the evidence for its history.

We are inevitably engaged in the piecemeal, cumulative assembly of information on buildings and should aspire to organise and preserve these records in a way which supports the advancement of knowledge and the development of understanding. This means recognising that work carried out for one purpose may be usable for another. Some sorts of data may need to be interpreted for the non-specialist. Publications, exhibitions, and – increasingly – television programmes are successfully used

to present such information in accessible forms. The experience of the NMR and of many other record repositories, however, suggests that a growing number of people are interested in doing their own research. They can and do make use of a wide range of original records. This enthusiasm and dedication should be encouraged and enabled by the provision of the tools required to understand buildings which are familiar or relevant to them.

The need for a national strategy

The absence of a national strategy for the archival deposit of buildings records and the provision of public access to them is culturally damaging. Current and future research programmes are limited by the lack of information and by the costs associated with the time it takes to locate material. Material that is lost through decay or failure to locate it constitutes a great waste of past efforts and potential resource. Effective planning and management decisions are largely dependent on knowledge of previous work, so are seriously constrained by the inaccessibility of comprehensive and current records. Public awareness remains skewed towards Grade I listed buildings, with little understanding of the vernacular and industrial heritage.

The effective provision of information to these various audiences depends on:

- the deposit of records in a repository which has the resources to catalogue, curate and provide access to them,
- the creation of an accessible, comprehensive and up-to-date index to records, giving an indication of the whereabouts of archive material and, ideally, supporting a degree of thematic enquiry,
- the accessibility of 'raw data' to those who can interpret it for others (teachers, writers, TV programme makers).

But who has ownership of this vision? And how – given the volume of data and the complexity of the circumstances in which it is produced – can it possibly be realised?

Archival deposit

There are a limited number of options. The tidiest solution is that a national repository takes responsibility for housing the records and for compiling and maintaining the index. The obvious candidates are the NMRs, with good archival and public access facilities, and expertise in the design and maintenance of information systems. However, the NMRs, like all public archives, are having to be increasingly selective about acquisitions and are unlikely to have the necessary resources to devote to new curation and cataloguing programmes of this scale.

A more practical solution is that records should be

housed locally. The principal advantages are that they would be more accessible (the majority of enquiries about small buildings emanate from the locality), would enhance local collections, thus contributing to a corpus of information, and would be better understood by local curators, and therefore of more use to enquirers. The selection of a repository is likely to be informed by the resources and commitment available locally or regionally. It is not necessarily an appropriate role for district planning offices or for SMRs, despite the fact that some are keen to encourage public access, a laudable aspiration voiced in a recent assessment of English SMRs (Baker and Baker 1999). Alongside their recommendation that SMRs be redefined as 'a definitive permanent general record of the local historic environment . . . publicly and professionally maintained, whose data is accessible and retrievable for a wide range of purposes', the authors note the urgent need for adequate resourcing of information management and public access facilities, and recommend the transfer of original archive material to appropriate repositories (Baker & Baker 1999, 3–5). There can be disadvantages in attempting to combine the interests of conservation and planning with curation and access, although in a few cases it has worked reasonably well. It may be more appropriate to consider institutions which are already experienced in and equipped for curation, cataloguing and public access – record offices and local studies libraries. In some counties, such resources are well developed. The Wiltshire Buildings Record, for instance, is a voluntary society and educational charity, conveniently housed alongside the county record office and local studies library. It holds a substantial archive on the county's historic buildings and promotes their study, offering guidance on recording practice as well as providing search room facilities and pursuing a publications programme. Plans for establishing an Oxfordshire Buildings Record are well advanced.

Terms of deposit and access may vary from archive to archive but issues likely to feature most prominently are quality, format and copyright. Good quality reports and drawings are desirable in any case, but for repositories with limited resources (the majority) high standards are critical. Most archives cannot afford to house, curate and catalogue poor quality material. Conventional paper formats are unlikely to present problems, but where digital formats are employed (for drawings, photographs or text) there might be difficulties; few archives have robust digital archiving policies as yet. In any case, a durable hard copy should be retained as an insurance against the loss of digital archives. The question of copyright is straightforward when a report has been produced by an independent researcher; the author retains copyright, but effectively licenses the repository to disseminate the information according to specified terms and conditions. When the report has been commissioned by a third party the copyright issue is more complex as the client generally has copyright. If the work

relates, however, to a planning application for listed building consent, it is deemed to enter the public domain.

Creating an index

If records are dispersed in a number of local and regional archives, the process of producing and providing access to one comprehensive index becomes more complicated although, given advances in database and internet technology, technically possible. There are compelling arguments – to do with efficiency, as well as with technical and data standards – for the ownership of such a database at a national level, but the viability of a 'national index' maintained by a single agency, is thrown into question by past experience.

One critical issue is that of cost. Another is the need to ensure that the design and scope of such a database is informed by a realistic assessment not only of user requirements but also of the resources available to compile and maintain it in the mid- to long term. It is true that technology provides all sorts of opportunities for the storage and analysis of data, but experience over the last 20 years shows that technology is a dangerous master, and that it will not provide all the answers. Many computer systems developed in the 1980s were characterised by the triumph of technician over user. Driven by the sophistication and potential of the technology, rather than by clear thinking about purpose and sustainability, many organisations ended up with databases which were over-complex, cumbersome, and offered possibilities for detailed indexing far beyond the capability of the associated human resource. There are far too many examples of half-filled databases, conceived with optimism and intended to record every imaginable level of detail in order to support the most sophisticated thematic analysis. When the money runs out all that remains is a partial data-set which does not even provide basic general information and whose lack of comprehensiveness defeats the whole object of thematic recording.

As a measure of the scale of the resource required to create and sustain a national record, it is worth noting that the Listed Buildings System (which comprises around 360,000 records) cost £3 million to design, build and compile. Records were input by 35 graduates over a period of three years. Since its completion in 1996 it has been necessary to devote a significant proportion of staff time to updating the content and software. Wherever databases are set up, there remains the need to invest in the prosaic business of information gathering, standardising, inputting and technical maintenance; all processes which can absorb vast amounts of time and money.

The business of updating the Listed Buildings System is at least made relatively easy by the fact that it is maintained by the organisation responsible for the creation of the original list entries. In instances where the records are produced outside the 'data curation' organisation a number of logistical challenges arise, although the resulting national overview is valuable. Such a model has been successfully implemented by the English NMR since 1978 in the shape of the Excavations Index, a database of archaeological interventions, which now comprises over 55,000 records. The index provides basic information on the location and results of fieldwork, and refers enquirers to holders of archives and finds. Information is derived from various sources, including pro-formas completed by planning archaeologists and project officers. It is worth noting, however, that despite the whole-hearted support of the Standing Conference of Archaeological Unit Managers (SCAUM 1997) it has been difficult to ensure consistent or comprehensive coverage. Although the database represents an invaluable tool for researchers, reliance on self-registration has produced an uneven record, with under-representation in areas where units and archaeological officers are not sympathetic to the project. In a parallel exercise English Heritage funded an annual data collection exercise to compile an index of archaeological investigations (AIP). Adopting a slightly different approach, researchers from Bournemouth University visited units and SMRs in order to identify and index reports. The results (*The Gazetteer of Archaeological Investigations in England*) are issued as annual supplements to the *BIAB*. There are now plans to combine the Excavations Index and AIP, and to provide on-line access to this enhanced dataset via the Archaeology Data Service. On-line input forms are also being developed. This project (OASIS) will encompass building recording reports produced by archaeological units and contractors in England since 1997. It is instructive that, in the wake of PPG 16, the archaeological community and English Heritage are now taking seriously the problem posed by the relative inaccessibility of an estimated 10,000 unpublished reports, particularly as syntheses by academics are perceived to be increasingly divorced from the latest archaeological discoveries made in the field.

Adoption of this model for the management of information about buildings may seem an attractive option. The principal databases of the NMR (including the Listed Buildings System) could at least provide basic information on every recorded building, including the location of the archive material. Index details could be submitted by authors or local curators and, with appropriate funding, entered onto the database by NMR staff. The coordination of such a scheme for architectural records, however, would undoubtedly be very complicated, involving the establishment of procedures that cut across professional and voluntary sectors as well as national, regional, and local interests. Another critical factor is the proliferation of recording bodies concerned with documenting and interpreting elements of the historic environment. Organisers of a seminar for those involved in national thematic surveys recently identified over 40 such projects in England, ranging in subject from war memorials to cinemas.[5] The results of these surveys are tremendously valuable and, like those produced on small buildings, deserve to be preserved and made accessible. The quantity of information involved, however, makes the twin tasks of ensuring archival stability and providing a national overview daunting indeed. A single institution – even a national agency – is unlikely to be able to find the resources required for the compilation of a high level index to all such projects.

Partnerships

The scale of this immense data resource poses a fundamental question about the role of the national agencies in relation to regional and local heritage bodies, and to individuals engaged in recording activity. How can the NMRs, for example, traditionally custodians of the national overview and recipients of much of this sort of data, cope with the increasing quantity of information? The growing recognition is that effective management of information relating to the historic environment can only be achieved through partnership, with the provision of common access to datasets compiled by diverse organisations. Developments in database and internet technology and increased levels of access to the world wide web mean that this concept, which has been in existence for some years, could now be realised.

In 1998 a statement of cooperation issued by RCHME, English Heritage and the Association of Local Government Archaeological Officers (ALGAO) aimed 'to ensure that the main custodians of heritage record systems in England progress in genuine partnership to meet society's requirement for information on the historic environment' (RCHME 1998a, 5). The document emphasised the potential for establishing, via SMRs, a computerised network providing a national information service for a diverse audience. As has already been noted, problems with consistency, quality and compatibility will need to be overcome. The SMRs are working – with the NMR and with the assistance of Lottery funding – towards a realisation of this vision. In this instance the NMR's role is primarily that of providing support and advice on recording practice, data standards and software design. This may be a more realistic approach in relation to other information resources.

Mapping Information Resources, the report produced for HEIRNET (Baker et al 1999), presents a vision in which a central internet register of records is maintained by the community of information providers, while the records themselves are compiled according to local or specialist requirements. The report identifies the opportunities and constraints presented by database and web technology and recommends the establishment of a technical advisory facility to promote the use of appropriate data standards, metadata standards and protocols, and technical standards.

The realisation of this vision is partly dependent on the resolution of strategic questions relating to the relative roles of national and local information providers. This, and the associated technical issues, may present a daunting prospect for individuals who are simply interested in finding ways to ensure that their work is accessible. As has been said, individual researchers and recorders have a responsibility to deposit copies of their records in a publicly accessible archive and many already do. Beyond this, those working as part of a recording group, or who have generated a significant corpus of material, could usefully begin to think about compiling a digital index to their records with a view to making it accessible via the world wide web. Umbrella recording bodies, such as the VAG, should certainly be exploring this area. The VAG already annually publishes national lists of tree-ring dates in *Vernacular Architecture*, and is currently seeking funds to complete computerisation of its ongoing bibliography for dissemination via the web. Preparing to coordinate an index of members' reports might be an appropriate next project. In the absence of the technical advisory facility recommended by the HEIRNET report, useful advice on data standards, technical standards and funding can be obtained from the NMR[6] and from the Archaeology Data Service (ADS).[7]

The adoption of common data standards is critically important and should be taken seriously by anyone compiling a digital inventory. As much work has already been done in this field, useful guidelines do exist. In 1989 a working group was formed under the aegis of the Council of Europe to explore the means by which cultural heritage information networks could be established. It was agreed that compatibility of data standards is most readily achieved at the level of 'core' information, ie those categories of essential, basic information, which are common to all. The *Core Data Index to Historic Buildings and Monuments of the Architectural Heritage* was produced following an international survey of architectural inventories and ratified by the Council of Europe in 1995. It provides for the classification of individual buildings and sites by name, location, functional type, date, architect or patron, building materials, techniques, physical condition and protection status. Its purpose is to 'enable the recording of the minimum categories of information required to make a reasonable assessment of a monument, whether for planning, management, academic or other purposes' (Thornes and Bold 1998, 8). In addition, it provides for the inclusion of references to further information held elsewhere. *The Core Data Index* and the *International Core Data Standard for Archaeological Sites and Monuments* (Thornes and Bold 1998) provided a basis for the NMR's own databases and for its continued work in data standards. In association with ALGAO, the *British and Irish Archaeological Bibliography*, English Heritage and the National Trust, the NMR recently published a monument inventory data standard, commonly known as *MIDAS* (RCHME 1998b),

which clearly explains the case for adopting common data standards, outlines relevant information schemes and provides a step-by-step guide to setting up an inventory. *MIDAS* was developed in response to the growing number of survey projects. It is specifically designed to support the work of independent researchers, thematic and local recording groups, professional heritage managers in national and local agencies. It is available on the English Heritage website (www.english-heritage.org.uk) and should be consulted by anyone thinking of creating an inventory.

Conclusion

It is undoubtedly the case that the funding and coordination of a national network of information resources, along the lines envisaged by HEIRNET, presents a considerable challenge. Nevertheless, the importance of addressing the challenge cannot be underestimated. It is hoped that the recommendations made in *Mapping Information Resources* (Baker *et al* 1999) will be implemented by the partner organisations. In the meantime anyone producing buildings records should be encouraged to take responsibility for ensuring the preservation and accessibility of their work, calling upon the national agencies for advice when needed. This is a critically important step if we are to ensure that the best possible planning and management decisions are taken, and if we are to provide for a better appreciation of our built environment.

Notes

1. The Royal Commission on the Historical Monuments of England was operationally merged with English Heritage on 1 April 1999.
2. England, Wales and Scotland each have their own NMR. The English NMR is part of English Heritage. The National Monuments Record of Wales and the National Monuments Record of Scotland are run by the Royal Commissions of Wales and Scotland respectively.
3. Sites and Monuments Records are maintained mostly by county councils, but in some cases by district, park, and unitary authorities. They contain information on the local archaeological (and in some cases, built) landscape. Their primary purpose is to support the conservation and management of the historic environment.
4. The NMR maintains an enquiry database, from which are derived these statistics about patterns of use.
5. Research carried out in preparation for a seminar 'Weaving the Tapestry' sponsored by the NMR and the ADS, and held at the Society of Antiquaries in November 1999.
6. Contact the Data Standards Unit, NMRC, Kemble Drive, Swindon, SN2 2GZ.

7   The ADS is funded by the Joint Information Systems Committee of the UK's Higher Education Funding Council and is managed by a consortium of UK institutions, including the CBA. Its aim is to collect, describe, catalogue, preserve and provide user support for digital resources that are created as a product of archaeological research. It also promotes standards and guidelines for best practice in the creation, description and preservation of digital records. Its web site address is http://ads.ahds.ac.uk/ahds/

Part V: Conclusions

13 Recording small buildings in a changing world
by Nicholas Cooper

This is the text of the report which Nicholas Cooper wrote for the Vernacular Architecture Group's Newsletter in January 1999, following the original conference on 'Recording small buildings in a changing world'. It has been reprinted here, with minor amendments, as it sums up most of the issues which were raised then and have continued to occupy the thoughts of the contributors to the present volume.

This very well attended conference provided a forum for the discussion of a wide range of current issues relating to the making and the use of records of smaller buildings. Eleven speakers gave formal contributions: Sarah Pearson (who gave the introductory talk), Nat Alcock, David Baker, Kate Clark, Jo Cox, Anna Eavis, Jane Grenville, Barry Harrison, David Martin, Bob Meeson and Edward Roberts, while the concluding discussion was chaired by Malcolm Airs. While each addressed a particular topic, there was a broad consensus about many of the ways in which building recording (and the recording of vernacular buildings in particular) had been affected by new research techniques and the emergence of new subject areas, changes in planning administration, demands for the protection of local character, changing requirements in further education, the emergence of professional building recorders, and problems in the archiving and retrieval of an ever-growing body of information, together with enduring difficulties in quality control and making sure that building records are used by those people – particularly planners, owners and building contractors – who often have the most immediate practical need for them.

In all meetings that are attempting to confront change, some reactions are pessimistic. This was particularly marked when considering the likely opportunities for 'pure' research, but there was recognition of both the need and the opportunities for the greater use of records and recorders in the areas of planning and protection. With so broad a range of subjects, and with so many topics impacting on others, no speaker-by-speaker summary is possible, but the principal topics that arose in the formal talks and in subsequent discussions were the following.

Research

New areas of research are opening up. These include the correlation of built forms and household composition; the many interactions of material and social cultures; the quantitative analysis of materials; the development of craft techniques and tools; the mechanics of craft transmission, and the influence these may have had on structural and formal possibilities. New kinds of explanation for buildings are being sought: environmental, economic and ideological. There remains a need for the fullest and most rigorous physical investigation of buildings, but records are means to an end rather than ends in themselves. Records must be interpreted in the light of their original purposes, but they may also be required to understand a building in ways not foreseen at the time of making, and any misinterpretation could invalidate later deductions.

Electronic recording of a fabric has limitations. Not only is it often no cheaper for a small building than is recording by conventional methods, but it may also lead to an undesirable separation between technician and interpreter.

In recent years the greatest single new research tool has been tree-ring dating. The volume of results that has by now accumulated is making possible the reassessment not only of individual buildings, but whole classes of buildings and structural forms. Close dating may show links between buildings which were not previously perceived as connected. It is also becoming possible to correlate buildings with documentary references, and to associate them with historical enquiries in which close dating is essential. The principal limitation remains the cost, which though not high, is generally beyond the means of private individuals.

There is a continuing shift in the character of research in that fewer resources are available to carry out coherent programmes of 'question-led' research into vernacular buildings, with a higher proportion now 'chance-led'. There is a continuing need for all types of investigation, but there are widening gulfs between 'pure research', commissioned recording, and the work of independent investigators. There is perceived to be declining institutional support for research by the Commissions (now English Heritage in England), universities, etc, although some local recording groups with limited objectives maintain their work, and beneficial, planning-led recording is increasing. As yet it is not clear what will be the effect in England of amalgamating RCHME with English Heritage, but the decline in broadly-based research will increasingly impact on the understanding of individual buildings and local ensembles. 'Chance-led' research may produce outstanding studies of individual structures, but lack of a wider programme means that syntheses from such work will probably take much longer to emerge.

Recording and planning

Since PPG 15 has enabled local planning authorities (LPAs) to require recording in connection with proposed works, the emphasis of emergency recording has shifted from retrospective to proactive. The purpose is to influence the planning process in respect of the building and to alert the owner and his contractor to its importance, while accumulated records have the potential to deepen the understanding of the local historic environment in LPAs and amenity groups. These objectives need the fullest support, but the process has its shortcomings.

Recording is too often confined to those parts of the building that are affected by the actual proposals, neglecting others. This may create a very partial understanding of the significance of the work proposed for the overall historic integrity of the building, as well as producing a record that is of very limited value for any other purposes. Recording should be used to make an informed decision about these proposals and to ensure that work is carried out as agreed. There may be problems over quality control; the LPA is often not in a position to assess the accuracy of the record, and the huge range of buildings that may need to be recorded means that an effective recorder must be a polymath. At the same time, there is often severe pressure, both financial and in timing, on the scope of the investigations, while whole classes of buildings which are perceived by LPAs as of little interest remain effectively outside the system.

Nor is it always easy to justify the procedure to the applicant; whereas under PPG 16 the developer may be prepared to pay for the investigation of features from whose destruction he will benefit, there is often no simple correspondence between loss and gain in the case of PPG 15 recording.

Education and publicity

In formal education, changing structures of extra-mural teaching and the need to service courses with systems of credit markings, means there is less flexibility for tutors to devise programmes of work that suit the specific needs of amateur or local groups with an interest in buildings. Teaching is increasingly carried out in urban centres. Course fees are rising beyond the reach of anyone who does not need to invest in a formal qualification. Any work outside the explicit requirements of the curriculum may have to be done in the tutor's own time and at his own expense, and teaching in any case is not well paid. For these reasons instruction about vernacular building may be harder for the informal group to find. Both the limitations and the potential of curiosity-led local groups need to be recognised. Their frequent reluctance to consider buildings outside their own locality may prevent them from understanding the full significance of the buildings they do

record, although local recorders may be able to gain access to buildings that are closed to representatives of official bodies.

Work on buildings may usefully be built into local history studies, and the involvement of professional historians may facilitate the exchange of information and interpretations between building studies and mainstream history. Historians make insufficient use of buildings as a source of information, and it would be mutually beneficial if students of vernacular architecture could be persuaded to present their findings in ways which historians can use.

Beyond this, vernacular buildings may still be studied at a post-graduate level, but here too there is a shortage of teachers as well as a lack of professional openings for those who have completed such studies.

Among the greatest needs is to teach non-specialists to appreciate the value of the buildings they are responsible for, and to show how recording and understanding can promote this appreciation. In addition to individual owners and the LPA, instruction is needed by builders, estate agents, conveyancers, surveyors and mortgage agents – among professional bodies the RICS has been notably and uniquely responsible in recognising the specialised needs of old buildings and their owners, and the responsibilities of practitioners. Besides obtaining informed analysis of their houses, owners should be encouraged to maintain log books recording changes, and these should be handed on to successive owners. It should be explained how such documentation may increase the value of the house. Technical and bureaucratic terms may inhibit understanding, so owners in particular must be helped to appreciate what is special about their property in non-technical language.

Archives and information retrieval

Problems arise from the volume of information, from its uneven quality, from differences in its organisation and format, from the different purposes for which and the processes through which it is generated, from the use of different vocabularies, from differences in ownership, and from the range of national and local, public and private, repositories. All these present difficulties of access and of indexing. While electronic access is the only practical means of handling so large a quantity of data, its volume already means that any retrieval system can only be at a high and potentially superficial level. The initial processing of data is labour intensive: to place the uniform and relatively straightforward 360,000 text entries of the national historic buildings lists on a database took 105 man-years.

The NMR, as the national archive, lacks resources to accept all the material offered to it, but while the problem of volume might be met by the establishment of a national cataloguing system which would direct users to local repositories, county sites and monuments records and record offices vary in their accessioning policies. Physical handling and access will remain formidable tasks wherever they are undertaken.

The non-standardisation of data remains a difficulty for any cataloguing system. Potential users, as well as those who make records, need to agree on what kinds of information they require from a retrieval system, and on formats in which information may be supplied. The employment of the European Core Data Standard may be a partial solution, but it would require agreement on a thesaurus of standard terms.

Conclusions

There was a high level of agreement about the problems raised, and although people differed about how easily these problems might be addressed, there was some satisfaction that they had been identified and generally closely defined. There was clear acknowledgement of the value of discussions about general issues and approaches, divorced from the immediate study of particular buildings. Delegates came from a variety of backgrounds and a diverse range of perspectives, which made the level of consensus the more valuable.

14 Some general conclusions *by Malcolm Airs*

To understand how far fieldwork in the recording of vernacular buildings has come over the last half-century, it is salutary to reflect on the national picture that W G Hoskins sketched in his pioneering essay on 'The rebuilding of rural England 1570–1840', first published in 1953. In support of his central thesis he claimed that 'from Cornwall up to Lancashire, and from Herefordshire across to Suffolk, the evidence . . . is abundant and inescapable . . . '. Yet the only active fieldwork that he was able to cite was that of Barley in Nottinghamshire and Lincolnshire, Fox and Raglan in Monmouthshire and Walton in the Yorkshire Dales. For the rest he relied on his own casual observations and the chance survival of documentary references for those areas which he knew best such as his beloved West Country, the Cotswolds and the East Midlands where he spent so much of his working life. There are shrewd comments on areas such as Lancashire, the Lake District and the Welsh Marches but Hoskins was never an active building recorder like his Oxford contemporary W A Pantin. With the benefit of hindsight, what is surprising is those parts of the country where there was no information to hand for Hoskins to use. Thus he was forced to write that in 'eastern England the evidence has yet to be examined in detail' and 'northern England for which the evidence is patchy'. Most astonishing of all is the unqualified comment that 'for southern and south-eastern England one has no evidence' (Hoskins 1953, 46–7).

All that was to change rapidly in the succeeding decades as the subject began to achieve academic respectability. The impetus came from three directions, united by a common belief that it was only through the discipline of recording buildings in a regional context that an understanding of the complex development of individual structures could be achieved. The vast and disparate collections that have accumulated were firmly based on the tape measure and the drawing board, wielded by enthusiasts from all walks of life. The academic questions and the increasing synthesis of knowledge came largely from a group of public servants employed as Inspectors and Investigators by central government, supplemented by a few historians working for a handful of the more enlightened local authorities such as the Greater London Council from the 1960s onwards. The contribution of the universities was largely concentrated in Manchester, where a steady stream of MA dissertations focused on regional recording and where Norman Foster first learnt to measure historic buildings. The weekly class programme of the further education departments in some universities also played an influential role in inspiring a whole generation of enthusiasts interested in commonplace building as well as the great set pieces of our architectural heritage. Many of them, both teachers and students, went on to instigate regional surveys or individual recordings in their own localities and some of them began to publish their results in local and national journals. These were the independent recorders whose investigations have formed the bedrock of the great upsurge in knowledge of our vernacular building stock over the last fifty years.

Representatives from all these strands were present at the Oxford Conference in 1998 which had been convened to debate the principal issues and new directions in the world of building recording which had emerged over the last decade, and which were causing a sense of bewilderment and anxiety for many practitioners. Despite the deliberate diversity of approach amongst the various contributors reflected in these pages there was a general consensus on the crucial importance of recording in both understanding and managing the historic environment. The main threads of the debate were admirably summarised by Nicholas Cooper in 1999 where he identified research, planning, education and information retrieval as the principal items on the agenda. It would be pointless to rehearse his observations here but it would be helpful to draw out some of the most significant elements.

The full title of the conference emphasised the changing world of building recording, and perhaps the greatest change that has taken place in recent years is the official recognition that recording listed buildings should be an integral part of the planning system as articulated by PPG 15. Because the PPG offers guidance rather than a mandatory obligation its potential is far from being comprehensively realised, but the onus is now clearly on the applicant to provide an informed assessment of the impact of any proposed work on the historic fabric. Consequently, it is reasonable to predict that in the fullness of time there will be a general acceptance of the desirability of statements of significance as well as a discrete record of the alterations following on from the grant of planning permission, in the same way that archaeological assessments and conditions blossomed in the wake of PPG 16. By the same token the growing acceptance of Conservation Plans as instruments of best practice in the management of the historic environment will have a complementary impact. Hitherto they have been exclusively confined to major monuments of acknowledged importance but there is no reason whatsoever why the concept of understanding prior to making decisions about change should not be extended to humbler buildings and promote the integration of recording and research.

Properly conducted, Conservation Plans constitute statements of significance, and their value should not be judged by their length or glossy presentation.

All of this will produce a prodigiously growing body of information and it is one of the greatest weaknesses of PPG 15 that it offers no guidance on how this accumulating archive should be deposited and curated. If the record is to provide a usefulness beyond its bureaucratic purpose it is essential that a mechanism is devised to make it accessible in the public domain and to ensure some form of consistent control over standards and quality. At one time one might have looked to the Royal Commissions to provide the initiative and the expertise to accept this challenge but the conference coincided with the administration of the last rites for the English Commission. In a sense, the amalgamation with English Heritage was simply another recognition of the central importance of recording in the planning process but there were legitimate fears that the integrity of the English Commission's independence would be fatally compromised in the new culture. So far, that does not seem to have happened and there have been hopeful examples such as the work on the Birmingham Jewellery Quarter, where the benefits of the integrated approach have been positively welcomed. Here, an enhanced understanding of the special character of the area based on a comprehensive survey carried out by the new English Heritage has led to an extended conservation area, the commissioning of a Conservation Plan and the forthcoming publication of a thematic volume in the established Royal Commission tradition (Cattell 2000; Cattell et al forthcoming).

One of the key functions previously undertaken by the Royal Commissions was the training of investigators in the full range of skills necessary for building analysis across a broad range of building types. There was a danger with the abandonment of the old county inventory volumes that some of these skills would be diminished, particularly with regard to medieval ecclesiastical buildings and country houses but, as far as smaller buildings are concerned, the new thematic surveys have continued to offer opportunities for investigators to widen their knowledge and to engage with new themes such as industrial buildings. The small outreach training programme of the English Commission has survived under the new English Heritage and the short courses in recording aimed at professionals and post-graduates continue to be offered at a number of centres. Other opportunities for training have also opened up in the last couple of decades. The national programme of resurvey of the list of buildings of special architectural and historic interest which partly sought to provide a better representation for vernacular buildings provided experience of rapid survey techniques for a large number of investigators on short-term contracts, many of whom have now found careers in both the public and private sectors. Listing is now concentrated on thematic issues and the historical research which is fundamental to this

approach has produced a number of background papers of high academic value which deserve to be disseminated more widely than just to the committee members who make recommendations to the Secretary of State. The best of them can be considered as a response to the sort of research agenda advocated elsewhere in these pages. This demand is also being addressed by English Heritage in its policy-making role as well. The inspiration for its comprehensive research project on thatching traditions was driven by the need to produce defensible guidance for conservation purposes, but the recent publication of the outcomes in three volumes is an initiative of exemplary scholarly value (Letts 1999; Moir and Letts 1999; Cox and Letts 2000; English Heritage 2000a).

The universities, too, continue to provide training across a broader front than might at first seem apparent. Where continuing education departments have survived the fad for mainstreaming of their activities which decimated so many of them in the 1990s, they now find themselves with renewed importance in current government thinking on life-long learning and part-time education. The traditional weekly class programme still has a role to play and although the pressure for accreditation might be changing the customer base in some subjects, building recording at least has the potential to encourage the production of work that can be assessed for every member of the class as part of the emerging credit framework. It is a hopeful sign that the consequences of this pressure were raised in the consultation papers on the Heritage Review published in June 2000 even if it did not go on to offer any solutions (English Heritage 2000b, paper 2, para 23).

However, the day and evening class is only part of a much wider programme of training in recording techniques and many other university-led initiatives are beginning to bear fruit in meeting the demand for professional expertise. In addition to summer schools and concentrated short courses, there are now a number of part-time undergraduate qualifications in vernacular architecture, regionally focused and based on the weekly class methods of teaching. The specialist post-graduate degrees in architectural history and the archaeology of buildings are complemented by a remarkable growth in historic building conservation qualifications, most of which contain an element of analysis and recording.

In a society which places a growing emphasis on vocational training, many of the graduates of these courses are taking their building skills into the market-place and the number of opportunities for professional building analysts is expanding at a marked rate. Driven by the demands of the planning system, most firms of archaeological contractors employ building specialists and a growing number of former local authority conservation officers have set themselves up as consultants offering building assessments as part of their range of services. At a time when a firm of consulting engineers like Alan Baxter Associates now employs more architectural historians than any public authority except for

English Heritage, it is probably safe to predict that the importance of the private sector will continue to grow. In its wake will come an urgent need to maintain standards, and professional bodies such as IFA and IHBC will come to exercise an increasing influence in this area.

The developing professionalism of building recording through the 1990s can be presented as a sign that the discipline is on the way to maturity in a healthy state. Some of the challenges that still need to be met are clear from the preceding chapters but it is equally clear that the voluntary recorder still has an important place in the overall picture. A changing world demands changing responses, but some things remain constant, and the desire to understand the fabric of their local communities will continue to hold a fascination for informed observers which will benefit us all.

Bibliography

Addy, S O, 1898 *The evolution of the English house.* Allen & Unwin

Alcock, N W, 1962 Houses in an east Devon parish, *Trans Devonshire Ass*, **94**, 185–232

Alcock, N W, 1969 Timber-framed buildings in north Bedfordshire, *Bedfordshire Archaeol J, 4,* 43–68 (in part with P V Addyman)

Alcock, N W, 1973 *A catalogue of cruck buildings.* Phillimore

Alcock, N W, 1981 *Cruck construction: an introduction and catalogue,* CBA Research Report, **42**. York: CBA

Alcock, N W, 1993 *People at Home: living in a Warwickshire village, 1500–1800.* Chichester: Phillimore

Alcock, N W, 1996a A stud-and-panel granary in Warwickshire, 1638/9, *Vernacular Architect,* **27**, 38–9

Alcock, N W, 1996b From Palladio to Potter's Bar: the evolution of the Georgian farmhouse, in N Burton (ed), *Georgian Vernacular*, 34–44

Alcock, N W, Barley, M W, Dixon, P W, & Meeson, R A, 1996 *Recording timber-framed buildings: an illustrated glossary,* CBA Practical Handbook, **5**. York: CBA

Alcock, N W, Braithwaite, J G, & Jeffs, M W, 1973 Timber-framed buildings in Warwickshire: Stoneleigh village, *Birmingham Archaeol Soc Trans,* **85**, 178–202 (also separately circulated under the title *Stoneleigh Houses*)

Alcock, N W, & Woodfield, C T P, 1996 Social pretensions in architecture and ancestry: Hall House, Sawbridge, Warwickshire and the Andrewe family, *Antiq J*, **76**, 52–72

Aldous, T, 1975 *Goodbye, Britain?* Sidgwick & Jackson

Alfrey, J, & Clark, C, 1994 *The landscape of industry: patterns of change in the Ironbridge Gorge.* Routledge

Arrowsmith, P, 1995 *Radcliffe Tower: an introduction to the Scheduled Ancient Monument.* Bury Metropolitan Borough

Arrowsmith, P, 1997 *Stockport: a history.* Stockport Metropolitan Borough Council

Arrowsmith, P, & Hartwell, C, 1989 Kersal Cell: a house of the lesser gentry, *Greater Manchester Archaeol J,* **3,** 71–93

Atchison, K, 1999 *Profiling the profession: a survey of archaeological jobs in the UK.* Council for British Archaeology/English Heritage/Institute of Field Archaeologists

Atkinson, F, & McDowall, R W, 1967 Aisled houses in the Halifax area, *Antiq J*, **47**, 77–94

Austin, D, 1990 The 'proper study' of medieval archaeology, in D Austin & L Alcock (eds), *From the Baltic to the Black Sea: studies in medieval archaeology.* One World Archaeology, **18**, Unwin Hyman, 9–42

Baker, D, and Baker, E, 1999 *An assessment of English sites and monuments records.* Bedford, ALGAO (available from Planning Department, County Hall, Chelmsford, Essex, CM1 1LF)

Baker, D, Chitty, G, Richards, J, & Robinson, D, 1999 *Mapping information resources.* Report produced for HEIRNET

Baker, D, & Meeson, B, 1997 *Analysis and recording for the conservation and control of works to historic buildings.* Chelmsford, ALGAO (available as above)

Barley, M W, 1961 *The English farmhouse and cottage.* Routledge & Kegan Paul

Barnwell, P S, & Adams, A T, 1994 *The house within: interpreting medieval houses in Kent.* RCHME/HMSO

Barnwell, P S, & Giles, C, 1997 *English farmsteads 1750–1914.* RCHME/HMSO

Berg, M, 1985 *The age of manufactures 1700–1820.* Fontana.

Beresford, M & Hurst J, 1990 *Wharram Percy, deserted medieval village.* English Heritage

Blair, J, 1993 Hall and chamber: English domestic planning 1000–1250, in Meirion-Jones & Jones (eds)

Bourdieu, P, 1973 The Berber house, in M Douglas (ed), *Rules and meanings.* Penguin, 98–110.

Boyns, R, 1999 Archivists and family historians: local authority record repositories and the family history user group, *J Soc Archiv*, **20** (1), 61–74

Britton, J, 1807–26 *Architectural antiquities of Great Britain*, 5 vols

Britton, J, 1814–35 *Cathedral antiquities of England*, 14 vols

Brown, F E, 1990 Analysing small building plans: a morphological approach, in R Samson (ed), *The social archaeology of houses.* Edinburgh University Press, 259–76

Brown, G Baldwin, 1905 *The care of ancient monuments.* Cambridge

Brunskill, R W, 1971 *Illustrated handbook of vernacular architecture.* Faber & Faber

Brunskill, R W, 1974 *Vernacular architecture of the Lake Counties.* Faber & Faber

Burke, T, & Nevell, M D, 1996 *The Buildings of Tameside.* Tameside Metropolitan Borough Council

Carr, E H, 1961 *What is History?* Macmillan

Cathedral Communications, 1999 *The Building Conservation Directory.* Tisbury: Cathedral Communications

142

Cattell, J, 2000 Birmingham's Jewellery Quarter, *Conservation Bulletin*, **38**, 18–19

Cattell, J, Ely, S & Jones, B, forthcoming *The Birmingham Jewellery Quarter*. English Heritage

Champion, T, 1996 Protecting the monuments: archaeological legislation from the 1882 Act to PPG 16, in Hunter 1996, 38–56

Chatwin, D, 1996 *The development of timber-framed buildings in the Sussex Weald: the architectural heritage of Rudgwick*. Rudgwick Preservation Society

Clark, G, 1934 Archaeology and the State, *Antiquity*, **8**, 414–28

Cleverdon, F, 1999 Cruck buildings in the Staffordshire moorlands: distribution and survival patterns in the medieval parish of Leek, *Staffordshire Archaeol Hist Soc Trans*, **38**, 49–58

Cooper, N, 1999 *VAG Newsletter*, **36**, 6–10

Cordingley, R A, 1961 British historical roof-types and their members: a classification, *Trans Ancient Monuments Soc*, **NS9**, 73–117

Council for British Archaeology, 1992–ongoing *British and Irish Archaeological Bibliography*

Cox, J, & Letts, J, 2000 *Thatching in England 1940–1994*. English Heritage/James & James

Croad, S J, & Fowler, P J, 1984 RCHM's first 75 years: an outline history, 1908–83, *RCHME Annual Review 1983–84*, 8–13

Currie, C R J, 1988 Time and chance: modelling the attrition of old houses, *Vernacular Architect*, **19**, 1–9

Darvill, T, Burrow, S, & Wildgust, D, 1995 *Planning for the past : v. 2 : an assessment of archaeological assessments*. Bournemouth University/English Heritage

Department of National Heritage, 1995 *Local government reorganisation: guidance to local authorities on the conservation of the historic environment*

Douet, J, & Saunders, A, 1998 *British barracks 1600 – 1914: their architecture and role in society*. English Heritage/HMSO.

Drury, P J, 1980 No other palace in the kingdom will compare with it: the evolution of Audley End, 1605–1745, *Architect Hist*, **23**, 1–39

Dunbar, J G, 1992 The Royal Commission on the Ancient and Historical Monuments of Scotland: the first eighty years, *Trans Ancient Monuments Soc*, **36**, 13–73

Dyer, C, 1997 History and vernacular architecture, *Vernacular Architect*, **28**, 1–8

English Heritage, 1992, 1998c, 2000 *Buildings at risk: sample surveys*

English Heritage, 1993 *Conservation area practice: guidance on the management of conservation areas*

English Heritage, 1995 *Development in the historic environment*

English Heritage, 1998a *Conservation-led regeneration*

English Heritage, 1998b *Dendrochronology: guidelines on producing and interpreting dendrochronological dates*

English Heritage 1999 *Conservation plans in action*

English Heritage, 2000a *Thatch and thatching: a guidance note*

English Heritage, 2000b *Review of policies relating to the historic environment*

Evans, R J, 1997 *In defence of history*. Granta Books

Fairclough, G, 1992 Meaningful constructions: spatial and functional analysis of medieval buildings, *Antiquity*, **66**, 348–66

Ferris, I M, 1989 The archaeological investigation of standing buildings, *Vernacular Architect*, **20**, 12–17

Ferris, I M, 1991 I am not a camera, *Vernacular Architect*, **22**, 1

Fowler, P J, 1981 The Royal Commission on Historical Monuments (England), *Antiquity*, **55**, 106–14

Fox, Sir C, & Raglan, Lord, 3 vols, 1951–4 *Monmouthshire houses*. Cardiff: National Museum of Wales

Froud, N Z, 1995 Bowes Morrell House, 111 Walmgate: an archaeological case study on aspects of private and public use of space in a timber-framed town house, unpublished MA dissertation, University of York

Fryde, E B, 1996 *Peasants and landlords in later medieval England, c1385–c1525*. Stroud: Sutton Publishing

Gilchrist, R L, 1993 *Gender and material culture: the archaeology of religious women*. Routledge

Giles, C, 1986 *Rural houses of West Yorkshire*. RCHME/HMSO

Giles, C, & Goodall, I, 1992 *Yorkshire textile mills 1770–1930*. London: RCHME/HMSO

Giles, K F, 1999a Guildhalls and social identity in York, c1350–1630, unpublished DPhil thesis, University of York

Giles, K F, 1999b The familiar fraternity: guildhalls and social identity in late medieval and early modern York, in S Tarlow & S West (eds), *The familiar past? Archaeologies of late-historical Britain*. Routledge

Giles, K F, 2000 An archaeology of social identity: guildhalls in York, c1350–1630, in *British Archaeological Reports British Series* **315**

Godelier, M, 1986 *The mental and the material; thought, economy and society*. Verso

Gould, S, 1995 Industrial archaeology and the neglect of humanity, in Palmer and Neaverson (eds), 49–53.

Gray, P, 1990 Dating buildings in the Weald, in J Warren (ed), *Wealden Buildings*. Horsham

Greatrex, J, 1978 *The register of the common seal of the priory of St Swithun, Winchester*. Hampshire County Council

Green, A, 1998 Tudhoe Hall and Byers Green Hall, County Durham: seventeenth and early eighteenth-century social change in houses, *Vernacular Architect*, **29**, 33–42

Grenville, J, 1994 Research strategies and priorities: an afterthought: the Chester Rows, in Wood (ed), 97–07

Grenville, J C, 1997 *Medieval housing*. Leicester University Press

Grenville, J C, 2000 Houses and households in late medieval England: an archaeological perspective, in J Wogan-Browne, R Voaden, A Diamond, A Hutchison, C Miele & L Johnson (eds) *Medieval women: texts and contexts in late medieval Britain. Essays for Felicity Riddy*. Turnhout: Brepols

Hall, L J, 1983 *The rural houses of North Avon & South Gloucestershire 1400–1720*. Bristol, City of Bristol Museum & Art Gallery, Monograph 6

Hall, L J, 1991 Yeoman or gentleman? Problems in defining social status in seventeenth- and eighteenth-century Gloucestershire, *Vernacular Architect*, **22**, 2–19

Hanson, J, 1998 *Decoding houses and homes*. Cambridge University Press

Harding, J, 1976 *Four centuries of Charlwood houses, medieval to 1840*. The Charlwood Society

Harris, R, 1977 Timber-framed buildings, *Architect J*, **165**, 797–800

Harris, R, 1989 The grammar of carpentry, *Vernacular Architect,* **20**, 1–8

Harris, R, 1994 Recording timber-framed buildings, in J Wood (ed), *Buildings archaeology: applications in practice*. Oxford: Oxbow, 235–48

Harrison, B, 1994 Review of Johnson 1993, *Vernacular Architect*, **25**, 45–6

Harrison, B, & Hutton, B, 1984 *Vernacular houses in North Yorkshire and Cleveland*. Edinburgh: John Donald Publishers Ltd

Hartwell, C, 1989 The Old Farmhouse Common Farm: a yeoman house in South Trafford, *Greater Manchester Archaeol J*, **3**, 95–101

Harvey, J, 1961 The origin of official preservation of Ancient Monuments, *Trans Ancient Monuments Soc* **9**, 27–31

Harvey, J, 1972 *Conservation of Buildings*

Hasler, P W, 1981 *The House of Commons, 1558–1603*

Hatcher, J, 1996 The great slump of the mid fifteenth century, in R Britnell & J Hatcher (eds), *Progress and problems in medieval England: essays in honour of Edward Miller*. Cambridge University Press

Hayden, R, 1995 Living and trading conditions in the Shambles, 1300 to 1600, unpublished MA dissertation, University of York

Heritage Lottery Fund, 1998 *Conservation Plans for Historic Places*

Hewett, C A, 1969 *The development of English carpentry, 1200–1700: an Essex study*. Newton Abbot

Hewett, C A, 1980 *English historic carpentry*. Chichester: Phillimore

Hillam, J, 1998 *Dendrochronology: guidelines on producing and interpreting dendro-chronological dates*. English Heritage

Hillier, B, & Hanson, J, 1984 *The social logic of space*. Cambridge University Press

Hingley, R, 1990 Domestic organisation and gender relations in Iron Age and Romano-British houses, in R Samson (ed) *The social archaeology of houses*. Edinburgh University Press, 125–47

Hobhouse, H, 1994 *London survey'd: the work of the Survey of London 1894–1994*. Survey of London

Holland, A, & Rawles, K, 1993 Values in conservation, *Ecos* **14** (1), 14–19.

Horton, M, *et al*, 1992 *Newdale: an industrial township of the mid 18th century*, Ironbridge Archaeological Series: **29**. Ironbridge: Ironbridge Gorge Museum Trust Archaeological Unit

Hoskins, W G, 1953 The rebuilding of rural England, 1570–1640, *Past and Present*, **4**, 44–59

Howard, M, 1994 The architectural and social history of the Tudor and Jacobean great house: new materials and new methods, in M Airs (ed), *The Tudor and Jacobean great house*. Oxford

Hunter, M, 1981 The preconditions of preservation: a historical perspective, in D Lowenthal & M Binney (eds), *Our past before us: why do we save it?* Temple Smith

Hunter, M (ed) 1996 *Preserving the past: the rise of heritage in modern Britain*. Stroud: Sutton Publishing

ICOMOS, 1990 *Guide to recording historic buildings*. Butterworth.

Impey, E, 1993 Seigneurial domestic architecture in Normandy, 1050–1350, in Meirion-Jones & Jones (eds)

Innocent, C F, 1916 *The development of English building construction*, reprinted 1999. Shaftesbury: Donhead

Jenkins, K, 1991 *Re-thinking history*. Routledge

Jennings, B, (ed) 1967 *A History of Nidderdale*, written by the Pateley Bridge local history tutorial class. Pateley Bridge

Johnson, M H, 1993 *Housing culture: traditional architecture in an English landscape*. University College London Press

Johnson, M, 1994 Ordering houses, creating narratives, in M Parker Pearson & C Richards (eds), *Architecture and order: approaches to social space*, 170–7

Johnson, M H, 1997 Vernacular architecture: the loss of innocence, *Vernacular Architect*, **28**, 13–19

Jourdain, M, 1924 *English decoration and furniture of the early Renaissance, 1500–1650*. Batsford

Lawrence, R J, 1983 The interpretation of vernacular architecture, *Vernacular Architect*, **14**, 19–28

Letts, J, 1999 *Smoke blackened thatch*. English Heritage/University of Reading

Locock, M, 1994 *Meaningful architecture: social interpretations of buildings*. Aldershot, Ashgate Publishing Ltd

MacCaig, N, 1969 *A man in my position*. Chatto & Windus/Hogarth Press

McCann, J, 1998 *The dovecotes of Suffolk*. Ipswich: Suffolk Institute of Archaeology and History

Machin, B, 1994 *Rural housing: an historical approach*. London: the Historical Association

McNeil, R, 1999 Staircase House Stockport, *Current Archaeol*, **165**, 346–54

McNeil, R, 2000 Building Spaces, *The Archaeologist*, **37**, 21–3

McNeil, R, with Arrowsmith, P, & Nevell, M, 1998 *Staircase House Stockport*, Design Development Study Report for Heritage Lottery Fund

MAP 2, 1991 *Management of archaeological projects*. English Heritage

Martin, D, & Martin, B, 1997 Detached kitchens in eastern Sussex, *Vernacular Architect*, **28**, 85–91

Mayer, A, 1992 The Bent, unpublished client report

Mayes, F, 1996 *Under the Tuscan Sun*. Bantam Books

Meeson, R A, 1989 In defence of selective recording, *Vernacular Architect*, **20**, 18–19

Meeson, R A, 1996 Time and place: medieval carpentry in Staffordshire, *Vernacular Architect*, **27**, 10–24

Meirion-Jones, G, & Jones, M (eds), 1993 *Manorial domestic buildings in England and Northern France*, Soc Antiq London Occasional Papers, **15**

Mercer, E, 1975 *English vernacular houses: a study of traditional farmhouses and cottages*. RCHME/HMSO

Miele, C, 1996 The first conservation militants: William Morris and the Society for the Protection of Ancient Buildings, in Hunter 1996, 17–37

Miles, D, 1995 The building accounts of the solar cross wing, in Roberts, 1995, 103–5

Miles, D, 1997 The interpretation, presentation and use of tree-ring dates, *Vernacular Architect*, **28**, 40–56

Miles, D, & Haddon-Reece, D, 1994 Tree-ring dates: list 56 *Vernacular Architect*, **25**, 28–30

Miles, D, & Haddon-Reece, D, 1995 Tree-ring dates: list 64, *Vernacular Architect*, **26**, 62–8

Miles, D, & Haddon-Reece, D, 1996 Hampshire dendrochronological project: phase 2, *Vernacular Architect*, **27**, 97–102

Miles, D, & Worthington, M, 1997 Hampshire dendrochronological project: phase 3, *Vernacular Architect*, **28**, 175–81

Miles, D, & Worthington, M, 1998 Hampshire dendrochronological project: phase 4, *Vernacular Architect*, **29**, 117–23

Miles, D, & Worthington, M, 1999, Hampshire dendrochronological project: phase 5, *Vernacular Architect*, **30**, 105–09

Moir, J, & Letts, J, 1999 *Thatching in England 1790–1940*. English Heritage/James & James

Moran, M, 1985 Padmore, Onibury, *Shropshire Archaeol. J*, **142**, 340–60

Moran, M, 1999 *Vernacular buildings of Whitchurch and area, and their occupants*. Logaston: Logaston Press

Morris, R K, 1994 Buildings Archaeology, in Wood (ed), 13–21

Morris, R K, 1997 Let culture and conservation co-reside, *Brit Archaeol*, **26**, 11

Murray, D, 1896 *An archaeological survey of the United Kingdom: the preservation and protection of our ancient monuments*. Glasgow

Muter, W G, 1979 *The buildings of an industrial community*. Chichester: Phillimore.

Nevell, M D, 1995 Onion Farm House, unpublished client report

Nevell, M D, 1997 *The Archaeology of Trafford*. Trafford Metropolitan Borough Council

Nevell, M D, 1998 Meal House Brow, unpublished client report

Nevell, M D, 1999 The Warburton archaeological survey and the vernacular buildings of a north-west township, *Archaeol North West*, **4**, 18–22

Oxford Brookes, 1999 *Local authority practice and PPG 15: information and effectiveness*. Unpublished report, School of Planning, Environmental Design and Conservation Research Group

Palmer, M, 1994 The Rolt Memorial Lecture, 1993. Industrial archaeology: continuity and change, *Ind Archaeol Rev*, **16**, 2, 135–56

Palmer, M, & Neaverson, P (eds), 1995 *Managing the industrial heritage*, Leicester Archaeology Monographs, **2**. Leicester

Pantin, W A, 1958 Monuments or muniments? The interrelation of material remains and documentary sources, *Medieval Archaeol*, **2**, 158–68.

Pearson, S, 1994a *The medieval houses of Kent: an historical analysis*. RCHME/HMSO

Pearson, S, 1994b Review of *People at Home* (Alcock 1993), *Vernacular Architect*, **25**, 52–3.

Pearson, S, Barnwell, P S, & Adams, A T, 1994 *A gazetteer of medieval houses in Kent*. RCHME/HMSO

Pearson, S, 1997 Tree-ring dating: a review, *Vernacular Architect*, **28**, 25–39

Peats, R, 1998 Liturgy and the medieval parish church: a study of St Helen's, Skipwith, unpublished MA thesis, University of York

Peats, R, forthcoming in *Internet Archaeology*, http://intarch.ac.uk

Peers, C R, 1931 The treatment of old buildings, *Journal Roy Inst Brit Architect*, 3rd ser **38**, 311–20

Pevsner, N, 1972 *Some architectural writers of the nineteenth century*. Oxford

Pevsner, N, & Neave, D, 1995 *The buildings of England: Yorkshire: York and the East Riding*. Penguin

Pevsner, N, & Wedgwood, A, 1996 *The buildings of England: Warwickshire*. Penguin

Phillips, E M, & Pugh, D, 2000 *How to get a PhD: a handbook for students and supervisors*. Buckingham: Open University Press

Platt, C, 1994 *The great rebuildings of Tudor and Stuart England.*

Powys, A R, 1937 *From the ground up*

PPG 15, 1994 *Planning Policy Guidance Note 15: Planning and the historic environment*. Departments of the Environment & National Heritage/HMSO

PPG 16 1990 *Planning Policy Guidance Note 16: Archaeology and planning*. Department of the Environment/HMSO.

Pugh, R B (ed), 1970 *The Victoria history of the counties of England. General introduction.* Oxford

Rahtz, P A, 1980 *The new medieval archaeology*, inaugural lecture, University of York, Department of Archaeology.

Rape of Hastings Architectural Survey, 1977–91 *Historic buildings of East Sussex*, **1–6** (work by D & B Martin)

Rapoport, A, 1990 Systems of activities and systems of settings, in S Kent (ed), *Domestic architecture and the use of space: an interdisciplinary cross-cultural study*. Cambridge University Press, 9–20

Reader, F W, 1941 A classification of Tudor domestic wall paintings, *Archaeol J*, **98**, 181–211

Rickerby, S, 1995 Scotson Fold, Radcliffe, Greater Manchester: report on the conservation and analysis of the 17th-century wall painting; unpublished report to GMAU & Bury Metropolitan Borough Council

Rickman, T, 1817 *An attempt to discriminate the styles of architecture in England from the Conquest to the Reformation*

Roberts, E, 1993 William of Wykeham's house at East Meon, Hants, *Archaeol J*, **150**, 456–81

Roberts, E, 1995 Edward III's lodge at Odiham, Hampshire, *Medieval Archaeol*, **39**, 91–106

Roberts, E, 1996 Overton Court Farm and the late-medieval farmhouses of demesne lessees in Hampshire, *Proc Hampshire Fld Club Archaeol Soc*, **51**, 89–106

Roberts, E, 1997 The Old Manor, Ashley, Hampshire, *Vernacular Architect*, **28**, 115–16

Roberts, E, & Gale, M, 1995 Henry Mildmay's new farms, *Proc Hampshire Fld Club Archaeol Soc*, **50**, 169–92

Roberts, E, & Miles, D, 1997 73–77 Winchester Street, Overton, Hampshire, *Vernacular Architect*, **28**, 120–1

Robertson, M, *et al* 1993 Listed buildings: the national resurvey of England, *Trans Ancient Monuments Soc*, **37**, 21–94

Rodwell, W, 1981 *The archaeology of the English church*, revised 1989 as *Church Archaeology*. Batsford/English Heritage

RCAHMW, 1998 *Glamorgan farmhouses and cottages*. HMSO

RCHME, 1991 *Recording historic buildings: a symposium*. RCHME

RCHME, 1993a *Salisbury: the houses of the Close*. HMSO

RCHME, 1993b 30a (Staircase Cafe) and 31 Market Place, Stockport, Manchester, unpublished historic buildings report

RCHME, 1998a *Unlocking the past for the new millennium*. Swindon: RCHME

RCHME, 1998b *MIDAS: A manual and data standard for monument inventories*. Swindon: RCHME

RCHME, 1999 *Recording historic buildings: a descriptive specification*. Swindon: RCHME

Ryan, P, 1993 A new house at Great Waltham, 1440–42, *Hist Build Essex*, **7**, 17–20

Saint, A, 1996 How listing happened, in Hunter (ed), 115–33

Saunders, A D, 1983 A century of ancient monuments legislation, 1882–1982, *Antiq J*, **63**, 11–33

SCAUM, 1997 *Recording information about archaeological fieldwork*. Standing Conference of Archaeological Unit Managers

Slocombe, P M, 1988 *Wiltshire farmhouses and cottages 1500–1800*. Stroud: Alan Sutton

Slocombe, P M, 1989 *Wiltshire farm buildings 1500–1850*. Stroud: Alan Sutton

Slocombe, P M, 1992 *Medieval houses of Wiltshire*. Stroud: Alan Sutton

Smith, J T, 1955 Medieval aisled halls and their derivatives, *Archaeol J*, **112**, 76–4

Smith, J T, 1958 Medieval roofs: a classification, *Archaeol J*, **115**, 111–49

Smith, J T, 1965 Timber-framed building in England, its development and regional differences, *Archaeol J*, **122**, 133–58

Smith, J T, 1989 The archaeological investigation of standing buildings: a comment, *Vernacular Architect*, **20**, 20

Smith, J T, 1992 *English Houses 1200–1800: the Hertfordshire evidence*. RCHME/HMSO

Smith, P, 1975 *Houses of the Welsh Countryside*. RCAHMW/HMSO

Smith, P, 1990 The RCAHM Wales in my time, 1949–89, *Trans Ancient Monuments Soc*, **34**, 29–83

Smith, W J, 1977 The Staircase Cafe, Stockport: an interim report, *Trans Lancashire Cheshire Antiq Soc*, **79**, 14–20

Smith, W J, 1998 Social pretensions in architecture: Scotson Fold, Radcliffe, Lancashire, unpublished report to GMAU & Bury Metropolitan Borough

146

SVBRG, 1996 *The vernacular buildings of Shapwick*. Somerset Vernacular Buildings Research Group

SSAVBRG, 1982 *Somerset Villages: Long Load and Knole, Long Sutton: their houses, cottages and farms, settlement and people,* Somerset & South Avon Vernacular Buildings Research Group

Steane, J, 1993 *The archaeology of the medieval English monarchy*

Stenning, D F, & Andrews, D D (eds), 1998 *Regional variation in timber-framed building in England and Wales down to 1550*. Chelmsford

Stocker, D, 1992 Broken toes or interdisciplinary ballet: architectural history, archaeology and the recording of buildings, *Fld Archaeol*, **16**, 302–3

Stocker, D, 1994 Understanding what we conserve, in Wood (ed), 1–9

Swain, H, 1998 *A survey of archaeological archives*. English Heritage/Museums and Galleries Commission

Taylor, C, 1991 Wythenshaw Hall and the Tatton family, *Trans Lancashire Cheshire Antiq Soc*, **87**, 1–5

Taylor, H, 1972 Structural criticism: a plea for more systematic study of Anglo-Saxon buildings, *Anglo-Saxon England*, **1**, 259–72.

Thornes, R, & Bold, J (eds), 1998 *Documenting the cultural heritage*. Los Angeles: The Getty Information Institute

Trinder, B, 1981 *The Industrial Revolution in Shropshire*. Chichester: Phillimore.

Turner, R, 1997 *Plas Mawr, Conw*, Cadw, Welsh Historic Monuments

UMAU, 1994 Kersal Cell, Salford: archaeological report; unpublished client report

UMAU, 1995 Staircase House: historic building survey, unpublished client report

Vernacular Architecture Group, 1972 (Hall, R de Z, ed) *A bibliography on vernacular architecture*. Newton Abbot: David & Charles

Vernacular Architecture Group, 1979 (Michelmore, D J H, ed) *A current bibliography of vernacular architecture 1970 – 1976*. York: Noel Richardson & Co Ltd

Vernacular Architecture Group, 1992 (Pattison, I R, Pattison, D S, & Alcock, N W, eds) *A bibliography of vernacular architecture*, vol III 1977–1989. Coventry: VAG

Vernacular Architecture Group, 1999 (Pattison, I R, Pattison, D S, & Alcock, N W, eds.) *A bibliography of vernacular architecture, vol IV 1990–1994*. Coventry: VAG

Victoria Histories of the Counties of England, 1900–14 *Hampshire and the Isle of Wight*, 5 vols. London

Wade, J (ed), 1986 *Traditional buildings of Kent,* **5**

Walker, J, 1998 Essex medieval houses: type and method of construction, in Stenning & Andrews (eds)

Walker, J, & Walker, P, 1998 review of Hillam, 1998, *Vernacular Architect*, **29**, 132–4

Waterson, R, 1997 *The living house: an anthropology of architecture in south-east Asia*. Thames & Hudson

Williams, P, 1995 *The later Tudors: England 1547–1603*. Oxford

Willis, R J, 1972, 1973 *Architectural history of some English cathedrals*. Chicheley, collective reprint

Wood, J, (ed), 1994 *Buildings archaeology:applications in practice*. Oxford: Oxbow

Wood-Jones, R B, 1963 *Traditional domestic architecture of the Banbury region*. Manchester

Wrathmell, S, 1990 Why the archaeologist is not a camera, *Scott Archaeol Rev*, **7**, 37–40

Index

Illustrations are denoted by page numbers in *italics*.